Reading and Writing Instruction *for*
SECOND- & THIRD-GRADE
Classrooms *in a* PLC at Work®

Sarah Gord
Kathryn E. Sheridan

EDITED BY
Mark Onuscheck
Jeanne Spiller

Solution Tree | Press

a division of
Solution Tree

555 North Morton Street
Bloomington, IN 47404
800.733.6786 (toll free) / 812.336.7700
FAX: 812.336.7790

email: info@SolutionTree.com
SolutionTree.com

Visit **go.SolutionTree.com/literacy** to download the free reproducibles in this book.

Printed in the United States of America

Library of Congress Cataloging-in-Publication Data

Names: Gord, Sarah, author. | Sheridan, Katie E., author.
Title: Reading and writing instruction for second- and third-grade
   classrooms in a PLC at work / Sarah Gord and Katie E. Sheridan.
Description: Bloomington, Indiana : Solution Tree Press, 2020. | Series:
   Every teacher is a literacy teacher | Includes bibliographical
   references and index.
Identifiers: LCCN 2019059163 (print) | LCCN 2019059164 (ebook) | ISBN
   9781949539172 (Paperback) | ISBN 9781949539189 (eBook)
Subjects: LCSH: Language arts (Elementary) | Professional learning
   communities. | Elementary school teachers--Professional relationships. |
   Second grade (Education) | Third grade (Education)
Classification: LCC LB1576 .G7217 2020 (print) | LCC LB1576 (ebook) | DDC
   372.6--dc23
LC record available at https://lccn.loc.gov/2019059163
LC ebook record available at https://lccn.loc.gov/2019059164

Solution Tree
Jeffrey C. Jones, CEO
Edmund M. Ackerman, President

Solution Tree Press
President and Publisher: Douglas M. Rife
Associate Publisher: Sarah Payne-Mills
Art Director: Rian Anderson
Managing Production Editor: Kendra Slayton
Senior Production Editor: Todd Brakke
Content Development Specialist: Amy Rubenstein
Copy Editor: Jessi Finn
Proofreader: Kate St. Ives
Text and Cover Designer: Abigail Bowen
Editorial Assistants: Sarah Ludwig and Elijah Oates

ACKNOWLEDGMENTS

It has been an honor writing this book with some of the best educators I know. Though writing is a passion of mine, writing a book was a dream that seemed like a far-off reality. Thank you, Jeanne, for the opportunity to be part of this experience. Your expertise and unwavering commitment to students' learning truly inspire me, and I am so fortunate to work in Kildeer Countryside District 96 alongside such dedicated professionals and educators. Thank you also to my three children—Lacey, Kendall, and Tanner—for inspiring me to continuously learn and grow as an educator so that I can make a difference in the lives of so many little ones just like you. Finally, thank you to my husband, Nelson, for being incredibly patient, encouraging, and supportive as this work unfolded.

—Sarah Gord

I am forever thankful for the opportunity to contribute to this series with this talented team. This opportunity to reflect on our craft and put our practice on paper has been some of my most valued professional learning. I loved every one of our conference calls, emails, texts, and wordsmithing sessions and am indebted to all of you for pushing forward our collective thinking about instruction. None of this would be possible without our connection through Kildeer Countryside District 96 and our engagement in professional learning communities. Thank you to D96 and Jeanne for everything. A huge thank-you to my four children—Everett, Liam, Graham, and Devin—for inspiring me to want to help all schools become places where I would want you to learn. Finally, a special thank-you to my wonderful partner and husband, Adam, for your support as this work unfolded in the midst of welcoming our fourth child.

—Katie Sheridan

Solution Tree Press would like to thank the following reviewers:

Denise Houghton
Director of Literacy
Park Avenue Elementary School
Stuttgart, Arkansas

Jane Losinger
Supervisor of Language Arts
Literacy
Howell Township Public Schools
Howell, New Jersey

Adrienne Wiggins
Third-Grade Teacher
Minnieville Elementary School
Woodbridge, Virginia

Visit **go.SolutionTree.com/literacy** to download the free reproducibles in this book.

TABLE OF CONTENTS

Reproducible pages are in italics.

ABOUT THE SERIES EDITORS

Mark Onuscheck is director of curriculum, instruction, and assessment at Adlai E. Stevenson High School in Lincolnshire, Illinois. He is a former English teacher and director of communication arts. As director of curriculum, instruction, and assessment, Mark works with academic divisions around professional learning, articulation, curricular and instructional revision, evaluation, assessment, social-emotional learning, technologies, and Common Core implementation. He is also an adjunct professor at DePaul University.

Mark was awarded the Quality Matters Star Rating for his work in online teaching. He helps to build curriculum and instructional practices for TimeLine Theatre's arts integration program for Chicago Public Schools. Additionally, he is a National Endowment for the Humanities grant recipient and a member of the Association for Supervision and Curriculum Development, the National Council of Teachers of English, and Learning Forward.

Mark earned a bachelor's degree in English and classical studies from Allegheny College and a master's degree in teaching English from the University of Pittsburgh.

Jeanne Spiller is assistant superintendent for teaching and learning for Kildeer Countryside Community Consolidated School District 96 in Buffalo Grove, Illinois. School District 96 is recognized on AllThingsPLC (www.AllThingsPLC.info) as one of only a small number of school districts where all schools in the district earn the distinction of model professional learning community (PLC). Jeanne's work focuses on standards-aligned instruction and assessment practices. She supports schools and districts across the United States to gain clarity about and implement the four critical questions of PLCs. She is passionate about collaborating with schools to develop systems for teaching and learning that keep the focus on student results and helping teachers determine how to approach instruction so that all students learn at high levels.

Jeanne received a 2014 Illinois Those Who Excel Award for significant contributions to the state's public and nonpublic elementary schools in administration. She is a graduate of the 2008 Learning Forward Academy, where she learned how to plan and implement professional learning that improves educator practice and increases student achievement. She has served as a classroom teacher, team leader, middle school administrator, and director of professional learning.

Jeanne earned a master's degree in educational teaching and leadership from Saint Xavier University, a master's degree in educational administration from Loyola University, Chicago, and an educational administrative superintendent endorsement from Northern Illinois University.

To learn more about Jeanne's work, visit https://livingtheplclife.com, and follow @jeeneemarie on Twitter.

To book Mark Onuscheck or Jeanne Spiller for professional development, contact pd@SolutionTree.com.

ABOUT THE AUTHORS

Sarah Gord is a reading specialist who also serves as an instructional coach at Kildeer Countryside Community Consolidated School District 96 in Chicago's northwest suburbs. In District 96, all schools in the district earn the distinction of model PLC, as recognized on AllThingsPLC (www.AllThingsPLC.info). As an instructional leader and literacy coach, Sarah focuses on curriculum design and the implementation of standards-aligned teaching and assessment practices. She supports teachers in applying the four critical questions of a Professional Learning Community (PLC) at Work® and leads professional learning focused on enhancing student achievement in the area of literacy. With more than fifteen years of experience in education, ranging from preK to eighth grade, she is passionate about and committed to helping students of all ages discover the power behind reading, writing, and communicating at high levels.

Sarah holds a bachelor's degree in English from Northern Illinois University, a master's degree in reading from Concordia University Chicago, and an additional master's degree in literacy education with an endorsement to support English learners from Northern Illinois University.

To learn more about Sarah's work, follow @SarahGord1213 on Twitter.

Kathryn E. Sheridan is the director of early literacy and language for Kildeer Countryside Community Consolidated School District 96 in Buffalo Grove, Illinois. School District 96 is recognized on AllThingsPLC (www.AllThingsPLC.info) as one of only a small number of school districts where all schools in the district earn the distinction of model PLC. Katie's work and passion center on supporting diverse learners through engaging educators in professional learning. She has experience participating in and leading the work of collaborative teams as a classroom teacher, instructional coach, middle school assistant principal, elementary school principal, and director. Katie received an Illinois Those Who Excel Award in 2008 for significant contributions to teaching and again in 2019 for contributions to the state's public and nonpublic elementary schools in administration.

Katie earned a bachelor's degree in education from the University of Illinois, a master's degree in educational leadership from National Louis University in Chicago, an educational administrative superintendent endorsement from Roosevelt University in Chicago.

To book Sarah Gord or Kathryn E. Sheridan for professional development, contact pd@SolutionTree.com.

Every Teacher Is a Literacy Teacher

The words *literacy* and *learning* possess an inseparable connection. In infancy, we learn to produce our first sounds; as toddlers, we sprawl paint across a page to communicate an idea; in elementary school, we learn the power of comprehension to unveil the essence of an author's words; in middle and high school, we learn to evaluate sources with a keen eye and construct arguments to defend our claims; and as adults, we strive to better our abilities to read widely, write clearly, and communicate articulately. In truth, the multiple facets of literacy surround all of us every day of our lives. Therefore, a literacy level that guarantees students will fully function and engage in society must be the reality for *every* student because, undeniably, illiteracy is not an option for any student. As educators, we recognize this reality and cannot afford to allow students to leave our care without guaranteeing they can read, write, and communicate as they move across grade levels.

While quality literacy instruction is critical at all grade levels, it is of particular importance in grades 2 and 3. By the end of third grade, students begin the pivotal transition from *learning to read* to *reading to learn*. They encounter complex texts with richer themes and dynamic characters and engage in *disciplinary literacy* (literacy instruction within a content area, such as science or social studies) as a way to learn about the world around them; they also learn through interdisciplinary units that classroom teachers design. Indeed, teachers in fourth grade and beyond expect students to be capable of applying strategies to independently navigate a variety of texts. But, if students' reading foundation lacks soundness, and second- and third-grade students do not receive the tools necessary for high-level comprehension, reading difficulties set in, triggering an unfortunate snowball effect that curtails individual student progress in other subject areas and later grade levels. In fact, students who are not reading proficiently by the end of third grade will struggle to comprehend as much as half the printed texts in the fourth-grade curriculum (Annie E. Casey Foundation, 2010). When readers struggle with material that is, to them, incomprehensible, they lose opportunities to gain knowledge, their confidence diminishes, and that snowball effect that began in the primary grades causes them to miss out on multiple occasions to strengthen their literacy skills.

Around age eight or nine, students begin to shape their own opinions about the subjects they study in school. They begin to recognize their personal strengths and weaknesses and become more self-aware of those skills with which they struggle, like reading and writing. When this happens, students who struggle with literacy skills may start to shut down and shy away from reading or writing, even declaring them their least favorite subjects or activities. These are the students who rarely, if ever, pick up a book unless told to; who fake reading at their desks, listlessly turning pages until the lunch bell rings; who stare at a blank page, uncertain what to write or how to craft ideas into sentences; and who tend to struggle with learning for many years to come. Research confirms that students who do not read proficiently by the end of third grade are four times more likely to drop out of high school, proving just how critical early literacy is to a student's long-term success (Hernandez 2011; Lesnick, Goerge, Smithgall, & Gwynne, 2010).

In this introduction, we consider what high-quality literacy instruction looks like in second and third grade, and we explore why this instruction needs to occur within the supportive and collaborative culture of a professional learning community (PLC). Also, we explain the structure of this book and its place in the *Every Teacher Is a Literacy Teacher* series.

What High-Quality Instruction Looks Like in Grades 2–3

Although research shows the woeful consequences of illiteracy (Cunningham & Stanovich, 1997; Dogan, Ogut & Kim, 2015; Hernandez, 2011), teams of teachers can positively counter this effect by setting high expectations and making instructional moves that assist students to rise to the rigor of grades 2 and 3 literacy. So, what exactly might one observe in a high-quality second- or third-grade literacy classroom?

Although the students who walk into the same classroom on the first day of school are roughly the same age, they have vastly different prior knowledge, skills, and interests. For this reason, it is important to assess and monitor their foundational skills. We teachers must ensure that students have a solid foundation in early literacy skills, like phonics and decoding, and we must continuously help students sharpen these skills so they can apply them independently as texts become increasingly rigorous. In teams, we must also place an instructional emphasis on fluency, knowing that fluent and accurate reading is linked to comprehension (Pikulski & Chard, 2005; Pinnell, Pikulski, Wixson, Campbell, Gough, & Beatty, 1995; Rasinski, 2014).

By second and especially third grade, we expect to listen to student readers that can proficiently read aloud with automaticity, expression and intonation, only periodically pausing to decode multisyllabic words given grade level text. With fluency as a focus, we must provide consistent opportunities for students to hear and practice what good reading sounds like. Through a variety of reading experiences, like echo reading, choral reading, partner reading, and read-alouds, teachers expose students to various genres and give them ample occasions to practice the skills they need to become fluent and confident readers.

As second- and third-grade teachers, we equip our students with the essential skills and strategies necessary for comprehension. By these middle-elementary years, students begin making more sophisticated, evidence-supported predictions and inferences from a wealth of sources. They start to study authors' craft—the words, details, purpose, strategies, and techniques authors use to develop a piece of writing. They investigate how authors support their central ideas and think critically to draw their own conclusions about a text.

Although the skills of reading fluently and making meaning are certainly essential, an integrated approach to literacy would not be complete without writing instruction. As any elementary teacher can tell you, second and third graders have vivid imaginations and rather entertaining stories to tell. Through teacher modeling and the use of mentor texts, students learn how to craft descriptive sentences and provide sensory details in a way that brings their stories to life. These learners also have some strong opinions to share! *Should second graders have a class pet? Should third graders have recess every day?* They are eager to share their opinions on these and other topics, and as we guide them through the writing process, these young authors begin to understand the power of language and written expression to convey their thoughts and ideas.

When providing high-quality literacy instruction, educators should teach reading and writing together and do so with an interdisciplinary mindset. There is an interconnectedness between the two that supports literacy development in students, and it is present not just in English language arts (ELA) but in every academic content area, from how students read and understand a story problem in mathematics to how they write notes about a science lab experiment. In their report *Writing to Read*, Steve Graham and Michael Hebert (2010) affirm the findings of multiple research-backed resources on the interrelated benefits of reading and writing. They maintain that writing has the potential to improve students' reading in three ways.

1. **Reading and writing are both functional activities:** Students combine these skills to accomplish specific goals, such as learning new ideas from a text and describing that learning (Fitzgerald & Shanahan, 2000). For instance, writing about information in a science text should facilitate comprehension and learning, as it provides the reader with a means for recording, connecting, analyzing, personalizing, and manipulating key ideas from the text.

2. **Reading and writing are connected:** Because they draw on common knowledge and cognitive processes (Shanahan, 2006), when students improve their writing skills, they simultaneously improve their reading skills.

3. **Reading and writing are both communication activities:** When writers create text, they gain insights about what they read. This deepens their comprehension (Tierney & Shanahan, 1991).

Just as critical to student success as reading and writing is the ongoing development of speaking and listening skills throughout literacy instruction. Daily academic discourse helps strengthen students' communication skills while embedding critical time for oral processing. As they share their knowledge and thinking with a partner or small group, students learn to organize and articulate ideas while gaining new insights from their peers. As added benefits, routine speaking and listening experiences enhance vocabulary knowledge, improve writing skills, and increase language development for all students, especially for students learning a new language. Indeed, as the National Governors Association Center for Best Practices and the Council of Chief State School Officers (NGA & CCSSO, n.d.a) state:

> Oral language development precedes and is the foundation for written language development; in other words, oral language is primary and written language builds on it. Children's oral language competence is strongly predictive of their facility in learning to read and write. (p. 26)

With this in mind, we teachers must constantly embed opportunities for students to think aloud about text that they read and rehearse or refine ideas that they plan to write about. To develop strong readers and writers, we have to engage and develop all four language domains the Common Core State Standards (CCSS) for English language arts identify: (1) Reading, (2) Writing, (3) Speaking and Listening, and (4) Language.

During instruction, let's not forget about the pervasive nature of technology at students' literal fingertips. As members of a digital world and as educators, we must provide high-quality literacy instruction to support students in utilizing technology for multiple realistic purposes. In "Why Personalized Learning Requires Technology and Thinking Humans," founder and CEO of ThinkCERCA Eileen Murphy Buckley (n.d.) writes:

> Let's face it, even the most basic Google search requires productive struggle and persistence. Eventually we will send our students out into the wild, where newspapers of record, college courses, bosses and colleagues, and increasingly, health care providers, bankers, and others will not provide them with accessible texts. Our grown-up students will be required to write evidence-based arguments in emails related to things like insurance or child care.

Further, not only do students need to learn how to appropriately find, comprehend, and evaluate digital resources, they must also understand the power and learning that come from their interaction with the information. It is the obligation of every teacher to ensure that students function at high literacy levels and learn to appropriately navigate complex digital and printed texts to prepare them for their pursuits in secondary school and beyond.

Second- and third-grade educators pave the way for future success and open new worlds for their students, especially in the area of literacy. They demonstrate how learners can visualize books, like animated movies inside their heads. They reveal how authors write for a specific purpose and use the power of language to express all kinds of important messages. They teach what good readers do when they get stuck because a particular sentence is not making much sense. Above all else, they teach with a passion and enthusiasm for literacy that models for students just how important and awesome it is to be skilled readers and writers.

The Value of the PLC Process in Literacy

As teachers, we must possess a repertoire of instructional strategies to build on the strengths and address the needs of a richly diverse classroom of students who have a range of reading, writing, speaking, and listening capabilities. The reality is that teachers rarely have all the skills, knowledge, and time necessary to meet the wide-ranging demands of literacy on their own. This complex and important process of teaching students literacy becomes more manageable and tangible as educators engage in the process together. Therefore, it truly makes a positive difference for all learners if collaborative teams effectively contribute to teachers making meaningful changes in classroom practices. When we integrate high-quality literacy instruction within the collective efforts representative of a PLC, literacy learning soars to new levels.

Those familiar with PLC culture know that the foundation of a PLC's work is built on three distinct big ideas: (1) a focus on student learning, (2) a collaborative culture and collective responsibility, and (3) a results orientation (DuFour, DuFour, Eaker, Many, & Mattos, 2016). Four critical questions guide educators as they collaborate to provide quality instruction for all learners (DuFour et al., 2016).

1. What is it we want our students to learn?

2. How will we know if each student has learned it?

3. How will we respond when some students don't learn it?

4. How can we extend and enrich the learning for students who have demonstrated proficiency?

The About This Book section (page 8) explains how the chapters and team action steps in this book align with these critical questions.

Within a PLC, teachers are organized into collaborative teams that "work interdependently to achieve common goals for which members are mutually accountable" (DuFour et al., 2016, p. 12). Together, they come to a clear understanding of the essential literacy skills that all students should know and be able to do, and they design assessments that align with the learning outcomes. They collaborate around sound instructional practices, sharing strategies that proved successful, and work as a team to develop differentiated lessons along the way. Further, they openly discuss and analyze student data as a way to make informed instructional decisions to move students' learning forward.

This book provides resources and tools to accomplish these critical tasks so teams can operate effectively and maximize their collective strengths in the service of students. Through these collective efforts, teachers establish a guaranteed and viable curriculum that ensures equal opportunities to learn. Thus, students are guaranteed access to the same content, knowledge, and skills, regardless of their teacher (Marzano, 2003). Put plainly, teachers within a PLC work *together* to ensure that every student, in every classroom, receives what he or she needs to master essential skills and pave the way for a promising future.

With collaboration as one of the three big ideas of a PLC, a concerted effort is no doubt essential. But what happens when you are the sole literacy teacher at your grade level? We often refer to these teachers as *singletons*—the one second- or third-grade teacher in an elementary school, for example. In these situations, it is important to collaborate with other professionals who can help support and guide you through the work of the PLC process. In many cases, a teacher from the preceding or following grade level can become a great working partner, as he or she has a wealth of knowledge about the skills students have acquired or will need to acquire for the next school year. Grade-level partners who teach other content areas can also be helpful as you work collaboratively to provide a guaranteed and viable curriculum for every student in every classroom across the school. Finally, take advantage of an online, interconnected world and reach out to grade-level teachers in other districts. Use technology to collaborate as you do the work of ensuring a consistent and viable literacy-focused curriculum.

When teachers collaborate to teach students literacy skills, the learning process becomes more manageable and tangible.

About This Series

This book is part of the *Every Teacher Is a Literacy Teacher* series, which provides guidance on literacy-focused instruction and classroom strategies for grades preK–12. The elementary segment of this series includes separate titles focused on instruction in grades preK–1, grades 2–3, and grades 4–5. While each of these books follows a similar approach and structure, the content and examples these books include address the discrete demands of each grade-level band. All the chapters are dedicated to the steps collaborative teams must take before engaging in instruction to ensure clarity about standards, assessment, learning progressions, mastery expectations, interventions, gradual release of responsibility, use of instructional time, instructional strategies, and diversity and equity. Each chapter also includes specific collaborative team exercises, paving the way for teams to engage in the work that the chapter describes.

The various secondary school books in this series each feature classroom literacy strategies for a subject area in grades 6–12, such as science or ELA. The expert educators writing these secondary-level books approach literacy in varying and innovative ways and examine the role every teacher must play in support-ing students' literacy development in all subject areas throughout their grades 6–12 schooling.

Woven throughout each book is the idea that collaboration plays a crucial role in the success of any school dedicated to building effective teams in a PLC culture. When experts collaborate, innovative ideas emerge in ways that support student learning and generate positive results. Further, schools that invest in a PLC cul-ture work in more unified and cohesive ways, prioritizing concerns and working together to innovate positive changes. In this series, we are excited to share ways a PLC can function to radiate change when thoughtful educators dedicate them-selves to supporting the literacy development of all students.

About This Book

We constructed this book to assist schools, and, more specifically, collaborative teams within a school, to design standards-aligned instruction, assessment, and intervention that support the literacy development of all students. We've focused it through the lens of PLC culture, with each of the first five chapters centered on how collaborative teams may begin to answer one or more of the four critical questions that drive the first big idea—a focus on learning (DuFour et al., 2016).

Chapter 1 addresses what collaborative teams want students to learn by intro-ducing the pre-unit protocol (PREP). This protocol assists teams in gaining clarity about student learning expectations before beginning a unit of instruction.

Chapters 2–4 address how teams can know what learning has taken place. Chapter 2 reviews the myriad assessment types, including how teams ensure a literacy focus. It features an example unit assessment continuum and ways teachers may use each type of assessment within a unit of instruction. Chapter 3 offers a process for creating an instructional learning progression for each learning stan-dard a team identified using PREP. The learning progression assists teams in the development of learning target–aligned assessments and high-quality instruction. Chapter 4 considers student proficiency, the various rubric types, rubric develop-ment, student checklists, and collaborative scoring.

Chapter 5 addresses how teams use data and determine next steps to support students who haven't achieved mastery or to extend learning for those who have. The chapter focuses on the data-inquiry process, scaffolded instruction, and exten-sion opportunities.

In chapters 6–9, we address instructional processes connected to literacy. Topics include using the gradual release of responsibility instructional framework (chapter 6), planning high-quality literacy instruction within the literacy block (chapter 7), selecting appropriate instructional strategies to facilitate high-quality literacy instruction (chapter 8), and considering diversity and equity in literacy instruction (chapter 9).

We also include an array of useful resources in this book's appendices. Appendix A consists of a variety of reproducible versions of tools from the book, including the PREP template. Appendix B expands on chapter 1's content related to priority standards by providing an effective process that teams can use to determine them. Appendix C offers extended details on Norman Webb's (1997, 1999) Depth of Knowledge (DOK) levels, which we introduce in chapter 1. Appendix D includes extra information about developing essential understandings and guiding questions when filling out the PREP template. Finally, appendix E provides a list of the figures and tables featured throughout the book.

The place to begin is gaining clarity as a team about what your students should know and be able to do. This is why, in chapter 1, we provide teacher teams with tools to arrive at a collective understanding of the literacy standards and the specific learning outcomes necessary for proficiency in grades 2 and 3. We provide a process to help your team examine and unwrap (also called *unpack*) the standards, and we share strategies for focusing conversations as you dig into the often complicated and ambiguous wording of your literacy standards. The critical work you do in chapter 1 will set the foundation for establishing a rich and robust plan for quality literacy instruction and assessment.

CHAPTER 1

Establish Clarity About Student Learning Expectations

The PLC process asserts that each student is entitled to a guaranteed and viable curriculum (DuFour et al., 2016; Marzano, 2003). *Guaranteed* expressly stipulates that schools grant all students the opportunity to learn a core curriculum to position them for success. To deliver this guaranteed curriculum, schools must ensure the curriculum is *viable*, meaning that schools ensure the necessary time is available as well as protected. With a deficit in students who excel in literacy, and by virtue of literacy contributing to lifelong success, there is a strong case for safeguarding essential literacy skills as guaranteed and viable.

The interesting challenge of setting learning expectations in second and third grade is maintaining consistent rigor for students across classrooms. As we established in the introduction, this is the critical juncture in which we support our students in moving from learning to read to reading to learn. It is imperative that collaborative teams have consistent expectations for students in terms of the standards, expectations for rigor relative to student performance, and achievement. As we work to transition students to read to learn, no student can lack in necessary and essential reading and writing skills that enable them to be independent learners.

The first critical question that drives the work of a PLC aligns with this promise by asking, *What is it we want our students to learn?* (DuFour et al., 2016). Put another way, *What do we want students to know and be able to do?* With regard to teaching literacy, this critical question means, for example, that before introducing a complex text, launching into a writing activity, or conducting an assessment, teacher teams must interpret language arts standards in the same way and use them to guide a robust and rigorous instruction and assessment plan. If teachers do not work together to analyze literacy standards and reach consensus on what each one means across the strands, they will not afford students access to the same content, knowledge, and skills. In essence, any lack of clarity we have as educators interferes with students' access to a guaranteed and viable curriculum.

Answering this first critical question requires careful consideration of the following components that work together to guide any effective instruction and assessment plan; in this text, we apply them to support students' literacy advancement.

- Standards
- Knowledge
- Skills
- Depth of knowledge
- Learning targets

To address these key components, teams of teachers must collaborate to become completely clear about the specific knowledge and skills that all students must know and be able to do by the end of a particular unit. Further, teachers need to balance designing instruction for the acquisition of foundational skills that enable students to crack the code and the acquisition of comprehension or analytic skills that give students the ability to digest and learn from text. To support this endeavor, we propose teams follow a pre-unit protocol (PREP) that they begin at least a week or more prior to instruction for a unit.

In this chapter, we take you through the six-step PREP process using the example of a third-grade unit titled Exploring Elements of Fiction. We use this unit as our core example throughout this book because it effectively illustrates a successful implementation of both reading and writing standards. Throughout this comprehensive unit, students utilize complex third-grade texts to examine elements of literature, such as plot, setting, character, and central message. Although our model details an ELA-focused example, teams can use this protocol with any unit of instruction across disciplines. Using it, they can identify the inherent literacy skills embedded in other content standards as unwritten expectations to demonstrate proficiency of learning. Teams can and should use this protocol for interdisciplinary units as well as to establish the essential elements of a unit of instruction that includes standards from multiple disciplines or content areas.

This chapter begins with an overview of the PREP steps and template and continues with a deep explanation of each step in the process.

PREP Process Steps

The PREP process features six steps we established to ensure teams accurately understand and unwrap the most important standards present in a unit of instruction, particularly those tied to literacy. This way, team members have a collective sense of the critical knowledge and skills that make up each standard. The six steps of the PREP process are as follows.

1. Enter unit standards onto the PREP template.

2. Indicate (or determine) priority standards.

3. Unwrap unit priority standards.

4. Identify knowledge items.

5. Determine skills.

6. Assign levels of rigor for learning targets.

When applying this process, teams can use the explanations and examples articulated in this chapter as tools to learn the significance of each component. Teams inclined to extend this process beyond the six steps can also build essential understandings and guiding questions. *Essential understandings* crystallize and articulate conceptual thinking for teachers to guide curriculum design more deeply, and *guiding questions* set the purpose for students' learning. For thorough definitions and rationales of these latter two components and information on where they reside within curriculum design, read appendix D (page 267).

Because mandated district, state, provincial, and national content-area standards can be complex and often lead to various interpretations among educators, adhering to this process protects student learning by establishing distinct expectations for learners across all grade-level classrooms. Participating in this protocol also sets the groundwork for subsequent collaborative efforts—building common assessments, critiquing the efficacy of existing units, and designing new lessons that guide students toward mastery of each learning standard.

Before beginning a unit of instruction, teacher teams must establish collective clarity around targeted literacy standards, which are the outcomes of instruction and expectations for student learning. It is most effective to accomplish this using a template that organizes priority standards, core learning strands, and ideas for unwrapped standards, key knowledge, and important skills.

Figure 1.1 features a completed PREP template. It displays the unit standards and priority standards for the Exploring Elements of Fiction unit, and it breaks down the specific knowledge and skills that our team wanted students to know and be able to use by the end of the four-week instructional period. (See page 246 for a blank reproducible version of this template.) Although it lists third-grade literacy standards, second-grade teachers can use this template and adjust to include their grade-level standards. Or they could adapt it to identify literacy-focused concepts and plan instructional units for content areas not traditionally associated with literacy instruction, such as science and mathematics.

Most likely, you have questions about the details and components in this protocol. In the following sections, we break it down piece by piece and explain how this protocol organizes and simplifies the process for teams to unlock the literacy content inherent in their curriculum. However, let's first examine the purpose of using this protocol.

Myriad knowledge and skills reside within a single standard. In an instructional unit that consists of multiple standards spanning more than one academic discipline and requiring literacy skills in a variety of contexts, the skill demands multiply. Taking a deep dive into a unit through the PREP process, grade-level teams can fully define and understand the nuanced standards most essential to a student's academic success. This allows the teams to establish a clear and consistent vision for student learning throughout the unit, one that includes an emphasis on core literacy skills. To honor the importance of identifying literacy-focused learning outcomes to steer instruction and assessment, teams engage in the PREP process so they can distinguish and unwrap essential learning standards and determine the knowledge and skills students must acquire.

A benefit of using this template is the way it facilitates teams' chunking curriculum content. In *The New Art and Science of Teaching*, Robert Marzano (2017) emphasizes that teachers need to chunk content when teaching new information. Breaking hefty content into digestible pieces helps students learn since they "can hold only small amounts of information in their working memories" (p. 30). This process also facilitates teams constructing a clear road map when creating learning progressions (see chapter 3, page 61) that empower them to select those important steps, thus creating chunks of comprehensible learning opportunities for students.

The following sections use the example unit articulated in figure 1.1 to detail the six steps in the PREP process.

Unit: Exploring Elements of Fiction | **Time Frame:** Four weeks | **Grade:** 3

Unit Standards (Priority standards are in bold and italic typeface.)

Strand: Reading Literature

- Ask and answer questions to demonstrate understanding of a text, referring explicitly to the text as the basis for the answers. (RL.3.1)

- *Recount stories, including fables, folktales, and myths from diverse cultures; determine the central message, lesson, or moral and explain how it is conveyed through key details in the text. (RL.3.2)*

- *Describe characters in a story (e.g., their traits, motivations, or feelings) and explain how their actions contribute to the sequence of events. (RL.3.3)*

Strand: Reading: Foundational Skills

- Know and apply grade-level phonics and word analysis skills in decoding words. (RF.3.3)

  • Identify and know the meaning of the most common prefixes and derivational suffixes. (RF.3.3a)

- *Read with sufficient accuracy and fluency to support comprehension. (RF.3.4)*

Strand: Writing

- Write informative/explanatory texts to examine a topic and convey ideas and information clearly. (W.3.2)

  • *Introduce a topic and group related information together; include illustrations when useful to aiding comprehension. (W.3.2a)*

  • Develop the topic with facts, definitions, and details. (W.3.2b)

Strand: Language

- Determine or clarify the meaning of unknown and multiple-meaning words and phrases based on grade 3 reading and content, choosing flexibly from a range of strategies. (L.3.4)

  • Use sentence-level context as a clue to the meaning of a word or phrase. (L.3.4a)

Figure 1.1: PREP example for grade 3—Exploring Elements of Fiction unit.

continued →

Unwrapped Unit Priority Standards	Knowledge Items	Skills (Learning Targets and DOK Levels)
RL.3.2: RECOUNT <u>stories</u>, including fables, folktales, and myths from diverse cultures; DETERMINE the <u>central message, lesson, or moral</u> and EXPLAIN <u>how it is conveyed through key details in the text.</u>	Stories consist of key elements like characters, setting, and plot. A recount is a recap of the key events and details in a text. The central message, lesson, or moral is what the author wants the reader to learn or understand from the story.	Recount the key events and details in a story. (DOK 1) Determine a central message, lesson, or moral. (DOK 3) Explain how key details convey a central message, lesson, or moral. (DOK 3)
RL.3.3: DESCRIBE <u>characters</u> in a story (e.g., their traits, motivations, or feelings) and EXPLAIN <u>how their actions contribute to the sequence of events.</u>	Traits are words used to describe a character. Motivation is the reason why a character acts a certain way. Characters' feelings and emotions are expressed through details in a text. Plot is the sequence of events in a story. Plot development is affected by the characters and their actions.	Describe characters by their traits, motivations, and feelings. (DOK 2) Explain how characters' actions contribute to the sequence of events. (DOK 3)
RF.3.4: READ with sufficient <u>accuracy and fluency</u> to support comprehension.	Reading smoothly helps a reader to make meaning End marks and punctuation give signals to the reader. Lines in poems require unique phrasing depending on the poem's structure.	Decode text to read words and make meaning. (DOK 2) Use context to make meaning of words and sentences. (DOK 2) Read with appropriate intonation, phrasing, and expression. (DOK 2)
W.3.2a: INTRODUCE a <u>topic</u> and GROUP <u>related information together</u>, include illustrations when useful to aiding comprehension.	Writers begin with topic sentences. Opening techniques include fact, quote, description, startling statement, and personal connection. There are a variety of organizational structures for writing that work to convey overall meaning.	Construct a topic sentence that states the main topic of the written task. (DOK 4) Organize details by logically grouping like information. (DOK 3)

Source for standards: NGA & CCSSO, 2010.

Enter Unit Standards Onto the PREP Template

At the start of the process, an essential part of a team's discussions centers on the targeted standards for a unit of study. A *unit* is a subdivision of instruction within a subject matter and, in second and third grade, might be interdisciplinary; it entails a series of standards-based interconnected lessons that share a common focus. For example, within ELA, teachers might conduct a narrative unit in which students read various fictional pieces and write their own stories or alternate endings to stories they have read. In social studies, teachers might introduce a thematic unit, such as one on community workers or conflict and cooperation.

Unit lengths vary from a mini-unit that can span a few days or a week to a comprehensive unit of perhaps eight weeks. During a unit, teacher teams conduct various formative and summative assessments that measure students' understanding of each standard in the unit. (For further information, see the discussion about assessments in chapter 2, page 39.) As specified in figure 1.1 (page 15), our third-grade team anticipated the Exploring Elements of Fiction unit lasting about four weeks.

To begin the first step, teams identify every standard they will address throughout a unit of instruction. Teams can determine the exact compilation of standards that compose a literacy unit of instruction by accessing teaching resources, like a literature textbook or packaged curriculum, referring to a curriculum-mapping or curriculum-pacing document, or designing their own unit. If the district or school has purchased a reading or writing program or textbook from a publisher, the content standards are typically indicated within the resource, which is organized by units or modules. When using a purchased program, teams should still review the standards to ensure which ones and how many are appropriate. Keep in mind that publishers often list more standards than teachers might address in any given unit.

In another scenario, some schools and districts have designed curriculum maps that outline the standards for a unit or cycle of instruction. If this is the case, teams use these standards. Or, teacher teams sometimes tap their collective professional expertise to design their own units of instruction and determine pertinent standards for the targeted unit. Whichever approach teams take—sometimes blending use of published resources, curriculum maps, and teacher-developed materials— identifying standards represents their initial step so that clarity about what students need to know and do to be proficient by unit's end guides the entire process.

Be cautious not to skip any steps, such as identifying knowledge items or determining skills, when transferring standards from a district or school list or from a purchased program. When educators use various resources to teach, such as published reading and writing programs, district curriculum materials, and teacher-generated units, teacher teams might conclude that because the curriculum is spelled out, these steps are unnecessary. However, the explicit and implicit skills embedded *within* the learning standards are what drive a well-designed and robust instructional plan and accompanying assessments, so teams must examine each learning standard and come to a collective agreement on its precise meaning and implications for instruction.

The sample PREP template (figure 1.1, page 15) contains the learning standards for a third-grade literacy unit on elements of fiction. It includes the CCSS for English language arts and is composed of the following three literacy strands: (1) Reading, (2) Writing, and (3) Language. If teams were using this template for interdisciplinary purposes, such as to identify literacy-critical aspects of a unit, including science and social studies content, they might identify one or more of these literacy-focused strands as crucial aspects of learning about, for example, weather and climate and their effects on society. Although we have used the CCSS to model the six-step process in this chapter, teams can complete the process using national, state, provincial, or school standards that they are obligated to implement.

It can seem overwhelming to consider teaching all the standards in a limited time due to their sheer number. Therefore, teams may feel compelled to prioritize the standards, choosing only those that are absolutely essential for students to learn. (Note the bold-italic text in the first section of figure 1.1, which signifies the prioritized standards.) Step 2 of this process will address these concerns. For now, teams enter *all* standards pertaining to a specific unit so they have a clear and comprehensive picture of the overall expected learning outcomes.

In looking at the sample template, you'll also notice that some standards are written as general learning goals with more granular standards beneath them. These granular standards provide more detailed expectations of student learning in relation to the overarching goal. Take, for example, the standard for writing W.3.2: "Write informative/explanatory texts to examine a topic and convey ideas and information clearly" (NGA & CCSSO, 2010). Although this is the general learning goal for this standard, we've listed two additional detailed standards, W.3.2a and W.3.2b, that specifically break down the targeted skills students need to master the overall standard. Our team of third-grade teachers chose to enter both the general standards and the specific granular standards into the template because we felt it was important for our team to access both the overall learning standards and the more granular standards as it worked through this six-step process.

EXERCISE
Enter Unit Standards Onto the PREP Template

To prepare for the six-step process, use a blank PREP template (page 246 and downloadable from **go.SolutionTree.com/literacy**) to input the entire set of standards for a unit your team has targeted. As your team reads about each step throughout this chapter, it may stop to participate in the included exercises and return to this template to record more information. Alternatively, your team can read the entire chapter and then work on all exercises in a fluid fashion.

Use the following questions to guide this exercise.

★ How can we work as a collaborative team to initiate and proceed with the steps outlined in this chapter?

★ Which roles will each of us assume to organize and complete work? For example, who will prepare the template? Which of us will be the note-taker? Who will reach out to others, such as special educators, to be sure they are included in the grade-level work?

★ If you are in a situation where you do not have a collaborative team in your building or district (you are a singleton teacher), who can you reach out to from another school or district? What opportunities exist to vertically articulate within your own school to create cohesion in expectations for students?

Indicate (or Determine) Priority Standards

So much to teach and not enough time. This seems to be a universal concern for teachers across all grade levels. With dozens of standards to address, a multitude of essential skills for students to learn, a sea of rich texts to introduce, and an array of lessons to deliver, one question lingers in the minds of educators everywhere: *How do I fit it all in?*

How to allot instructional time for every standard is a real concern. As second- and third-grade teachers race to cover the seemingly endless curriculum each school year, they soon realize that the race often does more harm than good. They may be running the distance, covering a lot of ground, particularly with reading and writing lessons, but their instruction lacks the depth needed to make real progress with their young readers and writers. So, although we'd love to say that we can most definitely and easily fit in every standard (and its embedded concepts and skills), the honest answer is we simply cannot—at least not with the fidelity and detailed attention required to make a significant impact on our students' learning.

Once teams enter all unit standards onto the PREP template, the critical next step involves indicating which of these standards qualify as priority standards—that is, the standards that are most vital for students to learn (DuFour et al., 2016). Note that some refer to priority standards as *power standards* or *essential standards* (Crawford, 2011); these are all interchangeable terms. Priority standards then become the basis for instruction. Teachers hold students accountable for learning priority standards as they emphasize these standards during instruction, design formal assessments around them, and plan interventions to ensure opportunities for all students to reach the expected outcomes. Other standards in the unit move to a more supporting role.

If your team has already identified grade-level priority standards for a unit of instruction, simply identify them on the PREP template by marking them in a way that sets them apart from nonpriority standards, such as through highlighting, bolding, underlining, or using a unique color. If your team hasn't yet identified these standards, it should carefully look at all the learning standards, combing through the precise language and identifying those that most significantly impact students' learning. The number of priority standards a team selects can vary depending on the number of calendar days teams allot for a unit; however, a specific number is not the place to start. Applying specific criteria for selection is the place to begin, which we address next. DuFour et al. (2016) write of standards prioritization:

> The process of prioritizing the standards has significant benefits. It creates greater clarity about what teachers will teach, which in turn, promotes more efficient planning and sharing of resources. Perhaps the greatest benefit of prioritizing the standards is that it encourages teachers to embrace more in-depth instruction by reducing the pressure to simply cover the material. (p. 117)

Collaborative teams within a PLC adopt a collective understanding of the priority standards most essential for students to master. However, with so many complex standards in a unit, how do teachers determine which standards to prioritize? Also, since English language arts standards encompass a multitude of expectations within the strands of reading, writing, speaking, listening, and language, how will teams identify literacy-critical aspects of these standards? To make this important decision, teams consider three key factors: (1) endurance, (2) leverage, and (3) readiness (Ainsworth & Viegut, 2015; Bailey, Jakicic, & Spiller, 2014; Reeves, 2002;). Additionally, they take into account the knowledge necessary for high-stakes exams. If your team has yet to establish priority standards for a unit, work together to review the following criteria that define the critical factors. (For more guidance, refer to the process for prioritizing standards in appendix B, page 257.)

▸ **Does the standard have *endurance*?** Are the skills and knowledge embedded in the standard critical for students to remember beyond the course or unit in which they are taught? For example, the ability to coherently summarize complex text is a skill that extends beyond a particular unit of instruction. Teachers expect students to be able to summarize key details from their reading throughout high school and even into their professional careers. To summarize is, therefore, an enduring skill worth teaching in grades 2–3.

▸ **Does the standard have *leverage*?** Are the skills and knowledge in the standard applicable across several disciplines? For example, summarizing complex text might be taught in language arts when students experience a literary work, but it is equally valuable when reading content in social studies and science. If the skills embedded in a standard are interdisciplinary—that is, if the skills have value in more than one content area—the standard has leverage and should become a priority.

▸ **Is the standard needed for student *readiness*?** Does the standard include prerequisite skills and knowledge necessary to prepare students for the next grade? For example, when students learn the structure and elements of an opinion paper, it equips them with the skills they need to tackle the more rigorous work of argumentation writing. Therefore, when prioritizing standards, consider the progression of skills from one grade level to the next, and choose those that build the foundation for future learning.

▸ **Is the standard needed for *high-stakes exams*?** Do students need to know and apply the skills and knowledge of the standard on external exams? For example, district, state or provincial, college, or vocational exams might include questions or writing prompts geared to this standard. Teachers should take this into consideration when discussing which standards are necessary for student preparedness.

To return to the example in figure 1.1 (page 15), bold-italic typeface indicates priority standards. While our team's unit encompassed three standards in the Reading Literature strand, we treated only two of those reading standards as priority standards. After thoughtful conversations on the endurance, leverage, and readiness of each reading standard, our team decided that targets RL.3.2 and RL.3.3 had the most impact on student achievement and lifelong learning. For example, during the discussions, one team member recognized how these two reading standards focus on strengthening students' basic reading comprehension, which leads to deeper analysis of texts down the road. She posited that these two standards meet the criteria for endurance, leverage, and readiness because they establish a foundation for comprehending fiction. Likewise, the team agreed that question items on high-stakes exams often assess the key literary ideas addressed in these standards.

Take standard RL.3.2, for instance: "Recount stories, including fables, folktales, and myths from diverse cultures; determine the central message, lesson, or moral and explain how it is conveyed through key details in the text" (NGA & CCSSO, 2010). This standard has endurance in that students must be able to recount the significant details of a text and determine an overarching theme throughout their educational careers (and beyond). In examining the progression of the CCSS, we recognized that the standards expect students to determine literary texts' themes at every successive grade level.

Similarly, this standard is necessary for student readiness, as the skills embedded within it prepare students for the next level of learning. In looking ahead at the standard RL.4.9, we found that fourth-grade students are expected to "compare and contrast the treatment of similar themes and topics (e.g., opposition of good and evil) and patterns of events (e.g., the quest) in stories, myths, and traditional literature from different cultures" (NGA & CCSSO, 2010). Certainly, students will likely struggle with the more complex skill of comparing and contrasting the treatments of themes across genres without first mastering the skills embedded in the third-grade standard RL.3.2.

Finally, our team had a conversation about standard RL.3.2's leverage, which sparked compelling questions and considerations: What value does this standard bring to other disciplines? Is it a universal skill that has the leverage to impact a student's overall academic success? While teachers noted that other academic disciplines, such as science and social studies, typically require reading skills to comprehend informational texts, they all noted that while this is a literature standard, the skills embedded also transcend to application with informational text as well. Therefore, they looked at the Reading: Informational Text standard under the same anchor (RI.3.2) to learn that standard states, "Determine the main idea of a text; recount the key details and explain how they support the main idea" (NGA & CCSSO, 2010). Therefore, when considering RL.3.2 for this fiction unit, the team concluded that, through it, students will acquire many of the skills they would also need to tackle informational text, such as reading closely to identify key details. This gives the standard leverage, and RL.3.2 became a priority standard for this unit of instruction.

As our team progressed through the prioritization process, an insightful dialogue emerged over writing target W.3.2a: "Introduce a topic and group related information together; include illustrations when useful to aiding comprehension" (NGA & CCSSO, 2010). The team unanimously agreed that introducing a topic and grouping related information are essential writing skills that meet the requirements of endurance, leverage, and readiness. However, after careful discussion, our team determined the standard's second half—which calls on students to utilize illustrations in their writing tasks—should not be all inclusive. While illustrations could certainly enhance a student's written expression and might even be a necessary scaffold for some students who need extra support with writing, they do not need to be present at all times in third grade. So, the team made a commitment to be clear that they are not looking for illustrations with every writing sample.

In almost all cases, teams will address all standards during the school year throughout the various units of instruction in which they apply. However, standards the team does not identify as priorities for a unit move to a supporting role that connects to or enhances the priority standards. "They are taught within the context of the priority standards, but do not receive the same degree of instruction and assessment emphasis as do the priority standards" (Ainsworth, 2013, p. xv). (You can learn more about this identification process in appendix B, page 257.) Supporting standards can, and often do, become priority standards later in the year. This most often occurs when teams do not emphasize a particular standard during initial units of study but then make it a primary focus for instruction and assessment during subsequent units.

After determining priority standards for the target unit, the team then unwraps these standards to examine the specific knowledge and skills embedded within each one. This helps teams develop assessments and design instruction.

EXERCISE

Indicate (or Determine) Priority Standards

Review the standards you entered onto the PREP template. If your team has already undergone a process for prioritizing them, merely distinguish priority standards from supporting standards by bolding, underlining, or color-coding them. If, however, your team has not yet prioritized standards, use the suggestions from this section along with the process articulated in appendix B (page 257) to do so. Then, return to the PREP template and mark the priority standards.

Use the following questions to guide this exercise.

★ Which standards will we deem priority; that is, which standards meet the criteria for endurance, leverage, and readiness to support students' academic and lifelong success?

★ Which priority standards are appropriate for our targeted unit of study?

★ Are all team members clear that we will be held accountable for students learning the priority standards? Are priority standards the focus for our teaching, assessment, and intervention?

★ Which standards serve as supporting standards and, as such, are subsumed under priority standards? Which priority standards subsume them?

★ Are there supporting standards that will become priority standards in a later unit?

Unwrap Unit Priority Standards

A common misconception among many teacher teams is that listing unit standards sufficiently represents the basis for all instructional decisions moving forward. One might think, *I've got a list of standards right here, so I'm ready to teach.* However, this is not the case. To fully understand each standard and guarantee a consistent curriculum for grades 2–3 classrooms, teams of teachers must examine each content-area standard and arrive at a collective agreement about its precise meaning and implications for instruction and assessment. When teachers do this, they will see standards are complex; many implicit knowledge items and skills are embedded in the standards. They will also notice that they may interpret standards differently. For example, the standard RL.3.1 refers to asking and answering questions, which is also the case for the second-grade standard and for the equivalent standards for reading informational texts. Initially, our team saw this as a standard to prioritize because it is a key reading strategy. However, once we unwrapped it (as explained in this section), we realized that skill is also embedded in many other, potentially more rigorous standards. Students frequently ask questions to comprehend a variety of texts, and they answer a number of text-based questions through formal and informal assessments during a unit. Therefore that skill is explicitly being taught and assessed through other avenues. As a result, we did not prioritize it.

When teams participate in the process of *unwrapping* (what some educators refer to as *unpacking*) standards, they critically examine and parse the words of a standard. By utilizing this strategy, teams can reveal fine-grain learning targets embedded within a standard to guide quality instruction, with an emphasis on literacy, and better support students' efforts to master that targeted standard. In *Simplifying Common Assessment*, Kim Bailey and Chris Jakicic (2017) write:

> The goal of the unwrapping process is twofold: first, to build shared or collective understanding of what the standard asks students to know and do; and second, to identify the smaller increments of learning, or learning targets, that will create a step-by-step path leading to that standard. (p. 21)

To give credence to unwrapping and to provide teachers with an authentic reason for participating in this critical step, teams talk about how they teach to a standard and what evidence of learning they ask students to produce. For example, prior to a team meeting, the three members of our third-grade team each located a student work sample from their respective classroom that they believed demonstrated a student's mastery of standard RL.3.3: "Describe characters in a story (e.g., their traits, motivations, or feelings) and explain how their actions contribute to the sequence of events" (NGA & CCSSO, 2010). The team's goal is to make sure all three members have the same interpretation and expectation of the standard. The following list details the student artifacts that each teacher brings to the team meeting.

▶ Teacher A presents a student work sample in which the student circled adjectives from a provided list to describe a story's main character. At the bottom of the page, the student wrote a one-sentence explanation of why she selected two of the character traits.

▶ Teacher B presents a paragraph that a student wrote to answer the following open-ended constructed-response question: *Choose a character from the story. Describe the character by his or her traits, feelings, and motivations. Then, explain how the character's actions contribute to the sequence of events.*

▶ Teacher C presents two separate student artifacts. The first artifact is a student drawing of a character from a story. Around the illustration, the student wrote adjectives that describe the character. The second artifact is a sequencing graphic organizer in which the student sequentially recorded events from the story.

All three examples are related to the overall reading standard, yet they do not all have the same rigor or require students to apply their thinking to the same depth. The following list examines the teacher-created assignments that led to these artifacts.

▶ Teacher A gave students a list of character traits from which to select appropriate responses; they did not need to name a trait on their own. Students explained why they chose certain traits from the list, but the assignment did not require students to demonstrate an understanding of how characters' actions affect the sequence of events.

▶ Teacher B required students to demonstrate proficiency at a rigorous level, as they constructed meaning on their own and crafted a paragraph to express their thinking. The writing prompt addressed both skills within the overall reading standard.

▶ Teacher C's samples show the teacher strongly intended for students to hit the standard's rigor but did not require students to synthesize their learning and demonstrate how a character impacts the sequence of events. The illustration and graphic organizer reflect student thinking in relation to the standard, but do not match the standard's rigor, which is a common misstep.

As you can see, the teachers had very different interpretations of the standard, and very different expectations of what students must do to demonstrate mastery.

By unwrapping standards, teachers on a team avoid translating and teaching a standard in their own highly variable ways. Rather, they ensure that team members will apply a more consistent approach to teaching and assessing student proficiency.

To unwrap a standard, teams can annotate the standard using a protocol like the one in figure 1.2. (See page 249 for a blank reproducible version of this figure.)

---

1. **What priority standard (or standards) are we targeting?** Record the priority standard in the space provided.

    (Describe) characters in a story (e.g., their traits, motivations, or feelings) and (Explain) how their actions contribute to the sequence of events. (RL.3.3)

2. **What will students need to do to be proficient?** Find and circle (or capitalize) pertinent verbs in the standard. The verbs—together with the content and context (step 3)—pinpoint the exact skills students need in order to achieve proficiency in this standard. List the verbs in the space provided.

    Describe   Explain

3. **With what content and context will students need to apply these skills?** Find and underline the nouns and phrases that represent the content and concepts to teach, and list them in the space provided.

    – Characters in a story
    – How their actions contribute to the sequence of events

Source for standard: NGA & CCSSO, 2010.

Figure 1.2: Protocol to unwrap priority standards—Exploring Elements of Fiction unit.

Since each standard contains several layers, teachers on a grade-level team may interpret the words differently (as illustrated in the scenario earlier in this section). If teachers misinterpret the intent of a standard, they inadvertently jeopardize a guaranteed curriculum as students across a school and district receive haphazard instruction with varying degrees of rigor. Therefore, during this portion of the PREP process, dedicate time to unwrapping priority standards and achieving collective agreement about them. Doing so requires teachers to closely examine and analyze every verb, noun, and conjunction to fully grasp the complexity and entirety of each ELA standard. This protocol provokes a serious conversation about the specific skills, knowledge, and concepts necessary for effective literacy instruction and assessment that will benefit grades 2–3 students.

In unwrapping the standard featured in figure 1.2 (page 27), our teachers recognized that this one learning standard has two verbs embedded within it: (1) *describe* and (2) *explain*. Once teams identify significant verbs, they convey the verbs' importance by either capitalizing or bolding them (if working electronically) or circling or highlighting them (if using hard copies). We circled the verbs in this example because our team completed the work using a hardcopy.

Once we identified the two verbs in this sample standard, our team realized that simply requiring students to *describe* a character's traits or feelings would not suffice when assessing student mastery; to meet the entire standard, students would also need to *explain* how a character's actions contribute to a story's sequence of events. This requires more complex and sophisticated knowledge and understanding. The ability to describe a character is one essential skill, and the ability to explain how that character's actions impact the progression of a story's plot is an entirely different student skill. Therefore, these two skills, along with the content and context of the standard, became the learning targets for the overarching standard—the incremental learning goals necessary for mastery of the full learning outcome.

After teacher teams identify the verb (or verbs) in a standard, they underline the nouns within the standard and note the nouns' significance. This allows teachers to pinpoint the knowledge items necessary for mastery. In the same standard shown in figure 1.2, teachers would underline the nouns *characters* and *actions* and the phrases they are part of (in total, *characters in a story* and *how their actions contribute to the sequence of events*). Although the latter phrase is lengthy, it defines a distinct and complex knowledge item that students must be able to explain, and therefore is an essential piece of the standard, in addition to the noun itself.

Finally, the team would also underline the words *in a story* to identify the context in which students will demonstrate their learning. When providing instruction for and assessing this standard, teachers engage students in reading a story. Alternatively, standards might present phrases like *in a poem* or *from illustrations* as a different context. The context becomes important when considering instructional implications, as well as the output through which teachers expect students to demonstrate proficiency.

As an additional consideration during the unwrapping process, teams should pay attention to these commonly used abbreviations within standards—*e.g.* and *i.e.* When a standard includes *e.g.*, the intent is to provide a list of examples. If a standard uses *i.e.*, what follows the abbreviation becomes an expectation. Teachers must take the time to scrutinize each standard to capture its intent and work in teams to help decipher and interpret what can sometimes be murky. For example, the second-grade literature standard RL.2.4 is written: "Describe how words and phrases (e.g. regular beats, alliteration, rhymes, repeated lines) supply rhythm and meaning in a story, poem, or song" (NGA & CCSSO, 2010) signaling each of those within the parentheses is an example but not a finite expectation. As you unwrap your state or district standards, pay particular attention to the language and abbreviations in the standard so that you honor and establish the true intention of each standard during the unwrapping process.

Unwrapping standards provokes an intentional conversation about the specific skills and concepts necessary for instruction and assessment. Prior to participating in the collaborative unwrapping process, a teacher might, at first glance, perceive a standard to require that students provide only basic character descriptions (standard RL.3.3 from figure 1.2, page 27). However, close examination and analysis of every noun and verb leads to deeper understanding of the complexity and entirety of the reading standard.

In *Yes We Can!*, Heather Friziellie, Julie A. Schmidt, and Jeanne Spiller (2016) write:

Unpacking standards enables every teacher who teaches the standard to develop a deep and consistent understanding of the standard and its component expectations. The outcome is that students will receive instruction that is truly aligned to the expected rigor and complexity of the standard. (p. 46)

After teachers annotate their standards through underlining, circling, bolding, or another method, they keep these standards readily available to use when they identify knowledge items in the following step.

EXERCISE
Unwrap Unit Priority Standards

As a collaborative team, work on unwrapping or unpacking priority standards to gain clarity about learning goals for your unit. To do so, refer to your PREP template and the protocol for unwrapping standards. (See pages 246 and 249 for reproducible versions of these tools.) Annotate standards according to the protocol steps to uncover smaller, incremental learning goals that exist within each overarching standard.

Use the following questions to guide this exercise.

★ What priority standards are we targeting for this unit?

★ What verbs and nouns within our priority standards indicate the skills students will need to learn or become proficient in for a particular context?

★ What smaller, incremental learning goals, or learning targets, exist within each overarching standard?

Identify Knowledge Items

After (or even while) teams annotate standards to deconstruct them, they focus collaboratively on identifying what students should *know*—the first part of the PLC critical question 1: *What do we want students to learn?* (DuFour et al., 2016). Or, put another way, *What is it we want students to know and be able to do?* The answer is largely factual information that forms the foundation for addressing standards and leads to understanding deeper concepts for those standards that are more sophisticated.

In this context, *knowledge* comprises facts, dates, people, places, examples, and vocabulary and terms—including concept words—although not all lessons or units necessarily include all of these. Teams can generate a list of these items. When doing so, they use nouns and noun phrases rather than line items that begin with verbs, which would reflect what we want students to *do*—the focus for the second half of the PLC question about skills (see the next section).

When compiling knowledge items, teams must consider the explicitly *and* implicitly stated information that students will need to know to meet a particular standard. As an example, refer to the third-grade reading standard RL.3.3: "Describe characters in a story (e.g., their traits, motivations, or feelings) and explain how their actions contribute to the sequence of events" (NGA & CCSSO, 2010). Team members may ask each other, "What will students need to know to successfully master the entirety of this standard?" While they will certainly list the explicitly stated nouns like *characters* and *actions* (students need to know these definitions), they will also add inferential knowledge items needed to describe characters and explain how their actions impact the sequence of events based on the details in the text. Figure 1.3 features an excerpt from our team's PREP template on exploring the elements of fiction; this excerpt shows the knowledge items our team generated for standard RL.3.3.

Unwrapped Unit Priority Standard	Knowledge Items
RL.3.3: DESCRIBE characters in a story (e.g., their traits, motivations, or feelings) and EXPLAIN how their actions contribute to the sequence of events.	Traits are words used to describe a character. Motivation is the reason why a character acts a certain way. Characters' feelings and emotions are expressed through details in a text. Plot is the sequence of events in a story. Plot development is affected by the characters and their actions.

Source for standard: NGA & CCSSO, 2010.

Figure 1.3: Knowledge items for a unit priority standard—Exploring Elements of Fiction unit.

To generate a list of knowledge items, teachers refer not just to standards but to multiple resources so all members of their team are aware of the foundational knowledge that leads to deeper, conceptual understanding. Along with tapping colleagues who have expertise in the targeted content of a unit, teachers can access available textbooks plus online and print resources and materials. Very often, these laser-focused conversations and collaborative exercises reveal new insights about knowledge items and implicit skills that even veteran teachers hadn't considered before.

At this stage, teams do not need to sequence the knowledge items; rather, they must just agree on what the knowledge items should be. During this exercise, teachers might find that generating knowledge items can take time, especially for those not altogether familiar with the content. Therefore, teachers who switch grades, who are new to the profession, or who are teaching new material will need to devote more time to this component.

Next, collaborative teams peruse the annotated, unwrapped standards and the new knowledge items to identify skills.

EXERCISE
Identify Knowledge Items

Work as a collaborative team to identify knowledge items aligned to your unwrapped priority standards. When ready, add the items aligned to each unwrapped standard onto your PREP template. Your team might generate a list, reference a page from a source (for example, a page in a textbook that features a diagram, a list of vocabulary, or the beginning of an engaging story), or create a graphic organizer. Be aware that sometimes a standard is lean and does not include all that it should to design effective instruction. These knowledge items are, therefore, implied.

Use the following questions to guide this exercise.

★ What will students need to know to successfully master the entirety of the priority standard?

★ What explicitly stated knowledge items do we expect students to know?

★ What implicit knowledge items does our team expect students to know?

Determine Skills

At this stage, teams review their annotation of unwrapped priority standards and their knowledge items (a list or graphic representation) to identify skills—what students actually must *do*. Educational consultant and author H. Lynn Erickson (2002) defines *skills* as:

> the specific competencies required for complex process performance. Skills need to be taught directly and practiced in context. For example, some of the skills required for doing the complex performance of research include "accessing information," "identifying main ideas and details," "note taking," and "organizing information." (p. 166)

Therefore, it is incumbent on teachers to plan learning experiences where they explicitly teach skills and directly assess them to ascertain students' levels of proficiency. Equally important is the idea that skills have transfer value so that they apply to new situations. Continuing Erickson's (2002) example, when second- and third-grade students learn to access information, identify main ideas, and take notes—perhaps when reading two texts on a topic, like severe weather in a science unit—they will be able to apply these skills in novel ways as they conduct research for other purposes.

The unwrapped, annotated priority standards serve as a guide to determine skills. Standards, like skills, begin with verbs. However, some of the verbs used in content standards are not necessarily observable but rather vaguely measurable mental verbs, such as *understand* and *know*. Instead of these verbs, teams should target using measurable action verbs like *define, analyze,* and *compare.* They must study the annotated standards and knowledge items to fashion skills that are sufficient to cover the intent of the standards as well as concrete enough to measure student aptitude. We refer to the skills that teams identify and define as *learning targets,* the incremental and specific skills that students must be able to do to achieve mastery of the entire learning standard. Throughout this book, you'll notice references to standards (overall learning goals) and learning targets (the skills embedded within the standards).

With a collective understanding of what students need to know (knowledge) and be able to do (skills), teams can design instruction that explicitly addresses these items. Figure 1.4 depicts an excerpt from our third-grade team's PREP template that adds skills (learning targets) to priority standard RL.3.3 and its knowledge items.

Unit Priority Standard	Knowledge Items	Skills (Learning Targets)
RL.3.3: DESCRIBE characters in a story (e.g., their traits, motivations, or feelings) and EXPLAIN how their actions contribute to the sequence of events.	Traits are words used to describe a character. Motivation is the reason why a character acts a certain way. Characters' feelings and emotions are expressed through details in a text. Plot is the sequence of events in a story. Plot development is affected by the characters and their actions.	Describe characters by their traits, motivations, and feelings. Explain how characters' actions contribute to the sequence of events.

Source for standard: NGA & CCSSO, 2010.

Figure 1.4: Skills for a unit priority standard—Exploring Elements of Fiction unit.

It is imperative that educators pay attention to the verbs associated with each skill so that the rigor of instruction matches the expectation for students. For example, consider the first item in the Skills column. Students need to be able to *describe*. That means the team must prioritize instruction that leads students to *describe*, and not just *identify*, a character's traits, motivations, and feelings. Teams can apply this kind of thinking across content areas when identifying important literacy-related skills inherent in other content standards.

Similarly, assessments need to match the exact skill the team intends to measure. In this case, students cannot simply select a multiple-choice answer to demonstrate that they know how to describe messages from a text. Essentially, they would be selecting a description that a multiple-choice question has already spelled out. Rather, the team should use an open-ended assessment, thereby allowing students to show that they can meet the rigor of the skill. We discuss types of assessments and how to match them to learning standards in chapter 2 (page 39).

After unwrapping priority standards, identifying knowledge items, and determining skills, collaborative teams are primed to consider the level of intended rigor for each learning target. This will help later when teams develop literacy-focused assessments they will issue for students to demonstrate understanding. To ensure a beneficial and rich learning experience, teams conscientiously assign the learning targets a level of rigor, the next component that guides curriculum design.

EXERCISE
Determine Skills

Using your team's unwrapped, annotated standards and knowledge items, collaborate on determining skills and enter them on your work-in-progress PREP template.

Use the following questions to guide this exercise.

★ What individual skills are embedded within the full learning standard? What must students be able to do to master the entire learning standard?

★ Are the verbs used to define each skill measurable? Do they match the rigor of the standard?

★ Do the skills have transfer value (leverage), or are the skills anchored to specific content?

Assign Levels of Rigor for Learning Targets

At this step, teams return to the unwrapped skills that serve as learning targets to examine their complexity. This scrutiny can lead to powerful team discussions regarding the intended rigor of the learning targets so teachers can match the challenge level in their instruction and assessments. We suggest Norman Webb's (1997, 1999) Depth of Knowledge, a thinking taxonomy, to identify the level of rigor in your learning targets. DOK is a scale of cognitive demand composed of the following four levels. (See appendix C, page 261, for a more extensive explanation of each level.)

1. **Recall:** Level 1 requires rote recall of information, facts, definitions, terms, or simple procedures. The student either knows the answer or does not.

2. **Skills and concepts:** Level 2 requires the engagement of mental processing or decision making beyond recall or reproduction. Items falling into this category often have more than one step, such as organizing and comparing data.

3. **Strategic thinking:** Level 3 requires higher-level thinking than levels 1 and 2 and could include activities or contexts that have more than one possible solution, thereby requiring justification or support for the argument or process.

4. **Extended thinking:** Level 4 requires high cognitive demand in which students are synthesizing ideas across content areas or situations and generalizing that information to solve new problems. Many responses in this category require extensive time because they imply that students complete multiple steps, as in a multivariate investigation and analysis.

Webb's (1997, 1999) DOK asks that teachers look beyond the verb used in the learning target, examine the context in which skills are to be performed, and determine the depth of thinking required. Although the verb choice helps indicate the level of complexity, teachers must consider the full context of the standard since the verb does not always give the complete picture of rigorous expectations. For instance, teachers can devise any of the following learning targets using the verb *describe*, but each carries a different level of expectation.

- ▸ Describe a character's physical traits.
- ▸ Describe what happens in the rising action of the story.
- ▸ Describe how the theme is developed throughout the story.

As an example, we refer to our third-grade team's analysis of the priority standard RL.3.2: "Recount stories, including fables, folktales, and myths from diverse cultures; determine the central message, lesson, or moral and explain how it is conveyed through key details in the text" (NGA & CCSSO, 2010). Our team identified three skills important to this standard.

1. Recount the key details in a story.

2. Determine a central message, lesson, or moral.

3. Explain how key details convey a central message, lesson, or moral.

When students recount the main events in a story, they participate in a task involving basic comprehension; thus, the first skill's cognitive demand falls under DOK 1. To determine a text's central message, lesson, or moral requires more mental processing, as students must make inferences. Drawing conclusions about a story's implicit theme requires strategic thinking; therefore, our team classified the second skill's cognitive demand as DOK 3. Similarly, when students cite key details from a story to explain how a central message is conveyed, they are again meeting the cognitive demand of DOK 3.

Knowing the complexity of the learning targets—identifying one target as DOK 1 and two as DOK 3—allowed our team to determine the types of assessments that would best measure students' abilities to meet expectations at the intended levels of rigor. Figure 1.5 illustrates (in bold text, for this example) how our team added these DOK levels to the PREP template, indicating the cognitive demand for each learning target. In addition to showing our team's work with RL.3.3, you will see the team's work for RL3.2 for a broader snapshot of the process. Chapter 3 (page 61) offers discussions about learning progressions and matching assessments to the rigor of skills.

When considering levels of expectations, educators must be careful not to change a target's intended rigor for students with special needs, English learners, or those struggling with the content or skills. Teams need to consider each of these students on a case-by-case basis—particularly for students with severe disabilities who may not function independently as adults—to determine an appropriate instructional plan. For other students, teachers should identify and implement instructional scaffolds and supports to ensure they can meet the intended rigor, as opposed to beginning instruction at a grade level lower than the students' age-appropriate placement. This decision demonstrates a PLC's commitment to closing learning gaps to ensure grade-level learning for all students (DuFour et al., 2016). You will learn more about responding to students' data for the purposes of intervention in chapter 5 (page 125).

Unit Priority Standard	Knowledge Items	Skills (Learning Targets and DOK Levels)
RL.3.2: RECOUNT stories, including fables, folktales, and myths from diverse cultures; DETERMINE the central message, lesson, or moral and EXPLAIN how it is conveyed through key details in the text.	Stories consist of key elements like characters, setting, and plot. A recount is a recap of the key events and details in a text. The central message, lesson, or moral is what the author wants the reader to learn or understand from the story.	Recount the key events and details in a story. (DOK 1) Determine a central message, lesson, or moral. (DOK 3) Explain how key details convey a central message, lesson, or moral. (DOK 3)
RL.3.3: DESCRIBE characters in a story (e.g., their traits, motivations, or feelings) and EXPLAIN how their actions contribute to the sequence of events.	Traits are words used to describe a character. Motivation is the reason why a character acts a certain way. Characters' feelings and emotions are expressed through details in a text. Plot is the sequence of events in a story. Plot development is affected by the characters and their actions.	Describe characters by their traits, motivations, and feelings. (DOK 2) Explain how characters' actions contribute to the sequence of events. (DOK 3)

Source for standard: NGA & CCSSO, 2010.

Figure 1.5: DOK levels for unit priority standards—Exploring Elements of Fiction unit.

E X E R C I S E

Assign Levels of Rigor for Learning Targets

Assign and input DOK levels to your team's chosen learning targets onto the work-in-progress PREP template. Refer to appendix C (page 261), as well as the examples in figure 1.5, for support in assigning these levels.

Use the following questions to guide this exercise.

★ Have we considered the full context of the standards rather than relying on the verbs alone, which sometimes gives an incomplete picture of rigor?

★ What is the complexity of each skill embedded within the full standard?

★ Have we keenly reviewed our learning targets to be sure we are not consistently aiming too low or even too high?

Summary

In a PLC, the first critical question is, *What is it we want our students to learn?* (DuFour et al., 2016). This question incorporates several components that begin with and derive from standards that determine what we want students to know and be able to do. All the components, which are embedded in the six-step PREP process articulated in this chapter, have a role and purpose, and together, they drive effective curriculum design.

As teams select priority standards to drive instruction, they also dig deeply into these standards to be crystal clear on what they mean. As teams uncover the implicit knowledge and skills, they learn a great deal about the standards. The *knowledge items* represent foundational information that is specific to content material, the *skills* reflect what students are expected to do, and *depth of knowledge* ensures appropriate rigor. As collaborative teams work on the PREP process, they afford their students the high-quality and effective curriculum they so rightly deserve.

In the next chapter, we explore how the PREP work teams engage in integrates with assessments, which consequently guide instruction for students. We discuss different types and formats of assessments that teams issue to measure student proficiency at various points in instruction, taking a close look at both formative and summative data collection. We also address specific assessment considerations relevant to literacy content. Keep exploring with us as we connect coherent and robust curriculum design to useful assessments for our second- and third-grade students.

CHAPTER 2

Examine Assessment Options for Literacy

In chapter 1, we took a deep dive into the first critical question of a PLC to establish precisely how teacher teams can use the six-step PREP process to determine what they want students to know and be able to do by the end of a unit. Through this process, teams can secure common learning expectations for every student in every classroom and solidify a foundation from which all subsequent unit planning can evolve. By clarifying the priority standards to be assessed *and* the specific knowledge and skills students must acquire to show proficiency, teachers set the groundwork for the second critical question of a PLC: *How will we know if each student has learned it?* (DuFour et al., 2016). Teams use assessments frequently, which come in a variety of formats, to help answer this question. Frequent monitoring of student learning is essential at the second and third grade level to continue the forward momentum of becoming a consumer of text and clear communicator in writing.

To provide the tools and guidance necessary to design literacy-focused assessments, this chapter examines assessment types and formats and their usefulness for achieving specific instructional goals. For example, teachers of students in second and third grade need to design assessments that will monitor the acquisition of foundational skills, reading comprehension skills, and the ability to synthesize and write about text. Therefore, we highlight the unique features of teaching literacy with assessments in mind. As a natural extension to these topics, the next two chapters focus on developing a learning progression (including making assessment choices and determining common assessments) and designing rubrics.

Assessment Types and Formats

Throughout an instructional cycle, effective teachers administer both common and individual classroom assessments to collect data on student progress that serve to drive learning forward. They design or find assessments, or revise existing ones, that give students multiple opportunities to demonstrate their learning in myriad ways. Whether creating assessments from scratch or planning to administer prepared assessments from a purchased literacy program, teacher teams must ensure that each assessment clearly measures students' understanding of the team's priority learning standards for a unit. Although the convenience of prepackaged assessments often entices teachers, teams need to review and sometimes revamp those assessments to make sure they evaluate precisely the right skills.

In truth, *assessment*—a term used pervasively in education—can cause confusion with its varied terminology of types and formats, such as *formative, summative,* and *performance; formal* and *informal; obtrusive, unobtrusive,* and *student-generated; selected-* and *constructed-response;* and so on. Ultimately, it's about how teachers "assess to gather information about student learning and either use that information *formatively* to advance learning or use it *summatively* to verify that it has occurred" (Schimmer, 2019).

Teachers judiciously choose an appropriate assessment, or even a combination of assessments, based on what will best measure students' proficiency with different learning targets. For example, teachers will collect frequent *informal data* as they observe students practicing the standards in class. To capture this data informally, a teacher might listen to a student read at the small-group table and record information about the student's fluency. In addition, throughout instruction, teachers also collect *formal data* by way of an assessment their team plans, creates in advance, and administers to students. What follows are explanations of assessment types along with example formats and methods to help clarify this somewhat murky topic. This includes explorations of the following.

- Formative and summative assessments
- Unobtrusive, obtrusive, and student-generated assessments
- Selected-response, constructed-response, and performance assessments
- Running records and reading fluency checks

If you choose to conduct your own search to collect information that will augment the discussion about assessment that follows, know that some resources might have slightly different definitions. This makes it important to ensure your team reaches a collective agreement on the academic language its members prefer. Always be mindful that assessments must match exactly what you intend to assess so they can inform your teaching and maximize student growth. We also list a variety of useful resources throughout this chapter.

Formative and Summative Assessments

Formative assessments are assessments *for* learning (Stiggins, 2005). They check for understanding and allow students the opportunity to practice skills and strategies in order to eventually master them. In other words, they guide and inform a teacher's instructional plan daily and weekly. According to assessment expert Dylan Wiliam (2018):

> An assessment functions formatively to the extent that evidence about student achievement is elicited, interpreted, and used by teachers, learners, or their peers to make decisions about the next steps in instruction that are likely to be better, or better founded, than the decisions they would have made in the absence of that evidence. (p. 48)

Formative assessments, when done well, provide meaningful information about how individual students are progressing throughout an instructional unit. This allows teachers to intervene with students who need a differentiated approach by providing scaffolded support and corrective instruction to those who are almost there, and even extending the learning of already proficient students. Robert J. Marzano (2017) identifies three types of formative assessments to track students' progress: (1) unobtrusive, (2) obtrusive, and (3) student-generated. Obtrusive and even student-generated assessments are more formal methods; in fact, selected-response and constructed-response items, which textbooks and other sources have aplenty, are technically obtrusive. We cover all these types and formats in the upcoming sections.

To check in on student learning, teams also collect data from *summative assessments*—assessments *of* learning (Stiggins, 2005). Traditionally, teachers issue summative assessments at the conclusion of a unit to ascertain what students learned. These assessments serve as the culmination of a comprehensive unit of instruction (or course), like a final writing product. At this grade level, students might read two science passages on the same topic and be expected to demonstrate their understanding in a constructed written response. This yields data for the classroom teacher about multiple comprehension and writing standards, including the science content. In this context, the data on the science topics serve as evaluative measures as the next unit of instruction is about to begin. Teams typically score and use summative assessments as evidence of student achievement. However, teams can consider some summative assessments to be formative, as well, based on the way teachers use the assessment data. For example, they can assess mastery of targeted learning objectives at different points within a unit. Carol Ann Tomlinson and Tonya R. Moon (2013) make this point in their book *Assessment and Student Success in a Differentiated Classroom*:

> Summative assessment can occur at the end of a unit when all of the learning objectives have been taught, at the end of several lessons that form a sub-set of meaning in the unit, or even at the end of a single lesson if the lesson objective has been fully met and students have had adequate opportunity to achieve mastery. Using summative assessments at the end of a lesson or set of lessons helps teachers ensure that students have developed the foundation on which subsequent lessons will build. Summative assessment takes its name from its purpose of "summing up" what students have learned at a logical point in time. (p. 92)

Think of the journey through a unit of instruction as a road trip, from an initial starting point to a desired end point. As teachers travel through their instructional unit from point A to point B, formative assessments are the quick pit stops along the way to check in on students' learning, while summative assessments can represent both the longer rest stops (perhaps for lunch) and the final destination. The latter provides evidence of what students have mastered during chunks of instruction plus how far they have traveled at the culmination of a unit of study. Whether teams administer and collect formative or summative assessments, they all reveal who has yet to demonstrate proficiency (and therefore needs additional support to progress toward mastery) as well as who needs extended opportunities to be further challenged. Figure 2.1 illustrates an assessment road trip.

Unobtrusive, Obtrusive, and Student-Generated Assessments

Unobtrusive formative assessments occur while students participate in the learning process and tend to be informal in nature. "In contrast to obtrusive assessments, unobtrusive assessments do not interrupt the flow of instruction. In fact, students might not even be aware that they are being assessed during [this kind of] assessment" (Marzano, 2017, p. 24).

During an unobtrusive assessment, teachers watch and listen for specific indicators of student learning, such as the kinds and quality of responses plus the level

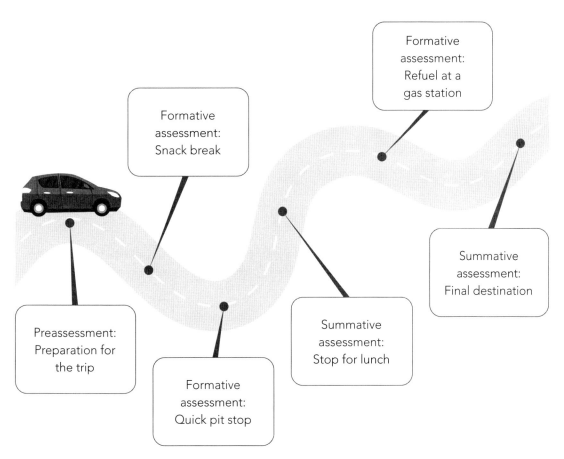

Figure 2.1: An Assessment road trip.

of engagement. For example, teachers circulate around the room listening in on small-group discussions or observe students as they complete a quick write or a graphic organizer. As needed, teachers approach students to redirect those who are off topic, pose questions to propel students to arrive at a new insight, or clear up any misconceptions. Additionally, teachers intentionally scan the room during instruction to be sure students actively listen to their teacher and peers, participate in discussions, or record key information when practicing literacy skills. Based on these observations, they make adjustments for individuals, groups, or the whole class on the spot.

Using a checklist or a recordkeeping sheet, teachers might opt to keep track of students' responses and take notes about their contributions, as in the example in figure 2.2 (page 44). As part of their daily classroom instruction, individual teachers informally and unobtrusively assess to check for understanding. However, because conducting a variety of assessments provides teachers with more information to

Data-Recording Tool

Unit: Exploring Elements of Fiction

Priority standard: Describe characters in a story (e.g., their traits, motivations, or feelings) and explain how their actions contribute to the sequence of events. (RL.3.3)

Concept or skill: Explain how characters' actions contribute to the sequence of events.

Student	Demonstrates mastery and can apply the concept or skill in an advanced way (4.0)	Demonstrates mastery of the concept or skill (3.0)	Has some understanding of the concept or skill (2.0)	Demonstrates limited understanding of the concept or skill (1.0)
John D.				Listed the characters; unable to identify actions ✓
Suzy S.			Identified only actions "playing" and "helping" ✓	
Darel J.	Ready for extension ✓			
Aditi V.			Could identify actions but is working to describe how actions inform the sequence of events. ✓	

Source for standard: NGA & CCSSO, 2010.

Figure 2.2: Sample unobtrusive data-recording tool.

Visit go.SolutionTree.com/literacy for a free reproducible version of this figure.

ascertain students' levels of proficiency on priority standards, teachers should also issue more formal assessments to determine how well students can demonstrate a skill.

When teachers assign *obtrusive* assessments, they interrupt classroom instruction and issue a task for students to complete or perform. Students can submit a quiz, written response, or another artifact that teachers read, provide feedback on, and sometimes score; however, there are a host of other obtrusive methods of assessment at varying degrees of engagement. Remember, though, that any assessment must match the purpose and the complexity of the standards it is measuring. Consider the following examples of obtrusive literacy assessments that are appropriate for grades 2–3 students.

▶ Annotate a short passage to identify the characters' traits.

▶ Complete a graphic organizer that captures the main idea and key details of a text.

▶ Write a summary of a complex text.

▶ Provide an outline for an opinion paper.

▶ Draw a setting based on a written or oral description.

▶ Orally explain the problem and solution of a text.

In addition to measuring content understanding through an application of literacy skills, each of these assessments are applicable to other disciplines. For example, students annotating a short text could examine a historical figure in social studies, while students writing an outline for an opinion paper might examine a passage related to littering and the environment.

Obtrusive assessments can be both formal and informal. The previous examples depict more formal options in that students produce something they submit to teachers for careful review and oral or written feedback. Teachers might also issue quick, informal check-ins that indicate their next instructional steps. For example, they can have students turn in an exit slip (also referred to as an *exit card*) on the way out of class to lunch or before a transition period to another subject, respond to questions on mini-whiteboards, or signal thumbs-up or thumbs-down to prompts (see Selected-Response, Constructed-Response, and Performance Assessments, page 48). For additional ideas suitable to multiple content areas, see figure 2.3; some entries can serve as formative or summative assessments depending on how teachers assign and use them.

A	B	C	D
Academic notebook entries	Billboard	Caption	Demonstration
Advertisement (newspaper, TV, internet, or magazine)	Biography	Cartoon	Descriptive writing (of a setting, character, individual, event, and so on)
Advice column	Blog	Chapter	
All-about book	Book	Character sketch	Diary entry
Alphabet book	Book cover	Comedy (play or script)	Dictionary with pictures
Analogy	Brochure	Comic strip	Drama
Anecdote	Bulletin board	Critique	
Annotation			
Argumentation essay			
Autobiography			

E	F	G	H
Editorial	Fable	Glossary	Handbook
Essay	Fairy tale	Graphic organizer	Headlines
Exit slip	Fan fiction	Graph with analysis	Historical fiction
Explanatory essay (how-to)	Fantasy story	Greeting card	How-to paper
Eyewitness account	Feature story		

I	J–K	L	M
Infographic	Job descriptions	Labeled diagram	Magazine article
Infomercial	Journal entries (for example, personal or historical accounts)	Legend	Manual
Informational essay or report		Lesson plan	Memoir
Interview		Letter (personal or business)	Menu
		Letter to the editor	Multimedia project
		List	Mural
		Literary critique or analysis	Mystery story
		Lyrics	Myth

N	O	P	Q–R
Narrative	Observation	Pamphlet	Questions and answers
Nature log	Opinion piece	Parody	Reader's theater
News story	Oral explanation	Personal narrative	

Newsletter Newspaper Notes	Oral presentation Outline	Poem Portfolio Poster PowerPoint Press release Program	Recipe Research report or project Review of a book, movie, or presentation
S	**T–U**	**V**	**W–Z**
Science fiction Scrapbook (annotated) Short story Sketch notes Speech Storyboard Student conference (with teacher) Summary	Tale Television script Timeline Travelogue	Venn diagram Verbal explanation Visual representation	Written response Year-in-review article or timeline

Source: Adapted from Glass & Marzano, 2018, p. 74.

Figure 2.3: Assessment options from A to Z.

When selecting an obtrusive assessment option, choose judiciously to ensure that the item students produce generates responses that will inform teachers whether—and to what degree—students have attained the knowledge and skills indicated in a standard. To achieve this (and avoid merely selecting activities that appear fun and yield little proof of mastery), teachers create a clear standards-based task and take caution to ensure that the assessment matches the purpose and the complexity of the standards they are measuring. For example, asking students to construct a dictionary with pictures would not appropriately measure students' knowledge of how readers describe characters by their traits. Instead, students might discuss this in a journal entry or annotate details in a story.

Student-generated assessment—a potentially valuable but underutilized form of assessment—involves students self-selecting ways in which they can demonstrate what they learn. To conduct this type of assessment, teachers lead a brainstorming session in which they ask students to generate a list of options that will show their understanding of a particular topic. For example, a student might wish to create a travel website to demonstrate his or her proficiency with literacy skills and knowledge of a recently studied geographic region. In contrast, another student might wish to create a travel brochure for the same purpose. Or, teachers can provide students with specific choices to support them in this endeavor and use ideas from other assessments, noting interests of students. As support, teachers can also pull ideas from figure 2.3 (page 47). The idea to get across to students is that they can demonstrate understanding in a way that they feel resonates with them and provides an opportunity to highlight what they have come to learn. All of the following three options would demonstrate mastery of the same skill of identifying the causes and effects of a historical event but allow for choice on behalf of the student.

1. Students might elect to annotate a text by underlining the causes and effects and using the margin to explain what they marked.

2. Other students might create or complete a graphic organizer showing the causes and effects of the event. (See chapter 8, page 205, to learn more about annotation and graphic organizers as instructional strategies).

3. Others might prefer to write a short essay to show awareness of the skill or utilize technology in some way.

This type of formative assessment promotes agency and engagement as students determine the best way to provide evidence of their learning. Further, the student that chose to demonstrate understanding through a short essay is likely doing so to highlight a relative strength the student has—writing. The student that chose to respond utilizing a graphic organizer might be communicating that he is still dependent on a visual scaffold to organize information, which may also signal to the teacher the student's need for differentiated instruction.

Selected-Response, Constructed-Response, and Performance Assessments

Sometimes teachers format an assessment by posing multiple-choice, matching, fill-in-the-blank, and true-or-false prompts that ask students to select an answer from a provided list. These *selected-response* assessments allow students to display knowledge of facts, main ideas, and basic skills that involve one correct answer, and they are obtrusive since teachers interrupt instruction to administer them. Students can take these assessments quickly, and teachers score them easily to obtain a broad overview of foundational information students know and don't know. However, with this assessment format, students can sometimes guess the answer, and it is not designed for students to demonstrate writing abilities or higher-level understanding of complex text (thinking at higher DOK levels). Therefore, teachers may couple selected response with other methods to gain a full impression of students' capabilities.

Students can complete formal selected-response items with pencil and paper or electronically and submit them for teachers to assess. Additionally, teachers can engage students informally by posing a selected-response question and asking students to respond on mini-whiteboards or with hand signals (thumbs or fingers). For thumb signals, teachers present a prompt, and students display thumbs-up to indicate *yes* or *true*, or thumbs-down to indicate *no* or *false*. For finger signals, teachers provide a key to show what each number—one, two, three, or even four fingers—means, and students respond accordingly for each prompt. For both hand and finger signals, students make a fist to signify *I am not sure*.

Figure 2.4 features a selected-response question for helping students identify if given traits describe a certain character. As a subsequent assessment option, students might provide additional traits of this character or provide traits of other characters either verbally with a partner or in a written format. As a further extension, teachers can ask students to explain their answers and share textual evidence signaling why they chose them. Since teachers should not teach literacy skills in isolation of text, these examples should originate from a complex text at the center of instruction; for example, our team used *Sarah, Plain and Tall* (MacLachlan, 1985).

Question: Do the following traits describe the main character of the story? (Have students respond to the items one at a time.)
a. Adventurous   b. Shy   c. Brave   d. Dishonest   e. Respectful   f. Independent
Thumbs-up: Yes, the trait describes the character.   **Thumbs-down:** No, the trait does not describe the character.   **Fist:** I am not sure.

Figure 2.4: Selected-response active-participation example.

Broadly speaking, unlike selected-response items—which have students choose a clear-cut answer to an objective prompt—*constructed-response* items require students to respond to open-ended reading and writing tasks. As the name denotes, this format requires students to construct either a relatively short response or an expanded response without the aid of suggestions or choices like in selected-response items. Teachers might ask students to simply produce a one- or two-sentence answer; develop an essay requiring analysis of information; make a graphic organizer or an outline; or write a summary or description of a setting or character, as we mentioned in the Unobtrusive, Obtrusive, and Student-Generated Assessments section (page 42).

To thoroughly and independently complete a constructed-response assessment, second and third graders typically require significant time set aside for literacy on the day of the assessment—perhaps twenty to forty minutes, depending on the task's requirements. Usually, students examine, read, study, watch, or listen to a stimulus—such as a text, graphic, short video, or audio recording—as the basis for their response. Their responses reveal how well they can apply knowledge and skills in general, and how well they can construct meaning and demonstrate understanding from the stimulus.

Unlike selected-response items, which teachers can expeditiously score to ascertain a right or wrong answer, students' constructed responses take more time to score, as they are more subjective and require teams' collective agreement about interpreting the rubric used for scoring purposes. (For more on rubrics, see chapter 4, page 101.) Also, a student who struggles with writing may find it difficult to accurately reveal what he or she has learned through a written constructed-response task. This does not necessarily reflect an inability to comprehend a text. To truly assess his or her ability to apply the assessed skill, you might need to consider a verbal response from this student and work with him or her toward demonstrating his or her learning in a written form. In this example, if the mastery expectation is that students can write to demonstrate their understanding, the student's proficiency level would be developing toward mastery. (See chapter 5, page 125, for more information about interventions.)

Performance assessments are more complex than the others, span a few days or a week or more, measure multiple learning outcomes, and promote critical thinking. Teachers gather extensive evidence about not only a product or performance that students complete, but also the process used to achieve the finished piece. Like constructed-response items, performance assessments are scored using a rubric. Students find this type of assessment highly engaging, as it allows them to apply knowledge and skills representative of what is happening in the real world. They can work collaboratively but ultimately generate individual products.

According to the Stanford Center for Assessment, Learning, and Equity (SCALE, 2015), a performance assessment requires students to think, produce a product, and demonstrate learning through work authentic to the discipline or real world, and it incorporates four key principles.

1. A performance assessment targets and improves knowledge and higher-order-thinking skills so, ultimately, students can apply what they learn to a novel situation (a hallmark of other assessments, as well). Additionally, it is an assessment *for* and *as* learning.

2. As students work on the assessment, they participate in myriad activities that present inherent learning opportunities. In this regard, they are assessments *for* and *as* learning. Teachers can collect information about the effectiveness of their teaching and can adjust, as needed, while students engage in various tasks.

3. A performance assessment is intrinsically linked to curriculum and instruction, rather than issued as an independent experience at the end of a unit.

4. The process students engage in while producing their products for a performance assessment presents a learning-by-doing situation.

Running Records and Reading Fluency Checks

In addition to collecting data about standards, teachers conduct *running records*, an assessment designed by Marie M. Clay (1993). Teachers should conduct these checks throughout second and third grade to investigate the distinct literacy strengths and needs of individual students. Fountas and Pinnell (2001), in their book *Guiding Readers and Writers Grades, 3–6*, reference running records as a way to observe students' oral reading behavior by learning about their processing strategies. These individually administered assessments monitor a student's reading progress and serve as an ongoing measure of oral-reading capabilities. They provide teachers with valuable formative data from which to make instructional decisions regarding reading instruction so they can increase the rate of students' development as readers in all content areas.

To conduct a running record, teachers record words students correctly and incorrectly read in real time as students read a text aloud. For each word a student reads accurately, the teacher records a checkmark on a blank form. When students mispronounce words or say other miscues, they enter a code that indicates the type of error. Afterward, teachers analyze the marks, look for patterns, and make instructional decisions regarding reading instruction. When considering students' reading needs based on the data, keep in mind that to read words adeptly, students need a strong foundation in phonics knowledge. If data from a running record shows that a student is making frequent errors, the teacher should further assess that student's foundational skills and put adequate interventions in place to close the gaps.

In an *Education Week* article on the science of reading, Sarah Schwartz and Sarah D. Sparks (2019) explain that "knowing how to decode is an essential step in becoming a reader. If children can't decipher the precise words on the page, they'll never become fluent readers or understand the passages they're reading." Although certain learning strategies work on some occasions, like using pictures to determine unknown words, second- and third-grade students (particularly third grade and up) will increasingly encounter texts with fewer pictures and visual supports. Therefore, teachers need to equip all students with a strong foundation to be able to read complex text across disciplines efficiently and independently.

With ongoing running records, teachers monitor reading factors that affect comprehension, such as the students' strategy use, rate, accuracy, errors, and ability to self-monitor. From there, "the analysis of running records should have a major impact on the teaching decisions the teacher makes while responding to and helping extend the beginning reader's literacy learning" (Fried, 2013, p. 5).

Also critical to assessment in second and third grade are frequent checks on reading fluency. In emphasizing the distinct connection between fluency and comprehension, John J. Pikulski and David J. Chard (2005) offer this definition of *fluency*: "Reading fluency refers to efficient, effective word recognition skills that permit a reader to construct the meaning of text. Fluency is also manifested in accurate, rapid, expressive oral reading and is applied during, and makes possible, silent reading comprehension" (p. 510).

To make meaning of the complex curricular materials used throughout instruction and assessment, and master rigorous reading standards, fluent reading is essential, especially in second and third grade. Additionally, as students transition to more independent reading, accuracy and automaticity become even more critical. When a student's "cognitive capacity is drained by the processing of decoding words, little or no capacity is available for the attention-demanding process of constructing and responding to the meaning of a text" (Pikulski & Chard, 2005, p. 511). By assessing and monitoring fluency frequently throughout the school year, teachers keep a close eye on second- and third-grade students' reading progress and use the formative data to design reading instruction and corrective instruction that bolster essential reading skills with the goal of building fluent and confident readers.

The Journey of Assessments

The field of assessment presents a vast amount of information, much of which this chapter covers. But for a more in-depth treatment, consider reading any of the following additional resources on designing quality-driven assessments. You might participate in a professional book study with team members and conduct a jigsaw activity. After or while reading a particular book, come together to discuss highlights with each other.

▸ *Design in Five: Essential Phases to Create Engaging Assessment Practice* by Nicole Dimich (Vagle, 2015)

▸ *Simplifying Common Assessment: A Guide for Professional Learning Communities at Work* by Kim Bailey and Chris Jakicic (2017)

▸ *Common Formative Assessments 2.0: How Teacher Teams Intentionally Align Standards, Instruction, and Assessment* by Larry Ainsworth and Donald Viegut (2015)

▸ *Designing and Assessing Educational Objectives: Applying the New Taxonomy* by Robert J. Marzano and John S. Kendall (2008)

▸ *Teacher-Made Assessments: How to Connect Curriculum, Instruction, and Student Learning* by Christopher R. Gareis and Leslie W. Grant (2015)

The assessments teachers and teams institute and administer—whether formal or informal, obtrusive or unobtrusive—are only part of the assessment journey. Throughout a unit, teachers repeatedly and continuously assess and collect data to determine how well students grasp specific skills and concepts. This informs their next steps in instruction and the feedback they give to students so that students can progress in their learning toward a target. So how can teachers choregraph assessment and instruction?

As a concrete example, consider figure 2.5 (page 54). Notice how this adapted sample from Kildeer Countryside Community Consolidated School District 96, a K–8 district in Buffalo Grove, Illinois, uses the notion of summative assessment to reflect an iterative process. Rather than call the end-of-unit assessment a *summative* assessment, the district elected to use *formative* to indicate that teachers can use

PLC critical question 1:
What is it we want our students to learn?*

*Team should engage in the pre-unit exploration protocol (PREP) before beginning the unit of instruction.

PLC critical question 2:
How will we know if each student has learned it?

Assessment Continuum and Data Analysis: Repeating Cycle for Units of Instruction

Optional preassessment with data conversation → Data-driven instruction → Formative classroom assessments → Data-driven instruction → During-unit common formative assessments with data conversation → Data-driven instruction → End-of-unit common formative assessment with data conversation

Preassessment
- Administered at least one to two weeks in advance
- Used to determine what students already know to tailor the instructional unit plan and differentiate to meet specific student needs
- May or may not be common

Formative Classroom Assessments
- Administered daily
- Used to make decisions in the moment or day to day (checklists, observations, conferences, and so on)
- May or may not be common

During-Unit Common Formative Assessments
- Administered during the unit of instruction within a defined window
- Used to check in on student progress toward mastery of essential learning outcomes
- Are common at the team or district level

End-of-Unit Common Formative Assessment
- Administered at the end of a unit of instruction within a defined window
- Used to assess students' current level of mastery after a significant amount of instruction
- Is common at the district level

PLC critical question 3:
How will we respond when some students don't learn it?

PLC critical question 4:
How can we extend the learning for students who have demonstrated proficiency?

Source: © 2016 Adapted from Kildeer Countryside Community Consolidated School District 96, Buffalo Grove, Illinois.

Figure 2.5: Example assessment continuum.

the information they glean from the culminating assessment to formatively further students' learning. Through this lens, assessment is a continuum—a recurrent cycle of instructing and assessing. Frequently administering a variety of assessments throughout the life span of a unit, particularly those formative in nature, correlates to student achievement (Marzano, 2006). Therefore, devising and committing to a continuum like the one in figure 2.5 will hold teachers and teams accountable to continuously gauge to what degree students are mastering standards, then act accordingly.

In figure 2.5, the horizontal timeline from the circle on the far left to the one on the far right represents assessments within one cycle or unit of instruction. Each circle reflects a different type of assessment that teachers administer throughout the unit to monitor individual and whole-class student progress both formally and informally. Although the diagram includes four circles, the instructional cycle certainly is not limited to just that number of assessments. Specifically, the second circle indicates several formative classroom assessments—obtrusive, unobtrusive, and student-generated—such as exit slips, observational data, student conference data, quick writes, journal entries, graphic organizers, or other artifacts of student work. In fact, a true depiction of a particular unit continuum may have six, eight, or even ten (or more!) assessment circles on the timeline. When teachers check in on student learning, they accumulate and examine data to monitor progress and respond in effective ways so they continually promote students' growth.

Between the circles on the continuum, the data that teachers collect from each prior assessment drive daily literacy and standards-based instruction. From data, teachers individually and with their teams can identify which students need additional support and which ones are ready to extend their learning. They then proceed to make informed instructional decisions, such as reteaching, introducing new information, scaffolding, increasing the rigor of tasks, or giving students additional opportunities to practice skills. (See chapter 5, page 125, for more information on responding to student data.) This continuous cycle of assessing and instructing ensures that each student receives precisely what he or she needs to progress toward mastery.

Even the end-of-unit assessment is used formatively, since teachers' work to support every student in mastering grade-level standards is never complete. Teacher teams may have taught the unit over the course of several weeks; however, if some students have not demonstrated mastery, teachers and teams must still discuss and find ways to provide differentiated support—hence the truly cyclical nature of an assessment continuum.

EXERCISE
Consider Assessment Types and Purposes

With your collaborative team, brainstorm and list various formative and summative assessments you might conduct for your unit. After reading about learning progressions in chapter 3 (page 61), return to this list and use it to identify specific literacy assessments that align with learning targets. For now, you should have a heightened awareness of the types of assessments and a healthy list of options to add to what you already conduct.

Use the following questions to guide this exercise.

★ What types of unobtrusive assessments can we conduct in our classrooms?

★ What formative and summative assessments can we administer to gain an accurate picture of what students can do?

★ What types of formal and informal data can we collect during instruction?

★ What does our journey of assessment look like, and what adjustments might we make to optimize data collection?

Literacy Assessment Considerations and Suggestions

Assessments are a steady and frequent factor in all effective instructional units, and each content area has unique considerations for evaluating students' understanding. A focus on enhancing students' literacy skills can play a role in any assessment. In mathematics, for example, grades 2–3 teachers may gauge students' learning by collecting responses to a word problem. During social studies, teachers can analyze students' understanding of how their home-state has changed through the years via a written description. In science, teachers use lab instructions and guides to foster hands-on learning and experimentation. When designing and scoring an assessment, teachers pay attention to various factors, such as lengths and types of texts used as the basis for a response, time parameters, and so forth.

Types of Text

When crafting assessments focused on reading and writing in different content areas, teachers make decisions about the lengths of texts students read for assessment purposes since they can experience both shorter and longer works. Teachers should tailor the qualities of a well-written assessment to the learning standards being measured, which can include complex text of various lengths. Specifically, in states that have adopted the Common Core State Standards:

> shorter, challenging texts that elicit close reading and re-reading are provided regularly at each grade. . . . Novels, plays, and other extended full-length readings are also provided with opportunities for close reading. Students should also be required to read texts of a range of lengths—for a variety of purposes—including several longer texts each year. (Coleman & Pimentel, 2012, p. 4)

Some reading assessments are based on students demonstrating an understanding of longer works—such as a chapter book, specifically in third grade—whereas other assessments may only necessitate the reading of a poem, a pair of poems, a short complex text, or an excerpt from a longer literary work. Additionally, teachers must consider the text used as the basis for a response and whether the task is meant to measure reading or writing standards, or both. We touch on this assessment consideration in chapter 3, in the section Discuss Options for Complex Texts (page 84).

Students also need exposure to texts from a range of literary and informational sources. This offers them a wealth of knowledge, content, and vocabulary to develop the "capacity to comprehend texts across a range of types and disciplines" (Coleman & Pimentel, 2012b, p. 1). By third grade, educators can expect students with grade-level reading skills to read and comprehend on their own. Therefore, second-grade teachers should begin to lessen the amount of teacher-directed read alouds for instruction and assessment by the end of the school year. This prepares students to meet this third-grade expectation. Also, in both second grade and third grade, teams need to match assessments' lengths to their purposes. Some assessments, for example, ask students to respond to an on-demand situation within a limited period. Others demand an extended time for completion as students learn and experience the steps of the writing process. Nevertheless, it is important that students participate in assessments of various lengths so they begin to learn how to pace their work on high-stakes assessments that have time constraints.

It's true that assessment tasks that align with the complex processes of reading and writing typically take longer to complete than those that don't require these core literacy skills. To meet the rigor of priority learning standards, students must employ a number of skills and strategies, often simultaneously, across literacy-focused strands. For instance, to explain the concept of how people and goods move from place to place around the world, students would need to identify specific examples of people and goods, consider their modes of transport, and explain how and why they move from place to place around the world.

Synthesizing a text using various reading strategies that aid in comprehension can understandably be time-intensive. Add on a writing task for students to demonstrate their understanding of the reading—and to do so with grammar and conventions intact—and the number of skills teachers are assessing multiplies. This is especially true if you are using an interdisciplinary assessment to yield data for multiple purposes. For example, you might be assessing the aforementioned list of literacy skills in addition to content knowledge that students have demonstrated through their produced work. We address the consideration of time for scoring in the next section.

Time for Scoring

Another assessment reality within literacy is the time it takes for teachers to score students' writing. You may have heard it said (or even said it yourself), "It is so much easier to assess students in mathematics because there's one right answer!" Additionally, the subjective nature of scoring certain skills—for example, *using sensory details to depict a character* or *constructing events to build suspense*—can present a challenge. Susan M. Brookhart (2013) refers to these types of items as *high inference*; they require assessors to make a decision and draw a conclusion about how to interpret criteria descriptions.

Having precisely scaled rubrics with scoring criteria and descriptions of each performance level addresses this type of subjectivity; these rubrics provide specific information not only for teacher teams but also for students and parents. In addition, participating in a collaborative-scoring process with grade-level teammates and establishing anchor papers—examples of student responses at each level of performance—will lead to more accuracy and consistency among teams when assessing and reporting on literacy tasks. (See chapter 4, page 101, for a detailed discussion of rubrics, collaborative scoring, and anchor papers.)

Assessment provides a clear snapshot of every student's progress at multiple points in an instructional unit. To demonstrate proficiency in the multifaceted areas of literacy, students need continuous practice to read and write well. As a result, teachers must purposefully conduct myriad assessments tied to standards. Assessments and data collection (see chapter 5, page 125) are invaluable because, without them, a teacher could not confidently identify the students struggling with specific concepts or the exact skills that present a problem. Similarly, the teacher would be unaware of those students who could benefit from learning extension.

Summary

With unwrapped priority standards, knowledge items, key skills, and levels of rigor determined via the PREP process, teacher teams are well positioned to begin determining which assessments they will conduct. For each learning target, they can start to decide which types of assessments are ideal for appraising students' proficiency. With an understanding of assessment options in place, teams can turn their attention to how they will teach the standards they've identified as priority.

In the next chapter, teams create a learning progression to map out the stepping-stones of knowledge and skills that students must acquire on their journey toward mastery of both content-area and literacy standards. *What will students need to learn first? How will teachers build on that knowledge? And what data will they collect along the way to determine if students learned the knowledge and skills necessary to eventually demonstrate proficiency?* Continue reading to grasp the importance of learning progressions and how they steer effective instruction and assessment.

CHAPTER 3

Create a Learning Progression to Guide Instruction and Assessment

During the PREP process articulated in chapter 1 (page 11), teams unwrap priority standards and determine the specific learning targets (skills) that they need to teach. As teams analyze and discuss their specific learning targets, they use Webb's (1997, 1999) Depth of Knowledge levels to distinguish the targets that represent simple skills or concepts from those that are more complex for students to understand or perform. In doing so, they naturally begin organizing the knowledge and skills into an instructional sequence. This work sets the stage for creating a *learning progression*, which James Popham (2011) defines as:

> a sequenced set of subskills and bodies of knowledge (*building blocks*) a teacher believes students must master en route to mastering a demanding cognitive skill of significant curricular importance (a *target curricular aim*). . . . formal, thought-through outline of the *key content of instruction*—what's pivotal to be taught and mastered, and in what sequence. As such, it's a foundation for sound instruction and effective planning. It's also the backbone of a sensible, *planned* approach to formative assessment. (p. 10)

By second and third grade, learning standards across disciplines become more complex, as does the cognitive demand of reading and making meaning of disciplinary texts. When digesting any type of material, whether a fictional story or nonfiction article, students must apply their recently learned knowledge of phonics and decoding, while adding the additional and critical layer of comprehension to their reading repertoires. Certainly, making meaning of text while also achieving mastery of a learning standard—and all the skills or building blocks embedded within it—can be quite a mental exercise for second- or third-grade students who recently learned to decode or read fluently in their primary years. Likewise, the demands for writing more detailed compositions and responses to text-based questions present additional growth-producing challenges. During this pivotal time in a student's literacy development, a specific and carefully-thought-out plan for instruction and assessment is most critical for navigating the complexities of a learning standard and ensuring adequate reading and writing growth. This type of detailed plan derives from a learning progression.

Through the process of unwrapping each priority standard, teams identify the building blocks (knowledge items and skills) embedded within it. By working together to sequence knowledge items and skills into a clearly articulated continuum of learning, teams essentially map out the step-by-step journey students will take toward mastering each standard. With rigor in mind, teachers list knowledge and skills in the order they will eventually teach them—from rudimentary to more complex—working up the proverbial ladder to mastery of the standard. In developing learning progressions, which are each guided by one or more complementary priority standards, teachers catalog and design target-aligned assessments for students to demonstrate their understanding of knowledge and skills. The team-compiled list of myriad assessments from chapter 2 (page 39) completes and fortifies the learning progression.

In developing learning progressions, teachers also distinctly identify and affirm all essential literacy skills that students must acquire to reach mastery of the overall standard. They assure that every literacy-based building block is accounted for in the progression of learning, knowing that reading and writing skills are critical to a child's success across all content areas. They then develop and catalog target-aligned assessments for students to demonstrate their understanding and plan high-quality instruction to move students forward in their learning.

This chapter provides a template your team can use to develop literacy-focused learning progressions for the priority standards your team has identified. We then use a literacy-based example to outline a six-step process that helps teams establish the foundational knowledge and skills the priority standards require. Finally, the chapter concludes with a section on how to set an instructional timeline for teaching learning progressions and assessing students' level of mastery in a unit.

A Template for Designing Learning Progressions

Teachers, and sometimes even collaborative teams, often neglect or overlook learning progressions as an essential step in instruction and assessment design. Despite the collaborative nature of a PLC culture, teacher teams often dedicate time to unwrap their standards, but jump to assessment writing without working together to determine the continuum of *how* learning develops as students strive to master a specific standard. Often, these teams lose sight of and unintentionally leave out the instruction of nuanced reading and writing skills that are critical for achieving a rigorous standard. However, when teachers develop learning progressions, they can use them to help design assessments that emphasize literacy, pinpoint students' performance, and choreograph their instruction at each step toward meeting a standard. Doing this sets the stage for differentiated instruction.

For those students who are missing essential building blocks, including those who have limited proficiency with essential literacy skills, teachers may need to backtrack along the continuum and reteach a concept or offer intervention on a particular skill. In other instances, students might already possess the knowledge and skills needed to advance further on the continuum, prompting teachers to increase the pace of instruction and provide extended learning opportunities for a target. In both situations, assessments guided by the learning progression provide data that allow teachers to appropriately match instruction to learners' specific needs (Heritage, 2008).

Teams can use the template featured in figure 3.1 (page 64) as a tool for designing a learning progression that drives assessment choices and recommended texts and resources. (See page 250 for a blank reproducible version of this figure.) Notice how it establishes a priority standard (dark gray shading) and then provides the option of identifying a learning target (skill; light gray shading) or knowledge item (no shading) for each step in the progression. The learning progression is distinctive, with teams customizing it to suit their specific needs and goals. As such, the number and order of knowledge and skills vary by standard and will depend on how your team sequences the learning. This figure shows a complete example based on the third-grade priority standard RL.3.3, "Describe characters in a story (e.g., their traits, motivations, or feelings) and explain how their actions contribute to the sequence of events" (NGA & CCSSO, 2010).

Priority Standard: Describe characters in a story (e.g., their traits, motivations, or feelings) and explain how their actions contribute to the sequence of events. (RL.3.3)

	Learning Progression Steps	Learning Progression Components	Assessments	Texts for Assessment
	Step 8	**Priority Standard** Describe characters in a story (e.g., their traits, motivations, or feelings) and explain how their actions contribute to the sequence of events. (RL.3.3)	***Common Summative Assessment: Short Constructed-Response Assessment** In a well-developed paragraph response, describe a character in a story and explain how one of the character's actions impact the sequence of events in the story. (Summative and formal)	*Brave Girl* (Markel, 2013)
	Step 7	**Learning Target (Skill)** Explain how characters' actions contribute to the sequence of events.	***Short Constructed-Response Assessment** In a two- to three-sentence response, explain what happens as a result of a character's action. (Formative and informal)	*The Sign* (Wrang, 2015)
	Step 6	**Knowledge** Plot development is affected by the characters and their actions.	**Constructed-Response Graphic Organizer** Complete a graphic organizer to show the cause-and-effect relationship between a character's action and what happens next in a story. (Formative and informal)	*The Sign* (Wrang, 2015)
	Step 5	**Knowledge** Plot is the sequence of events in a story.	**Teacher Observation** Arrange details from a story into the correct sequence of events using a flowchart. (Formative, informal, and unobtrusive)	
	Step 4	**Learning Target (Skill)** Describe characters by their traits, feelings, and motivations.	***Common Formative Assessment: Short Constructed-Response Assessment** In a two- to three-sentence response, describe a character from a story and use evidence from the text to support your thinking. (Formative and formal)	*The Sign* (Wrang, 2015)

		Knowledge	**Teacher Conference**	Excerpt from *Sarah, Plain and Tall* (MacLachlan, 1985)
	Step 3	Motivation is the reason why a character acts a certain way.	Meet with the teacher to describe characters and their motivations in a story. (Formative and informal)	
	Step 2	**Knowledge** Characters' feelings and emotions are expressed through details in a text.	**Teacher Observation** Identify traits that describe characters in a story, and determine a character's feelings based on story details. (Formative, informal, and unobtrusive)	Excerpt from *Sarah, Plain and Tall* (MacLachlan, 1985)
	Step 1	**Knowledge** Traits are words used to describe a character.		

Optional texts to consider for instruction or assessment:

- Excerpts from *Charlotte's Web* (White, 1980)
- *The 13 Clocks* (Thurber, 1978)
- *Poppleton in Winter* (Rylant, 2008)

*Grade-level teams will analyze and discuss data collected from common formative and summative assessments.

Source for standard: NGA & CCSSO, 2010.

Figure 3.1: Unit learning progression and assessments—Exploring Elements of Fiction unit.

Teams might elect to add or remove rows as necessary for their specific priority standard. For example, if, after unwrapping a priority standard, a team identifies three knowledge items and two skills needed to meet the entirety of the standard, the learning progression would contain five steps (or rows), with the sixth and final step being the overall priority standard. The number of knowledge items and skills a team identifies as it unwraps a standard determines the number of rows in a learning progression.

Ultimately, teams in the primary grades typically design a learning progression for each priority standard and may opt to develop learning progressions for supporting standards as well; however, in upper elementary and beyond, sometimes teams deem it necessary to combine aligned standards within a single progression. In the PREP template in chapter 1 (figure 1.1, page 15), our third-grade team identified four priority standards for the example unit on exploring elements of fiction, so it developed four separate learning progressions to support them.

In the next section, we use this learning progression example to examine the steps teams should follow when developing their own learning progression.

Suggested Learning Progression Process

With so many options for and approaches to instruction, teachers might wonder, *How will we know that we got it right? Is our sequence for instruction correct?* According to W. James Popham (2007), with few exceptions, "there is no single, universally accepted and absolutely correct learning progression underlying any given high-level curricular aim" (p. 83). Popham (2007) argues that separate teams of committed educators can unwrap identical standards and generate diverse learning progressions, and that is perfectly acceptable. Some teams are new to creating learning progressions and don't feel as confident with their final product. Indeed, teams continue revising learning progressions over time. What matters most is that when collaborative teams take the time to think deeply about learning and discuss each learning target's nuances, it benefits students more than those who do not make the attempt. Therefore, read this section for guidance to create a learning progression suitable for students at your site.

If your team uses a purchased literacy program that includes a prepared sequence of lessons, review the document together to ensure that the program addresses the unwrapped priority standards and aligns with the true intentions of the unit your team plans to teach. If it doesn't, make the necessary adjustments to achieve your team's predetermined learning outcomes. For example, if you've identified a knowledge item or specific skill embedded within a priority standard that is not explicitly addressed throughout your program's instructional sequence, your team will want to make adjustments to ensure that students are provided opportunities to acquire each increment of learning. This may require embedding additional mini-lessons and opportunities for assessment throughout the unit or altering the lesson sequence to better prepare students to achieve the priority standard.

With the completed PREP template and a blank version of the learning progression and assessments template (pages 246 and 250) accessible—plus any accompanying resources to support the unit, such as textbooks, complex text, and internet links—the team begins to construct a learning progression.

1. Select priority standards.

2. Sequence the learning targets (skills).

3. Sequence the knowledge items.

4. Determine all assessments.

5. Identify and design common assessments.

6. Discuss options for complex texts.

As teams of teachers work through this six-step process, they will keep in mind the unique aspects of literacy learning in grades 2 and 3. Though decisions the team made on the PREP template drive steps 1–3, teams collaboratively complete steps 4–6 as they determine types of assessments, identify and design common assessments, and choose complex texts suitable for second- and third-grade students.

The following sections detail each step using our third-grade team's development of a learning progression for reading standard RL.3.3: "Describe characters in a story (e.g., their traits, motivations, or feelings) and explain how their actions contribute to the sequence of events" (NGA & CCSSO, 2010). Using this progression, the team developed assessment ideas and identified texts for assessment purposes. Teacher teams should choose assessment texts ahead of time so that they preserve those texts and prevent students from using them prematurely. This way, students access them as new texts at the scheduled assessment time, which allows the students to demonstrate their independent level of proficiency with the standard and ensures consistency in the assessment experience across all classrooms. Also, keep in mind that these sections detail a learning progression for only *one* of the four priority standards that exist for this third-grade unit. Your team will need to develop literacy-focused learning progressions for *each* of your identified priority standards, regardless of content area. As we stated earlier in this chapter, your team may also choose to develop learning progressions for supporting standards.

Select a Priority Standard

When our third-grade team discussed the priority standard about describing characters and their impact on story sequencing, we kept in mind that we could not adequately address the standard in isolation. Rather, it comprises many skills, and it works in concert with other unit priority standards (and their corresponding learning progressions). Together, our team ultimately aimed to develop students' comprehension of the key elements of fiction. As such (and as mentioned previously), the team would eventually develop four total progressions, each focused on a priority standard within the elements of fiction unit.

Since a learning progression builds in sophistication to meet the curricular outcome of one or more priority (and likely some supporting) standards, teams record their selected standard or standards in the top row of the template to represent the overarching goal. They input it again on the top rung of the learning progression ladder (the last step in students' learning) because an eventual summative assessment will align to it. Although summative in nature, teams still use the data they collect for formative purposes to drive future instruction and ensure students, as necessary, receive additional practice and intervention to master each standard throughout the duration of the unit and, in some cases, even after a unit ends. At the culmination of the unit, teams may opt to have students demonstrate their understanding of all priority standards in a comprehensive end-of-unit summative assessment should they want or need additional evidence of student learning. Students that are not yet proficient should still receive practice until they achieve mastery even as a new unit begins. Figure 3.2 illustrates the top-level step for the learning standard RL.3.3 using dark gray shading. We continue to expand on this figure over the rest of this chapter.

	Learning Progression Steps	Learning Progression Components	Assessments	Texts for Assessment
Priority Standard: Describe characters in a story (e.g., their traits, motivations, or feelings) and explain how their actions contribute to the sequence of events. (RL.3.3)				
	Step ____	**Priority Standard** Describe characters in a story (e.g., their traits, motivations, or feelings) and explain how their actions contribute to the sequence of events. (RL.3.3)		

Source for standard: NGA & CCSSO, 2010.

Figure 3.2: Establishing the priority standard for a learning progression.

Sequence the Learning Targets (Skills)

When our third-grade team unwrapped the reading priority standard, we identified two specific skills that would serve as learning targets. Figure 3.3 shows an excerpt from the original PREP template we featured in chapter 1 (page 11). For now, focus on the information in the Skills column.

Unwrapped Unit Priority Standard	Knowledge Items	Skills (Learning Targets and DOK Levels)
RL.3.3: DESCRIBE <u>characters</u> in a story (e.g., their traits, motivations, or feelings) and EXPLAIN <u>how their actions contribute to the sequence of events</u>.	Traits are words used to describe a character. Motivation is the reason why a character acts a certain way. Characters' feelings and emotions are expressed through details in a text. Plot is the sequence of events in a story. Plot development is affected by the characters and their actions.	Describe characters by their traits, motivations, and feelings. (DOK 2) Explain how characters' actions contribute to the sequence of events. (DOK 3)

Source for standard: NGA & CCSSO, 2010.

Figure 3.3: Excerpt of priority standard RL.3.3 from the PREP template.

To determine how to sequence these items, we started by examining the depth of knowledge of each target. During the PREP process, the team labeled the first target as DOK 2 because it requires students to do more than simply recall facts, definitions, terms, or simple procedures from the text. Instead, students must describe the characters within a story by making inferences about their traits, motivations, and feelings. We listed the second target as DOK 3 due to an increase in the depth of thinking required of students. In addition to describing the characters, students have to explain how the characters' actions contribute to the sequence of events. The students must understand and explain the relationship between the characters and the development of the plot, which requires in-depth thinking. Since the learning targets' complexity levels differ, our team agreed that students would first need to learn to describe the characters before they could explain how the characters' actions contribute to the sequence of events throughout a story. Based on this analysis, the team could begin formulating a learning progression.

Mindful that the learning progression ascends in a sequential fashion from the bottom up, with the simpler skills or concepts listed below more complex skills, we input these two skills on the learning progression ladder in the order we would teach them. Again, this progression all leads up to the priority standard. Because learning targets represent crucial skills needed for mastering the priority standard, our team lightly shaded any steps containing learning targets to indicate their significance, as shown in figure 3.4 (page 70).

Priority Standard: Describe characters in a story (e.g., their traits, motivations, or feelings) and explain how their actions contribute to the sequence of events. (RL.3.3)			
Learning Progression Steps	**Learning Progression Components**	**Assessments**	**Texts for Assessment**
Step ___	**Priority Standard** Describe characters in a story (e.g., their traits, motivations, or feelings) and explain how their actions contribute to the sequence of events. (RL.3.3)		
Step ___	**Learning Target (Skill)** Explain how characters' actions contribute to the sequence of events.		
Step ___	**Knowledge or Learning Target (Skill)**		
Step ___	**Learning Target (Skill)** Describe characters by their traits, motivations, and feelings.		
Step ___	**Knowledge or Learning Target (Skill)**		

Source for standard: NGA & CCSSO, 2010.

Figure 3.4: Learning progression work in progress—Learning targets.

At this point in the process, teams have not yet added knowledge items, so the learning progression shown here reflects a work in progress. Once teams enter all items onto the template, they will know the exact configuration or number of learning progression steps. When working through the remaining steps, teams might decide to shuffle the order of what they input in light of any new thinking or ideas.

As stated earlier in the chapter, there is no ideal learning progression for a given priority standard. Teams can fashion their learning progression in various ways, so the key is to engage in discussion to arrive at a plan that supports your students and your team members' teaching style. For this reason, wait to number the learning progression steps until team members agree with the sequence of all the learning targets and knowledge items. Constructing the progression using a shared electronic document assists with manipulating the entries to reorganize them or add and delete rows, as needed.

Sequence the Knowledge Items

As shown in figure 3.4, our third-grade team left blank rows between the two learning targets as placeholders for inputting knowledge items. As a reminder, knowledge comprises facts, dates, people, places, examples, and vocabulary and terms (including concept words). Knowledge items are items students should know so that they can perform the skills (learning targets) a teacher team wants them to have. Popham (2008) refers to these items as *building blocks*:

> Each of the building blocks you identify . . . should be so unarguably important that a student's status regarding every building block must be and will be verified via formal or informal assessment. You are not trying to locate "nice to know" building blocks here. Rather, you are isolating "need to know" building blocks. (p. 37)

Because knowledge items indicate important steps on students' learning journey, teachers need to refer again to the PREP template (figure 1.1, page 15) and discuss how to sequence them in a way that enables students to achieve the learning targets.

Our discussions led our team to further probe our thinking by asking questions such as, "How should we sequence knowledge items to enable students to achieve the learning targets?" and "What must we explicitly teach, and in what order must we teach it?" By answering these questions, our team agreed that an important first step in the sequence of instruction would be for students to know that traits are words used to describe a character. Once teachers have explicitly taught students what constitutes a well-defined character trait, they can then focus their instruction on helping students describe characters by their traits. Therefore, the team made the following knowledge item the first step on the learning progression: *Traits are words used to describe a character.*

Our team then identified two additional knowledge items students must acquire before they can meet the rigor of the learning target that requires them to describe characters by their traits, feelings, and motivations. Students need to know and understand that (1) authors use details to express characters' feelings and (2) motivation is the reason why characters act certain ways. Therefore, we made these knowledge items the next two steps in the learning progression, indicating that students must obtain this knowledge before moving toward mastery of the learning target and, eventually, the overall standard.

When we added these knowledge building blocks in sequential order to the bottom of the learning progression, a strategic instructional plan emerged, unveiling how to move students, step by step, toward proficiency of the learning target (the target skill). With the prerequisite knowledge in place, the learning target, *Describe characters by their traits, motivations, and feelings*, became the fourth step of the learning progression. Figure 3.5 illustrates how these knowledge items (rows with no shading) build up to the learning target.

Priority Standard: Describe characters in a story (e.g., their traits, motivations, or feelings) and explain how their actions contribute to the sequence of events. (RL.3.3)			
Learning Progression Steps	Learning Progression Components	Assessments	Texts for Assessment
Step ____	**Priority Standard** Describe characters in a story (e.g., their traits, motivations, or feelings) and explain how their actions contribute to the sequence of events. (RL.3.3)		
Step ____	**Learning Target (Skill)** Explain how characters' actions contribute to the sequence of events.		
Step ____	**Knowledge or Learning Target (Skill)**		
Step ____	**Learning Target (Skill)** Describe characters by their traits, motivations, and feelings.		

		Knowledge Motivation is the reason why a character acts a certain way.		
	Step ____			
	Step ____	**Knowledge** Characters' feelings and emotions are expressed through details in a text.		
	Step ____	**Knowledge** Traits are words used to describe a character.		

Figure 3.5: Learning progression work in progress—Knowledge items.

Our team next discussed the knowledge items needed to reach the remaining learning target for this priority standard (*Explain how characters' actions contribute to the sequence of events*) and agreed on a sequence to input on the template. Figure 3.6 (page 74) shows what this looks like. With this prerequisite knowledge in place to support learning targets, teachers can number the remaining steps. This sequenced learning progression establishes a thoughtfully articulated and logical plan for tackling the next stage of the learning progression—assessment design.

Determine All Assessments

At this stage, teams must identify the assessments for each step on the ladder that will allow students to demonstrate what they have learned. This requires that teams ask questions like the following.

▸ "What types and formats of assessments can we use?"

▸ "What evidence will each assessment yield that will reveal whether students are achieving mastery?"

▸ "What types of classroom assessments can we issue that will provide actionable data about students' learning?"

As we detailed in chapter 2 (page 39), teachers use a variety of formative assessments to collect data on student progress that serve to drive instruction forward. They administer many of these check-ins through obtrusive classroom assessments as they ask students, for example, to complete exit slips, quick writes, or graphic organizers. Unobtrusively, teachers also observe and listen to students

Priority Standard: Describe characters in a story (e.g., their traits, motivations, or feelings) and explain how their actions contribute to the sequence of events. (RL.3.3)

	Learning Progression Steps	Learning Progression Components	Assessments	Texts for Assessment
	Step 8	**Priority Standard** Describe characters in a story (e.g., their traits, motivations, or feelings) and explain how their actions contribute to the sequence of events. (RL.3.3)		
	Step 7	**Learning Target (Skill)** Explain how characters' actions contribute to the sequence of events.		
	Step 6	**Knowledge** Plot development is affected by the characters and their actions.		
	Step 5	**Knowledge** Plot is the sequence of events in a story.		
	Step 4	**Learning Target (Skill)** Describe characters by their traits, motivations, and feelings.		
	Step 3	**Knowledge** Motivation is the reason why a character acts a certain way.		
	Step 2	**Knowledge** Characters' feelings and emotions are expressed through details in a text.		
	Step 1	**Knowledge** Traits are words used to describe a character.		

Figure 3.6: Learning progression work in progress with all knowledge items and skills.

participate in a group activity, engage in a discussion with a partner, or practice a task independently.

Teams are most successful when they brainstorm these ideas together, as this collaborative and collective inquiry furthers thinking and learning. As they consider assessments, teams should keep in mind key factors for assessing literacy skills, such as choosing an appropriate response type (oral, written, or performance assessment) to adequately measure student understanding. An assessment must also elicit clear evidence of the student's knowledge of literacy concepts or his ability to perform a literacy skill. For example, suppose that after reading a science text about earthquakes, students are asked to respond to the following prompt: *After reading the text about earthquakes, write an informational paragraph about this type of natural disaster.* At first glance, this seems to be a suitable constructed-response question for an assessment. However, after collecting the data from students, teachers may find it difficult to distinguish those students who gleaned information from reading the text closely from those who supplied mostly background knowledge they already had about earthquakes. Though background knowledge is surely important, and we will certainly celebrate those students who have such rich knowledge about the world around them, their responses won't provide the type of infallible data teams need to measure their students' abilities to read and comprehend. Instead, teachers might tweak this prompt to read something like: *After reading the text about earthquakes, explain how the author supports his point that earthquakes are dangerous. Use evidence from the text to support your answer.* (For reference, this question aligns to the second-grade standard RI.2.8: "Describe how reasons support specific points the author makes in a text;" NGA & CCSSO, 2010.)

Teams must carefully consider each assessment's role along the learning progression so that they can use the resulting data efficiently and effectively. To accomplish this task, they can return to the brainstormed list of formative and summative assessments that they generated as a result of the exercise in chapter 2 (page 39). Figure 3.1 (page 64) lists the assessments our team chose for the progression we designed for the priority standard RL.3.3. However, even if your team were designing a progression for this specific standard, it is not a given that it would come to the same consensus about assessments that ours did. Even within a single collaborative team, teachers may opt to choose how they want students in their classroom to meet a particular skill or knowledge item. As the team plans together, team members might decide to each issue all the same classroom assessments, but that is not mandatory in all cases. Team members also decide how long they spend on a particular step since students in some classrooms might progress at a faster or slower pace than those in another. This exemplifies the flexibility—or loose aspect—of PLC culture (DuFour et al., 2016). The tight, non-negotiable aspect of PLCs means that all team members must collaboratively develop and issue common formative assessments as well as a common summative assessment at the end of the learning progression. Typically, these common assessments are more formal, consisting of selected-response items, constructed-response items, a combination of both, or sometimes a performance assessment. We explore how teams identify which assessments are common in the next section.

To design valid assessments for each learning progression step, teams must consider the level of rigor (DOK) for the intended learning target and choose an assessment method that matches the cognitive demand of the learning. They take into account the knowledge items and design pertinent assessments to measure students' takeaway of factual information, as well. For example, if teachers use only the selected-response format (multiple-choice and true-or-false items) to assess the learning target, *Describe characters by their traits, motivations, and feelings*, it wouldn't allow a teacher to sufficiently and confidently ascertain that students can *describe* a particular character. Because this format asks that students merely identify a trait from a list or acknowledge a trait as true or false, it is too narrow and misses the mark in giving students a proper avenue with which to demonstrate their understanding of the rigorous task this particular learning target requires.

A constructed-response format, however, could more aptly assess to what degree students can *describe* a text by requiring detailed information. A combination of selected- and constructed-response items, or a constructed-response task alone, would allow students to paint a more exact picture of their capabilities in meeting the standard's rigor.

Selected-response items are best suited for students to display knowledge of basic factual information. Remember that an assessment is valid and reliable only if it measures what it is intended to measure; therefore, align the learning target's rigor with the assessment format. Reliable assessments mean teachers can trust that the results indicate which students have and have not reached proficiency on the learning target they are meant to gauge. Bailey and Jakicic (2017) highlight two approaches that contribute to an assessment's reliability.

1. **Always include a sufficient number of questions for each learning target:** Researchers Christopher R. Gareis and Leslie W. Grant (2008) assert that "at least three to four selected-response questions per learning target will eliminate lucky guessing" (Bailey & Jakicic, 2017, p. 70). For

constructed-response questions, one well-written question should give a team confidence that it can decide on next steps.

2. **Write the questions or task in language accessible to students so they clearly understand what they are asked to do:** If the assessment directions hamper a student's ability to answer the questions, that can skew the results. In this case, the assessment assesses not his or her knowledge of a learning standard or associated skills, but his or her lack of understanding of the questions.

To determine where students within a classroom and across the grade level might experience hurdles, teachers can assume the role of the student and take the assessment that they created. The entire team should engage in this work, and each teacher should bring his or her findings to a team meeting to discuss what he or she notices. Looking at the assessment in this way implies more than a glance or preview. By simulating what students will do to demonstrate mastery, teachers can fully understand and appreciate the expectations for students. Acting as a student and participating in the assessment helps teachers uncover mistakes or unclearly written tasks or directions. Additionally, this exercise pinpoints where students might struggle the most so teachers can align their instruction accordingly.

Identify and Design Common Assessments

With a list of assessments determined, the collaborative team reviews it and identifies which ones become the common formative assessments (CFAs) and the common summative assessments (CSAs) that all grade-level teachers will administer at agreed-on steps in the learning progression. Although individual teachers issue formative assessments that provide timely feedback and valuable data to both teachers and students, these data alone "cannot become a catalyst for improvement" (DuFour, DuFour, Eaker, & Many, 2010, p. 184).

For teachers to use the data to spur students toward growth and achievement, there must be a basis for comparison. Therefore, teams collaboratively take the following steps for grading calibration.

1. Design common assessments.

2. Collect students' work (data).

3. Analyze students' work together against a common rubric.

When determining which assessments to use or create along the learning progression, teams might ask themselves, "Which assessments from our list will be common assessments that we create and administer as a team?" That the final assessment should be common is a given, but teams must collaborate to determine which other assessments should be common.

To accomplish this, teams should carefully consider which steps along the learning progression require the focus and attention of a common formative assessment and which ones teachers can individually assess. Most likely, teams will choose to develop common formative assessments to measure student progress on critical and more complex learning targets that students often find difficult to learn, rather than on knowledge items, which teachers can typically measure using informal check-ins. Often, these are literacy-rich targets that require the integration of various reading and writing skills, such as applying comprehension strategies to determine the relationship between scientific ideas in a text or performing a close read of an excerpt to determine a story's central message. In addition, teams consider the realistic conditions of how frequently they can meet and how much time they have available to review outcomes because engaging in data analysis and collective reflection takes dedicated, uninterrupted time together. We address making time to meet in this chapter's Learning Progression Timelines section (page 89), and you will find comprehensive information about data analysis in chapter 5 (page 125).

Figure 3.7 illustrates the assessments our team assigned for each step of the learning progression. As a reminder, the data collected from all assessments informs next steps for instruction as students work toward mastery of the standard throughout a unit of instruction. A summative assessment is listed at the top row of the progression since it measures students' understanding of the full standard toward the end of the progression, but teachers will still respond to the data to assure that all students have opportunities to learn these key concepts. Detailed team discussions unfolded as we brainstormed assessment ideas and determined those that would become common (steps 4 and 8 in the progression).

Although it may appear from figure 3.7 that all teachers on the team chose to administer the exact same assessments, that is not the case. As a reminder, aside from the common assessments in steps 4 and 8, the ideas we record here serve as options for teachers to use in their classrooms. While they may choose alternative assessment methods for learning progression steps that do not denote a common assessment, teachers must take caution to ensure all assessments match the rigor of the standard or learning target. To make these sorts of assessment decisions, we find it highly beneficial to have a record of assessment ideas they generated during team discussions, as teachers often reflect in isolation and need to remember conversations.

	Learning Progression Steps	Learning Progression Components	Assessments	Texts for Assessment
Priority Standard: Describe characters in a story (e.g., their traits, motivations, or feelings) and explain how their actions contribute to the sequence of events. (RL.3.3)				
	Step 8	**Priority Standard** Describe characters in a story (e.g., their traits, motivations, or feelings) and explain how their actions contribute to the sequence of events. (RL.3.3)	***Common Summative Assessment: Short Constructed-Response Assessment** In a well-developed paragraph response, describe a character in a story and explain how one of the character's actions impact the sequence of events in the story. (Summative and formal)	
	Step 7	**Learning Target (Skill)** Explain how characters' actions contribute to the sequence of events	***Short Constructed-Response Assessment** In a two- to three-sentence response, explain what happens as a result of a character's action. (Formative and informal)	
	Step 6	**Knowledge** Plot development is affected by the characters and their actions.	**Constructed-Response Graphic Organizer** Complete a graphic organizer to show the cause-and-effect relationship between a character's action and what happens next in a story. (Formative and informal)	
	Step 5	**Knowledge** Plot is the sequence of events in a story.	**Teacher Observation** Arrange details from a story into the correct sequence of events using a flowchart. (Formative, informal, and unobtrusive)	
	Step 4	**Learning Target (Skill)** Describe characters by their traits, motivations, and feelings.	***Common Formative Assessment: Short Constructed-Response Assessment** In a two- to three-sentence response, describe a character from a story and use evidence from the text to support your thinking. (Formative and formal)	

Figure 3.7: Third-grade learning progression with assessments.

continued →

	Learning Progression Steps	Learning Progression Components	Assessments	Texts for Assessment
	Step 3	**Knowledge** Motivation is the reason why a character acts a certain way.	**Teacher Conference** Meet with the teacher to describe characters and their motivations in a story. (Formative and informal)	
	Step 2	**Knowledge** Characters' feelings and emotions are expressed through details in a text.	**Teacher Observation** Identify traits that describe characters in a story, and determine a character's feelings based on story details. (Formative, informal, and unobtrusive)	
	Step 1	**Knowledge** Traits are words used to describe a character.		

The following sections use the full learning progression shown in figure 3.7 (page 79) to highlight our third-grade team's discussion points and assessment ideas at each step of the learning ladder. These sections provide a glimpse into our thought process and collective decision making around assessment choices at each step.

Learning Progression Steps 1 and 2 (Knowledge Items)

Step 1 represents the bottom rung of the learning progression and contains the knowledge item, *Traits are words used to describe a character.* The team decided that this basic knowledge item, which requires low cognitive demand, is easy to assess using a quick teacher observation. While we were brainstorming how to collect these data after instruction took place, one teacher suggested gathering students on a carpet and asking them to determine if a trait describes a character from a story they read aloud in class. In this selected-response activity, once the teacher reveals a word that is a trait and discusses its meaning, he or she asks students to provide a thumbs-up to answer *yes* ("This trait describes the character") or thumbs-down to answer *no* ("This trait does not describe the character"). Students who don't know may opt to provide a fist to indicate *I am not sure*, rather than guessing. As students flash their answers, the teacher records quick anecdotal notes on which students are on track and which need more support. Or, the teacher might find it easier and quicker to collect these data using a copy of their student roster, on which they simply put checkmarks by the names of students who respond incorrectly.

Although step 1 is a knowledge item—a key concept that students must know before continuing their learning journey—teachers assess it by way of a skill. To demonstrate their understanding of character traits, students must do something to show what they know. This simple activity provides quick, unobtrusive data that inform the teacher's plan for intervention before the teacher moves too far ahead in the learning progression.

As we discussed assessment options, team members noticed that the knowledge item in step 2 (*Characters' feelings and emotions are expressed through details in a text*) is similar to the one in step 1, and that we could likely assess them at the same time. Therefore, we decided to merge the two for assessment purposes, recognizing that we could concurrently obtain data on students' knowledge of character traits and character emotions. In this case, we decided that after the initial thumbs-up or thumbs-down activity, the teacher might ask the students to discuss evidence from the story that highlights characters' emotions.

When assessment opportunities for multiple learning progression steps can blend into one, teachers should take advantage of it to maximize classroom time. The more efficiently and effectively teachers can collect data, the more responsive the entire team's instruction and interventions will become.

Learning Progression Step 3 (Knowledge Item)

After collecting data during whole-group instruction, the team was eager to collect more precise data on individual students. To assess the knowledge item associated with step 3—*Motivation is the reason why a character acts a certain way*—the team decided that students would confer with teachers during small-group instruction to describe characters and their motivations in a story. During this small-group time, teachers can collect precise data on students' understanding in order to drive further instruction and plan for remediation or extension.

Learning Progression Step 4 (Learning Target)

Our team concluded that step 4 is critical to students' overall mastery of the priority standard, so we agreed to create and administer a common formative assessment at this point in the learning progression. This way, we collect more formal data. We agreed to commonly assess using a short constructed-response activity in which students draft two to three sentences in response to an open-ended text-based question. Through their written responses, students demonstrate their proficiency with the reading skill and show their ability to support their conclusions with text-based evidence.

Although the written assessment is more formal in nature, the formative data the team collects in this step can continue to drive each teacher's instruction and intervention plans, just like the preceding steps' data. Moving from an oral assessment during small-group instruction to a written assessment also allows the team to gauge if students can both determine an answer and express their thinking through writing. Additionally, since the team identified step 4 as a common formative assessment, we also discussed collective plans for administering the assessment, developing a common analytic rubric, preparing students' data, and meeting for data analysis.

Learning Progression Steps 5 and 6 (Knowledge Items)

As we continued our discussion, we decided to use a pair of graphic organizers to measure knowledge items at both step 5 (*Plot is the sequence of events in a story*) and step 6 (*Plot development is affected by the characters and their actions*). At step 5 we chose to observe students as they arranged story details in a flowchart to demonstrate their ability to sequence story events; at step 6, students complete a graphic organizer to show the cause-and-effect relationship between a character's action and what happens next in a story.

Learning Progression Step 7 (Learning Target)

As our team continued brainstorming assessment ideas, we chose to include short constructed response at step 7 to determine students' understanding of the learning target: *Explain how characters' actions contribute to the sequence of events.* As you may recall from chapter 1 (page 11), the team agreed that this learning target's level of rigor is DOK 3 due to the complex thinking required for students to interpret text and support their ideas. Therefore, the team decided a short constructed-response assessment would be appropriate for demonstrating this level of thinking.

Learning Progression Step 8 (Priority Standard)

Finally, with the building blocks of knowledge and skills strategically mounted in place, students embark on the final rung of the ladder. For this final step, they demonstrate their understanding of the full standard—"Describe characters in a story (e.g., their traits, motivations, or feelings) and explain how their actions contribute to the sequence of events" (RL.3.3; NGA & CCSSO, 2010). Students do this by partaking in a formal common summative assessment that requires them to compose a well-constructed and detailed response that highlights their proficiency with the standard.

Though step 8 is the final step of the progression, and we classify its assessment as summative, team members still use it for formative purposes. Very likely, students will need several opportunities to practice and demonstrate their understanding of the full standard, and therefore the data collected will be used to respond to student learning, provide additional instruction and opportunities for practice, and move back down the ladder to provide interventions if needed.

Our third-grade team designed the common summative assessment for this learning progression to allow students to tap into all the knowledge and skills they accumulated by responding to the following prompt: *Choose a character from the story. Describe the character by his or her traits, feelings, and motivations. Then, explain how one of the character's actions contribute to the sequence of events in the story.* As with all common assessments, the team had to design the prompt, discuss how to administer it, and create a common rubric for assessment and instruction.

As we have discussed, a learning progression gives teams a framework for assessment that allows teachers to systematically collect data, adjust their instruction, and respond to the ever-shifting instructional needs of students as they strive for mastery of a standard. This framework for gathering data helps teachers check on student learning and also serves as a guide for preparing students for the common summative assessment at the end of the progression. Essentially, by the time students reach the end of a learning progression, they should have the background knowledge, skills, and experience necessary to demonstrate a comprehensive understanding of the full standard.

The learning progression we present in this chapter allowed our team to use a variety of formative assessments to check in on student progress. However, formative assessment data do little good in improving student achievement if teachers don't develop a collaborative plan of action to respond to the resulting data. When data from these formative assessments indicate that students already have prior knowledge of a concept, teachers should move them up to the next step on the progression, forging ahead to new learning experiences. If students need more time to work through a skill, teachers should slow their pace or try a different approach to instruction.

Although we refer to assessments at the end of a learning progression as *summative*, a teacher team's work to support every student in mastering grade-level standards is never complete. Your team may have taught a unit over the course of several weeks, but if every student has not demonstrated mastery, each team member must find other ways to provide differentiated support until all students master the unit's priority standards. Throughout the school year, teams may choose to apply those same standards to more rigorous texts or teach them in combination with other standards to create new learning experiences. Summative assessments provide evidence of what students have mastered at the culmination of a unit of study, and teachers must use these data to determine next steps for every student.

E X E R C I S E

Develop a Learning Progression and Assessment Plan

Your team should sequence the unpacked knowledge items and skills from your PREP template into a learning progression by starting at the simplest concepts and working up to the most complex skills. Each step in the learning progression acts as a touchstone for formative assessments and an opportunity for teams to discuss the best type of assessment to check in on student learning.

Use the following questions to guide this exercise.

★ What priority standard in the unit is the basis for the learning progression we will build first?

★ How can we sequence the skills and knowledge items?

★ What types and formats of assessments will we conduct?

★ What common formative assessments will we issue? What will we use for a common summative assessment?

Discuss Options for Complex Texts

Teams must consider text complexity when creating or choosing texts that will support students' learning of knowledge items and learning targets as they progress toward proficiency of a priority standard. Students should experience rich, grade-level text throughout instruction; therefore, teachers should pay particular attention in choosing text at the appropriate complexity level.

When choosing a text they will use in an assessment, teacher teams must ensure the text will yield valid data for determining students' proficiency and mastery of grade-level learning targets. For example, a student might be able to apply a skill when using simpler text; however, when he or she applies it to a grade-appropriate complex text, the student may actually struggle to demonstrate proficiency on his or her own. Using texts at an appropriate complexity level will help avoid inaccurate results, such as these. Use the "Tool for Measuring Text Complexity" in appendix A (page 252) to support your selection of text.

To choose such texts for instructional and assessment purposes, teams consider three criteria that gauge a text's complexity level: (1) the quantitative features of the text, (2) the qualitative features of the text, and (3) the reader and task considerations (NGA & CCSSO, n.d.a).

1. *Quantitative* refers to text features and properties that can be counted, like word length and frequency, word difficulty, sentence length, and number of syllables. To calculate a text's quantitative readability level, schools typically rely on computer programs, for example, the Flesch-Kincaid Grade Level test or the Lexile Framework for Reading by MetaMetrics.

2. *Qualitative* refers to text features that include the sophistication of the language (literal and clear language versus figurative, archaic, or unfamiliar language); the knowledge demands concerning the extent of readers' life experiences, subject-matter content (typically for informational texts), and depth of cultural and literary knowledge (mostly for literary texts); and the text's structure, levels of meaning, and purpose. Refer to appendix A for rubrics teams can use to ascertain the qualitative nature of literary and informational texts.

   Quantitative and qualitative measurements are closely aligned; one without the other will render measurement incomplete and perhaps invalid when selecting the right text. For example, the quantitative text features of John Steinbeck's (1939/1993) *The Grapes of Wrath* measure at a second-to third-grade level, yet clearly, the qualitative and reader considerations would dictate that this text be read at a much higher grade level due to its sophisticated content.

3. *Reader and task considerations* refers to the particular composition of the students in a classroom (specifically, these readers' cognitive abilities, motivation, knowledge, and experiences). It also entails the purpose for reading, including the task students complete based on the text. Teachers use their professional judgment and expertise, coupled with what they know about their students, when attending to this area of text complexity. (Refer to chapter 9, page 227, for a discussion about equity and culturally relevant texts.)

In addition to considering grade-appropriate text complexity features, teams should also be cognizant that students must understand texts of steadily increasing difficulty as they progress through grade levels. By the time they graduate, they must be able to independently and proficiently read and comprehend the kinds of complex texts commonly found in college and the workplace. Therefore, beginning in early elementary school, teams should take text complexity into account during the assessment-writing and assessment-selection process.

As teams secure the learning progression for students, they should discuss and commit to complex text that would best address the demand of the knowledge and skills they will assess. Since our featured third-grade reading standard requires students to discuss characters and plot, our team purposefully selected stories that have a variety of well-developed characters, rich details, and a coherent plot sequence. We recorded these texts in the learning progression template's Texts for Assessment column (see figure 3.1, page 64). To support them in selecting appropriately challenging text, teams can search for potential titles in the following resources (Glass, 2015) and then check any contenders using the three complexity criteria described in this section.

- **The California Department of Education's Recommended Literature List (www.cde.ca.gov/ci/cr/rl):** This webpage features a list of recommended preK–12 literature across content areas. A customizable search tool aids users in finding appropriate texts to suit their criteria.

- **Appendix B of the Common Core State Standards for English language arts (www.corestandards.org/assets/Appendix_B.pdf):** This appendix includes complex text suggestions for grade-level bands (including 2–3) across content areas and categorized by text type. Some entries appear as titles only and others are excerpts taken from whole works, so educators can find and expose students to the original text sources. In addition, this source includes sample performance tasks that educators might issue.

- **National Council of Teachers of English award winners (NCTE, https://ncte.org/awards/ncte-childrens-book-awards):** Each year, the NCTE grants the Orbis Pictus Award (for children's nonfiction) and the Charlotte Huck Award (for children's fiction) and lists the winning titles on its website.

- **The International Literacy Association's Choices Reading Lists (www .literacyworldwide.org/get-resources/reading-lists):** This organization offers three collections of reading lists: Children's Choices (grades K–6),

Teachers' Choices (grades K–8), and Young Adults' Choices (grades 7–12) each year. Each resource provides annotated lists of literary titles.

Realistically, for a four-week unit, grades 2–3 teacher teams would select anywhere from two to five texts, depending on the length of the text and the purpose of the assessment. Often, teams can use various sections of the same text for different assessments at various steps of the learning progression. For example, in our sample learning progression in figure 3.1 (page 64), you'll see that we elected to use the same text to assess steps 1, 2, and 3 of the learning progression. As teams discuss text options, they may elect to list additional texts as optional materials for teachers to use for instruction or assessment purposes at their discretion. Our third-grade team listed these at the bottom of the progression template for easy accessibility after the team discussion. As teams generate ideas and suggestions about the types of texts and tasks to use when assessing the steps along their learning progressions, they can jot down and visually display any notes in the learning progression template.

EXERCISE
Consider Options for Complex Texts

Teachers must be aware of what qualifies a text to be complex. Review this chapter's three criteria for text complexity—and the "Tool for Measuring Text Complexity" in appendix A (page 255)—to ascertain the complexity level of any text your team has under consideration for classroom instruction. Make plans as a team to select appropriately challenging texts or review current texts for this purpose.

Use the following questions to guide this exercise.

★ What texts do we already use? Should we re-evaluate any texts for complexity?

★ Have we considered using culturally responsive texts? (See chapter 9, page 227.)

★ Which complex texts can we use as mentor texts (exemplary models) to illustrate learning targets in the unit? (See chapter 7, page 165, for a detailed discussion about mentor texts.)

Learning Progression Timelines

After completing a learning progression and selecting or designing assessments, teams begin planning the execution of the unit. In doing so, they generate a team calendar that pinpoints dates for instruction and assessment (both formal and informal) around the standards. Some building blocks might take two or more days to teach; if this is the case, teams reflect this in the team calendar. Additionally, they reserve time for intervention—offering corrective instruction for students who have yet to master standards and providing extension for those who have achieved mastery. Teams anticipate these assessment and intervention dates and incorporate them within the unit's time frame.

As mentioned in the Identify and Design Common Assessments section (page 77) and described more thoroughly in chapter 5 (page 125), assessments guided by the learning progression provide data that allow teachers to appropriately match their instruction to their learners' specific needs. It stands to reason that the more common assessments teams conduct, the more data they collect and analyze together. But the team calendar must also reflect a *realistic and attainable* timeline of instruction, interventions of corrective instruction and extension, and all that pertains to assessment, such as team meetings devoted to writing an assessment, developing a rubric, and analyzing data. To accomplish this, team members must take into consideration aspects of the unit, such as its length, the number of priority and supporting standards, and the complexity of those standards.

As a reminder, units will have a limited amount of priority standards to allow for thorough and intentional teaching of a few standards, rather than surface-level teaching of several. The total number of priority standards will typically depend on the length of the unit. Essentially, every unit should have mid-unit check-ins, and longer units will have more, but brief, check-ins. For example, if a unit is twelve weeks long, the team might issue a common formative assessment every three weeks. For a short three-week unit, issuing a common formative assessment each week may not work. Additionally, team members should recognize time issues, such as how often the team meets and the length of these meetings. If a team has limited opportunities to convene, it needs to take that into account when creating a timeline.

Using its PREP template for the Exploring Elements of Fiction unit (figure 1.1, page 15), along with the completed learning progressions for all unit priority standards and the District 96 assessment continuum (figure 2.5, page 54) as a resource, our third-grade team strategically mapped out instruction, assessment, and intervention for the entire unit onto the team calendar shown in figure 3.8. This calendar reflects all priority standards, all supporting standards, and all assessments that guide

Unit: Exploring Elements of Fiction

Time Frame: Four weeks in October   **Grade:** 3

Today's Date: September 16 (two weeks prior to unit)

Monday, 9/16	Tuesday, 9/17	Wednesday, 9/18	Thursday, 9/19	Friday, 9/20
Instruction for the current unit takes place while the team engages in the PREP process for the upcoming Exploring Elements of Fiction unit beginning on 9/30.				

Monday, 9/23	Tuesday, 9/24	Wednesday, 9/25	Thursday, 9/26	Friday, 9/27
Instruction for the current unit takes place while the team engages in the PREP process for the upcoming 9/30 Exploring Elements of Fiction unit.		Preassessment	Instruction for the current unit takes place while the team engages in the PREP process for the upcoming 9/30 Exploring Elements of Fiction unit.	

Monday, 9/30 Day 1	Tuesday, 10/1 Day 2	Wednesday, 10/2 Day 3	Thursday, 10/3 Day 4	Friday, 10/4 Day 5
Instruction on Priority Standards: RF.3.4 (LP steps 1 and 2) W.3.2a (LP step 1) **Instruction on Supporting Standards:** RL.3.1 **Assessment:** RF.3.4 (informal and unobtrusive for five students based on a common rubric)	**Instruction on Priority Standards:** RL.3.3 (LP steps 1 and 2) RF.3.4 (LP steps 3 and 4) W.3.2a (LP step 2) **Instruction on Supporting Standards:** RL.3.1 L.3.4a **Assessment:** RL.3.3 (LP steps 1 and 2; informal and unobtrusive) RF.3.4 (informal and unobtrusive for five students based on a common rubric) **Team Literacy Meeting**	**Instruction on Priority Standards:** RL.3.3 (LP step 3) RF.3.4 (LP step 5) W.3.2a (LP step 2) **Instruction on Supporting Standards:** RL.3.1 **Assessment:** RL.3.3 (LP step 3; informal) RF.3.4 (informal and unobtrusive for five students based on a common rubric)	**Instruction on Priority Standards:** RL.3.3 (LP step 3) RF.3.4 (LP step 6) W.3.2a (LP step 3) **Instruction on Supporting Standards:** L.3.4a **Assessment:** RF.3.4 (informal and unobtrusive for five students based on a common rubric)	**Instruction on Priority Standards:** RL.3.3 (LP step 4) RF.3.4 (LP step 7) W.3.2a (LP step 3) **Instruction on Supporting Standards:** RL.3.1 **Assessment (Team CFA):** RL.3.3 (LP step 4; formal CFA) W.3.2a (LP step 3; formal CFA) RF.3.4 (informal and unobtrusive for five students based on a common rubric)

Figure 3.8: Team calendar for the Exploring Elements of Fiction unit.

continued →

Monday, 10/7 — Day 6	Tuesday, 10/8 — Day 7	Wednesday, 10/9 — Day 8	Thursday, 10/10 — Day 9	Friday, 10/11 — Day 10
Instruction on Priority Standards: RL.3.3 (LP step 5) RL.3.2 (LP step 4) RF.3.4 (LP step 7) **Instruction on Supporting Standards:** W.3.2b RF.3.3a **Assessment:** W.3.2a (LP step 4; informal and unobtrusive)	**Instruction on Priority Standards:** RL.3.3 (LP step 5) RL.3.2 (LP step 1) **Instruction on Supporting Standards:** W.3.2b **Assessment:** RL.3.3 (LP step 5; informal and unobtrusive) **Team Literacy Meeting** **Team Data-Inquiry Meeting:** Discuss RL.3.3 and W.3.2a CFA data from 10/4 and running-record data collected for RF.3.4.	**Instruction on Priority Standards:** RL.3.3 (LP step 6) RL.3.2 (LP step 1) W.3.2a (LP step 5) **Instruction on Supporting Standards:** W.3.2b RF.3.3a **Assessment:** RL.3.2 (LP step 1; informal and unobtrusive) **Corrective Instruction or Extension for RL.3.3 and W.3.2a (based on data inquiry)**	**Instruction on Priority Standards:** RL.3.3 (LP step 6) RL.3.2 (LP step 2) W.3.2a (LP step 5) **Instruction on Supporting Standards:** L.3.4a **Assessment:** RL.3.2 (LP step 2; informal and unobtrusive) W.3.2a (LP step 5; informal and unobtrusive) **Corrective Instruction or Extension for RL.3.3 and W.3.2a (based on data inquiry)**	**Instruction on Priority Standards:** RL.3.3 (LP step 6) RL.3.2 (LP step 3) W.3.2a (LP step 6) **Instruction on Supporting Standards:** None **Assessment:** RL.3.3 (LP step 6; informal)

Monday, 10/14 — Day 11	Tuesday, 10/15 — Day 12	Wednesday, 10/16 — Day 13	Thursday, 10/17 — Day 14	Friday, 10/18 — Day 15
Instruction on Priority Standards: RL.3.3 (LP step 7) RL.3.2 (LP step 3) W.3.2a (LP step 6) **Instruction on Supporting Standards:** RL.3.1 **Assessment:** RL.3.2 (LP step 3; informal and obtrusive)	**Instruction on Priority Standards:** RL.3.3 (LP step 7) RL.3.2 (LP step 4) **Instruction on Supporting Standards:** None **Assessment:** RL.3.3 (LP step 7; informal and unobtrusive) RF.3.4 (informal fluency check based on common rubric for	**Instruction on Priority Standards:** RL.3.2 (LP step 5) **Instruction on Supporting Standards:** RF.3.3a **Assessment:** W.3.2a (LP step 6; informal and obtrusive) RF.3.4 (informal fluency check based on common rubric for	**Instruction on Priority Standards:** RL.3.3 (LP step 8) RL.3.2 (LP step 5) **Instruction on Supporting Standards:** None **Assessment:** RL.3.3 (LP step 8; formal and obtrusive CSA) RL.3.2 (LP step 4; formal and obtrusive CFA)	**Instruction on Priority Standards:** RL.3.2 (LP step 6) RL.3.3 (LP step 8) W.3.2a (LP step 9) **Instruction on Supporting Standards:** L.3.4a **Assessment:** RL.3.2 (LP step 5; informal and unobtrusive)

RF.3.4 (informal fluency check based on common rubric for students that have not yet mastered)	students that have not yet mastered.) **Team Literacy Meeting:** Begin to look ahead at the next unit.	students that have not yet mastered)

Monday, 10/21 **Day 16**	**Tuesday, 10/22** **Day 17**	**Wednesday, 10/23** **Day 18**	**Thursday, 10/24** **Day 19**	**Friday, 10/25** **Day 20**
Instruction on Priority Standards: RL.3.2 (LP step 7) W.3.2a (LP step 6) **Instruction on Supporting Standards:** L.3.4a **Assessment:** RL.3.2 (LP step 6; informal and unobtrusive)	**Instruction on Priority Standards:** RL.3.2 (LP step 7) **Instruction on Supporting Standards:** W.3.2b **Assessment:** Determine assessment based on corrective instruction or extension provided to students. **Team Meeting** **Team Data-Inquiry Meeting:** Discuss RL.3.2 and RL.3.3 data from 10/17.	**Instruction on Priority Standards:** Provide corrective instruction or extension based on all previous assessments. **Assessment:** Determine assessment based on corrective instruction or extension provided to students.	**Instruction on Priority Standards:** Provide corrective instruction or extension based on all previous assessments. **Assessment:** W.3.2a and RL.3.2 formal and obtrusive CSA.	**Instruction on Priority Standards:** Provide corrective instruction or extension based on all previous assessments. **Assessment:** Determine assessment based on corrective instruction or extension provided to students.

LP = Learning progression

instruction. Alongside each priority standard, you will see the learning progression step for that standard that the team will instruct on that day. For example, *LP step 1* stands for the first step in the learning progression for that standard. As your team reviews this sample calendar, consider how you and your team members might use it as a model for developing your own team calendar.

While teaching the unit, teachers make notes about possible calendar adjustments as they are teaching, and they discuss suggestions for revisions at a team meeting. We recommend your team use or adapt the following four steps when devising a calendar.

1. Begin constructing a unit calendar by indicating any days off school or other important events like field trips.

2. Note the days when team literacy meetings will be held. This will help to appropriately pace common formative assessments since data-inquiry conversations will take place at these meetings. Our team met formally each Tuesday during collaborative team time our school provides in our schedule. However, we also met frequently and informally each day.

3. Indicate when to administer a pre-assessment prior to the unit to plan instruction.

4. Fill in standards and assessments based on learning progressions in a realistic time frame for the unit.

In the next two sections, we examine factors teams should consider when developing their own calendars and provide tips teams can use to enhance their calendars.

Considerations for Team Calendars

Our third-grade team discussed many factors when planning for and pacing the four-week unit calendar in figure 3.8 (page 89). The following list notes some key aspects of our team's decision making in creating this sample calendar. Use it to guide your own team's thinking about its calendar.

▸ **Sequencing unit standards:** Because several priority and supporting standards typically exist within a single unit, teams must carefully decide how to map out all the learning taking place. On the sample calendar, our team chose to begin with supporting standard RL.3.1— "Ask and answer questions to demonstrate understanding of a text, referring explicitly to the text as the basis for the answers" (NGA &

CCSSO, 2010)—so it could quickly collect data on this standard. That way, the team could glean information about who might struggle with subsequent priority standards because the skills embedded within the supporting standard are necessary to adequately reach proficiency on priority standards RL.3.2 and RL.3.3. These data can also help teachers plan future whole-group and small-group lessons. RL.3.1 persists as a focus while instruction on the other priority standards occurs, as students use the skill of asking and answering questions about a story to fully master RL.3.2 and RL.3.3.

▸ **Pacing assessments:** Notice that there are assessment opportunities listed on every day of the team calendar in figure 3.8 (page 89). At first glance, this may seem overwhelming or unmanageable. However, remember that assessing students is a natural part of the learning process, and most of the assessments listed in the calendar are informal and unobtrusive. They are simply a way to check-in on students as they are participating in the day's work to ensure students are on track. These observations help teachers make decisions about next steps for instruction (sometimes right in that very moment). Also, you'll notice that the calendar in figure 3.8 specifically lists only assessments for priority standards. Though not indicated on the calendar explicitly, teachers will also be sure to informally assess students on supporting standards as well to ensure understanding and adjust instruction as needed.

▸ **Assessing fluency:** Our team decided to monitor fluency priority standard RF.3.4—"Read with sufficient accuracy and fluency to support comprehension" (NGA & CCSSO, 2010)—from the onset of the unit so that the acquisition of this standard could support all future literacy learning. We committed to assess fluency through unobtrusive running records for every student (a few at a time) throughout the first five days of the unit. Teachers would have fluency data on each student by the end of the first week. Our team would then analyze the data from the running records and discuss them at the team data-inquiry meeting on day 7. You'll notice fluency checks scheduled for later in the unit, which allow teachers to further monitor those students who need additional differentiated support

▸ **Pacing and assessing writing:** On the calendar, notice that the team immediately begins the unit with instruction on the writing priority standard W.3.2a—"Introduce a topic and group related information together" (NGA & CCSSO, 2010)—as writing instruction is a daily staple of literacy instruction. This standard becomes the prime focus of whole- and small-group writing instruction throughout the four-week unit (and can be reinforced in other content studies as well). Instruction aligned with both the priority and supporting writing standards continues throughout the unit calendar.

▶ **Repeating learning progression steps:** As you skim the calendar's pacing, notice that some learning progressions' steps repeat for both reading and writing standards. For example, students receive instruction for step 5 of standard RL.3.3's learning progression on day 6 and day 7. A team may repeat a learning progression step for one of two reasons: (1) preassessment data indicate that students will need more than one lesson on the step in order to adequately learn it or (2) the team has concluded the step is complex and will take longer to teach and assess than others.

▶ **Considering time constraints:** When determining unit pacing, teams must consider time issues such as how long it typically takes students to complete standards-aligned classwork and assessments. For example, teachers might keep in mind the rate at which third graders can produce written compositions or whether students should type or handwrite those compositions. Teams must also understand that the timeline for each learning progression step should be swift but not so swift that it is unproductive.

▶ **Scheduling common formative assessments:** Our team scheduled the first common formative assessment for the fifth day of the unit. We specifically designed this assessment to check on students' proficiency on step 4 of reading standard RL.3.3's learning progression. We planned for our teachers to also issue a common formative assessment on that day so they can measure students' progress throughout the week with priority standard W.3.2a. The team will eventually analyze the data from both these common formative assessments and discuss these data at the team's scheduled literacy meeting the following week. All of this appears on the calendar. During any team data-inquiry conversation, team members must determine next steps for instruction based on common assessment data.

We scheduled our team's next common assessment for day 14. For this check-in point, our team created a common assessment that assesses learning progression steps for two standards at once: RL.3.2 (formatively) and RL.3.3 (summatively). Because both standards address elements of fiction, our teachers decided to maximize assessment time by having students demonstrate their proficiency on both skills at once even though whole class instruction has reached a culmination for one standard and not the other. They carefully crafted the assessment items so that the team can glean precise data to measure each skill distinctly.

▸ **Reserving time for corrective teaching and extension:** Finally, our team decided not to plan instruction on priority standards for the day preceding and following the common summative assessment on day 19. Our team felt it necessary to leave a small window of time for additional corrective teaching or extension of student learning prior to and following the common summative assessment. Providing this window at the end of the unit gives teachers a final opportunity to reteach or refine the learning of all priority and supporting standards. Additionally, this time helps account for any necessary calendar adjustments due to emergency closing days, newly scheduled assemblies, or other unforeseen events. After providing a few days of corrective teaching and extension, teams should strive to adhere to the agreed-on unit end point so they do not reduce the instructional days planned for subsequent units.

As Alice Furry and Lexie Domaradzki (2010) of the National Reading Technical Assistance Center assert, "Implementing a pacing schedule commits the district, school, and classroom to teach reading every day . . . from the first day of school to the last day of school, days before and after holidays, testing and assessment days, and special days." The team calendar is a team's commitment to ensuring high-quality, sequenced, and well-paced instruction throughout the duration of a unit. Additionally, as teams build unit calendars, team members must always be mindful that, while all students need to learn the material, they won't all consistently learn purely through whole-class instruction or at the same rate. Teams must address some students' individual needs through other avenues, including intervention and extension, as we discuss in chapter 5 (page 125). While planning instruction, a team needs to acknowledge that if most students struggle at any point during the learning progression, the team will re-evaluate its original timeline to cater to students' needs in real time.

Tips for Team Calendars

The following points may help teams generate their own calendars.

▸ One to two weeks before a unit starts, teams should engage in the PREP process articulated in chapter 1 (page 11) to gain clarity and prepare for teaching the unit, plus design a preassessment. Teams might even elect to work together in the summer to plan.

▸ Not all instruction within the instructional time frame will center on priority standards. Teams will want to build in instructional opportunities for nonpriority (supporting) standards as well.

▸ For more robust learning progression steps that take two days or more to teach, teams should enter the assessment on the step's last day since that is when teachers will assess the standard.

▸ In a well-functioning PLC culture, teams meet for different purposes. Teachers need time to participate in a team data-inquiry meeting (see chapter 5, page 125) where they can analyze and discuss the collected results from common formative assessments. Teams also get together to collaboratively score assessments (see chapter 4, page 101), which helps inform the data-inquiry meetings. During some units of instruction, teams will input collaborative scoring on their calendars to be sure they carve out time to interpret the rubric uniformly and collect anchor papers. This helps ensure they are consistent in their scoring, which contributes to accurately analyzing data.

▸ *Intervention* and *responsive teaching* are interchangeable umbrella terms that encompass both corrective instruction and extension. *Corrective instruction* speaks to PLC critical question 3, as it services students who have yet to master a standard. *Extension*, which appeals to critical question 4, refers to those who have successfully mastered a standard and thus need extended opportunities. Although teachers responsively teach in that they cater to students' needs and provide necessary support daily based on classroom formative assessments, corrective instruction and extensions are built into the team calendar. This ensures teachers directly make the instructional moves that need to occur based on the data-inquiry meeting's review of the common formative assessment.

▸ While providing an intervention, which could last one to three days, teachers continue to teach other standards within the learning progression unless they determine that most students have not shown mastery. If this is the case, teachers must critically examine their instruction and teaching practices to provide alternative strategies that will help students succeed. Just because they have taught a standard does not necessarily mean that students have learned it.

▸ Teachers also calibrate the common summative assessment, take it to a team meeting for data analysis, and account for corrective instruction of this assessment in the subsequent unit's calendar.

▸ Teams should group together standards as makes sense for assessment purposes. This serves to maximize class time. While assessments are both valuable and essential to student growth, teachers must aim to provide and protect ample time for instruction and intervention, when the learning and growing takes place. Ultimately, we want students to be able to synthesize information, make connections between the standards, and think critically to draw conclusions about the unit's overarching concepts. In grouping standards—especially in the common summative assessment—teachers give students opportunities to demonstrate a wealth of new knowledge and skills.

EXERCISE

Map Out Instruction and Assessment Dates

At this junction, work with your team to produce a team calendar. Consider the suggestions in the preceding list to assist each other in completing this work.

Use the following questions to guide this exercise.

★ In what ways might we prepare for our team meeting to make efficient use of our time? (For example, teachers can research preassessments to share with the team, draft ideas for the assessment tasks, research a tool or format for the team calendar, and so on.)

★ Who will be responsible for creating a calendar template that the team can fill in together during discussion? Where will this document live for all to access?

★ In which order should we address priority and supporting standards so we can build on each of them during instruction?

★ How can we pace instruction so that we account for data-inquiry meetings, enabling us to be responsive in our teaching?

Summary

It is critical that teacher teams carefully design a learning progression that sequences the step-by-step instructional moves teachers take to teach the skills and knowledge necessary for students to attain mastery of priority standards in any given unit. This crucial aspect of curriculum design also provides teachers and teams with guidance in developing assessments, gathering evidence of student performance, and adjusting instruction to meet the specific needs of students.

When teams develop a learning progression, they also take into account the complex text students will experience as the vehicle to meet expectations. Such works can also serve as reading and writing mentor texts. Since choosing complex text can prove challenging, teachers implement a three-part model to assist them in selecting appropriate fiction, nonfiction, and cross-curricular texts. It involves examining the quantitative and qualitative aspects of prose or even poetry, as well as considering students' characteristics and the tasks the team will ask students to perform.

Once teams build a learning progression and determine assessments, they fashion a team calendar. On it, they record dates for instruction, assessments, interventions, and data analysis. Individual teachers can duplicate the team calendar and input their classroom assessments on it, as well, to be sure to intentionally map out all that is required to assist all students towards mastery of priority standards.

After teams participate in the exercise to map out instruction and assessment dates, the next chapter supports teams in understanding and designing rubrics and student checklists and using them as instructional tools. Additionally, teams will learn a process for consistently scoring student work so all teachers assess uniformly.

CHAPTER 4

Develop Collective Understanding of Mastery Expectations

With a solid learning progression in place, teachers position themselves to deliver a guaranteed and viable learning journey for every student. Thus far, teams have mapped the steps students will take to acquire the knowledge and skills needed to master targeted literacy standards. Additionally, they have determined how to assess students along the way. In doing this work as a team, teachers put in place a secure progression of literacy-focused learning in all classrooms. Yet as part of a PLC culture, the commitment to collaboration continues. Teachers must collectively understand what it means for a student to master each standard and not just what type of data to collect to measure students' progress. Without this collective understanding, there is no assurance that teachers will evaluate all students similarly and hold them to the same learning expectations. What does mastery look like? How will teachers know when a student has mastered a learning standard? How will teachers measure student proficiency and do so uniformly?

Despite the necessity of discussing and scoring student work together, many teams fail to collaborate on this critical aspect of PLCs. Teams successfully prepare for instruction, but often, each teacher evaluates student performance in isolation. Consequently, teachers come to realize that, just down the hallway, colleagues lack clarity on what mastery looks like. Or, they happen into a conversation that reveals a notable difference in their and other teachers' evaluation of student performance. Upholding a commitment to collaboration helps teams avoid this common setback as they work together to promote continued clarity and solidify consistent expectations in specific ways. As teachers implement literacy standards across content areas, this work is important for evaluating reading comprehension and writing in social studies, science, and other disciplines so that all high-inference rubric items are also interpreted and scored uniformly.

This effort is the focus of this chapter, which covers rubrics (understanding rubric types, rubric development, and using them as instructional tools), student checklists (creating a list of items an assignment requires), and collaborative scoring (scoring consistently and collecting anchor papers).

Rubrics

Teachers of any grade likely come across a medley of rubrics—also called *rating scales*—with different point scales, formats, and purposes used to assess students' performance on a variety of artifacts. As Susan M. Brookhart (2013) articulates the value of rubrics by stating:

> Rubrics are important because they clarify for students the qualities their work should have. This point is often expressed in terms of students understanding the learning target and criteria for success. For this reason, rubrics help teachers teach, they help coordinate instruction and assessment, and they help students learn. (p. 11)

When teams construct and use rubrics well, it benefits both teachers and students. Rubrics help to actualize expectations for mastery and allow students to view their progress in a concrete way. With a rubric, students understand their current level of proficiency of a standard in any content area and also discern the exact criteria necessary to achieve at the next level. Moreover, they improve literacy-skill outcomes by distinguishing the distinct reading or writing skills associated with each level of proficiency. With clear literacy outcomes defined, teachers and students can specify individualized areas of strength and areas for growth.

With these factors in mind, this section examines types of rubrics, common analytic rubrics and their development, and the use of rubrics as an instructional tool.

Types of Rubrics

The most common types of rubrics are holistic and analytic, although sometimes educators use other kinds, like task-specific rubrics. In *The Fundamentals of (Re)designing Writing Units*, author Kathy Glass (2017) describes holistic rubrics:

A holistic rubric might include a broad entry about the use of proper writing conventions instead of specifying which particular convention is the focus (such as proper use of subject-verb agreement or quotation marks in dialogue). Usually, holistic-scoring systems are used with an on-demand prompt for a school, district, or state summative assessment. They are efficient and useful when scoring student products on a large scale and can even work well for some classroom assessments to determine how the class performs as a whole to inform instruction. Although these rubrics do reflect students' strengths and weaknesses, they often provide a single score without feedback to identify specific areas that need attention or demonstrate where a student shows mastery. (p. 60)

Holistic rubrics typically group more than one skill, revealing a general picture of student performance. For a concrete example, review the following grade 3 narrative writing rubric excerpt from the Smarter Balanced Assessment Consortium (2014):

The organization of the narrative, real or imagined, is fully sustained and the focus is clear and maintained throughout:

- an effective plot helps to create a sense of unity and completeness
- effectively establishes setting, and narrator/characters
- consistent use of a variety of transitional strategies to clarify the relationships between and among ideas; strong connection between and among ideas
- natural, logical sequence of events from beginning to end
- effective opening and closure for audience and purpose

This excerpt groups a series of skills together as meeting level 4 out of four levels for the trait (category) Organization/Purpose. A list of these skills at level 3 includes the same number of items but with descriptors reflecting an *adequate* and *generally maintained* performance.

Unlike holistic rubrics, *analytic* rubrics are educative in that each criterion is devoted to a specific skill that students need to master. Consequently, these rubrics provide teachers, as well as students, with feedback for improvement. In this regard, analytic rubrics are a highly effective tool for conducting classroom instruction, gauging students' literacy-skill development, and scoring both formative and summative assessments.

A *task-specific* rubric details criteria specific to a particular assignment, such as the following items for a science writing task: *accurately details the characteristics of ecosystems, thoroughly reveals the differences between two ecosystems*, and *correctly explains the similarities between ecosystems*. This type of rubric assesses knowledge pertaining to a specific unit topic; it measures performance for a single point in time, and it is often only applicable to one assignment. Due to its temporary application to one assignment or one unit, the feedback provided to the student doesn't typically allow for the tracking or monitoring of long-term goals. The student knows how he or she performed on this one assignment but has limited information about how to improve his or her skills for the next unit of study. Given these limitations, we focus our efforts in this chapter on analytic rubrics, which can be used for common and in-class assessments.

Common Analytic Rubrics

Since analytic rubrics target and isolate specific skills that are typically taught and assessed, teacher teams benefit from using this type of rubric. When they agree on adopting the same analytic rubric, it's called a *common* analytic rubric, which, not surprisingly, they use to score *common* assessments. With this tool, teams collect information for gleaning strengths and weaknesses in students' performance to move their learning forward (Jonsson & Svingby, 2007).

Anytime teams assess certain skills within and across content areas, as appropriate, they can use either the same analytic rubric or applicable line items from it. This allows teams to gain comparative data and students to observe their own progress. Both groups can then identify skills for students to work on and even set personal growth goals. Generally, common analytic rubrics ensure teams have several data points from which to assess students' proficiency, check their progress over time, and thoughtfully plan instruction and interventions. They are also especially useful in monitoring students' literacy-skill development because they allow teachers and students to delineate specific strengths and areas for growth in reading and writing. For example, writing itself is intricate and has many unique features that an analytic rubric can clearly define and distinguish as separate criteria. Instead of receiving one cumulative and vague score for an overall writing piece, teachers can individually assign scores relative to distinct features, such as organization, content, supporting details, word choice, grammar, or mechanics. This type of transparency enhances collaborative scoring, allows students to know precisely what they need to work on, and provides targeted feedback for revisions and continued growth.

So, it should come as no surprise that common analytic rubrics fit the bill of addressing the second critical question of a PLC: *How will we know if our students have learned the knowledge and skills we want them to?* (DuFour et al., 2016). Teams use this type of rubric to assess student performance based on set criteria that align to standards. Relative to our discussion of learning progressions in chapter 3 (page 61), rubrics set the learning expectations for students so the success criteria that they need to achieve are transparent. In this way, teachers also utilize the rubric as an instructional tool so students can be advocates for their learning. (See the section Rubrics as an Instructional Tool, page 111.)

Regardless of its visual format, an analytic rubric encompasses three common components: (1) scoring criteria (standard or skill), (2) levels of performance, and (3) criteria descriptors. With these components decided, teams can then test the rubric. Figure 4.1 (page 106) depicts an example analytic rubric with these components. It addresses two learning targets from a single standard and two different writing criteria. Our team gleaned the specific reading skills from the full standard during the unwrapping process in chapter 1 (page 11) and arranged them into the learning progression of knowledge and skills leading up to the overarching standard in chapter 3 (page 61). This more granular rubric is helpful when assessing and collecting data specific to those targets or verbs that are embedded within the overall standard. And because students will be demonstrating proficiency of the targets by way of a written task, the two additional writing criteria provide feedback on all aspects of the task. For teachers and students, this sort of rubric offers more explicit feedback since the scoring criteria and criteria descriptors are broken down by skill rather than by the full overarching standard.

In reviewing this rubric, notice how the criteria descriptors illustrate the justification behind a particular score and indicate to students what they can do to improve and move closer to mastery. Also, recognize how this rubric indicates the opportunity to assign half-values for students who demonstrate some characteristics found in two adjoining columns. In that case, teachers may prefer to assign and mark on the rubric an in-between score to reflect the student's performance in each of the two adjacent columns. Teams collaboratively make the decision whether to utilize a half-value, and as such, all members should consistently implement this option (or not implement it) for scoring and reporting purposes.

The following section explains and explores each of the three sections we highlight in this rubric.

Levels of Performance

Scoring Criteria

Criteria Descriptors

Scoring Criteria	4.0 Extends	3.5	3.0 Mastery	2.5	2.0 Developing Mastery	1.5	1.0 Novice
Describe characters in a story. (RL.3.3a)	Makes inferences about characters that go beyond the explicit details of the story		Accurately describes a character in a story (his or her traits, motivations, or feelings) Uses descriptive language to provide a thorough description.		Provides a partially accurate, limited, or vague description of a character		Has missing or inaccurate character descriptions
Explain how characters' actions contribute to the sequence of events. (RL.3.3b)	Analyzes how the actions of two or more characters propel a story forward or impact the plot		Accurately explains how a character's actions contribute to other events in the sequence of a story		Demonstrates a limited understanding of how characters contribute to the sequence of events Explains a character's actions, but does not connect them to the story sequence		Does not explain how a character's action relates to an event in a story
Introduces the text or topic of the writing task	Introduces the text or topic by providing a preview of the big ideas or using a hook to capture the reader's attention		Includes a topic sentence that clearly introduces the text or topic		Attempts to introduce the topic Text or topic is not completely clear to the reader		Does not introduce the text or topic of the writing task
Organizes information and ideas clearly	Uses a unique organizational structure to effectively convey ideas and connect		Groups like information together to clearly convey ideas Includes a variety of transition words to link ideas		Attempts some form of organization Contains some unclear or off-topic information		Contains ideas that are unclear or difficult to follow

Source for standards: NGA & CCSSO, 2010.

Figure 4.1: Rubric for analyzing student performance of learning targets within a standard.

Common Analytic Rubric Development

When teachers collaboratively design a common analytic rubric, they must clarify and agree on expectations for student mastery, in addition to descriptors for other performance levels. The goal of creating an analytic rubric is to create a rubric that teams can repeatedly use in multiple assessment situations as students demonstrate their understanding of particular standards throughout the year. Providing various opportunities for students to show to what degree they master standards (and the degree to which they've mastered essential literacy skills inherent in the standard) allows for practice and the assurance of proficiency. For example, if the target standard requires students to use key details to identify a text's main idea, teachers can assign tasks involving various complex texts across content areas while utilizing the same common rubric to measure student understanding of the standard as well as literacy skills students must employ to achieve it.

To make rubrics instruments that guide them in fairly and accurately measuring students' performance and achievement, teachers participate in calibration sessions, which are discussed later in this chapter (see Collaborative Scoring, page 116). For now, review the following four general steps for rubric generation. As you read these steps, consider the example rubric in figure 4.1 as a guide while designing rubrics or revising existing ones.

1. **List the scoring criteria:** For standards-aligned rubrics, the learning targets (or skills) are the elements to be measured, so list them on the rubric's left-hand side to indicate the scoring criteria. Some discrete literacy-focused criteria might include *draw inferences using key details*, *use sensory details to describe a setting*, *differentiate between fact and opinion*, and *use correct punctuation*.

   To avoid overlap, which would only create confusion when scoring, ensure that each criterion is dedicated to a separate skill and positioned in its own row. For example, in figure 4.1, the focus is on describing characters and their actions, so the learning targets our third-grade team chose align with this topic of study. When students complete a summative assessment demonstrating their overall understanding of elements of fiction, teachers will use a comprehensive rubric with more criteria items. For a unit common formative assessment, teams—as well as teachers in their classrooms—will chunk the discrete standards into a manageable group of learning targets.

2. **Determine the levels of performance and the terminology:** Most rubrics have between three and six levels of performance. If possible, teams should use the same number system as reflected in the school or district report card. This is particularly important in a standards-based grading system where report cards list the same learning standards to report on learning outcomes (Townsley & Wear, 2020). Some rubrics include numbers and terms; others include one or the other. If using terms, just as the point scale should reflect the school's or district's grading system, so, too, should the terms coupled with each score, such as *advanced* or *extends* for level 4; *proficient* or *mastery* for level 3; *developing mastery* or *partially proficient* for level 2; and *basic* or *novice* for level 1. Some schools may need to revise their rubrics to adopt growth language, so that they avoid judgmental language (for example, *excellent*, *fair*, and *poor*), or create terms, if desired, where they currently are absent. For performance label ideas or suggestions, consult curriculum products or standardized tests. Enter these performance levels across the top row of the rubric, as shown in figure 4.1 (page 106).

3. **Craft criteria descriptors:** With the assessment criteria and performance levels in place, teams collaborate to write descriptors that match each level of performance. Rubric designers begin in one of two ways. In one approach, begin with the Mastery (proficient) column, which represents the grade-level expectations and aligns with the standard. Then build up or down from there. Others take the approach of beginning with the Extends column, describing what student work looks like when they move beyond the grade-level mastery expectation, which is more sophisticated. From this point, describe performance levels moving down. Later in this section, we provide some tips for writing descriptors. Use the descriptors in figure 4.1 as a reference while perusing these suggestions.

4. **Test the rubric:** Once done, teams should test the rubric by analyzing and scoring actual student work or teacher-created exemplar pieces. The goal is to ensure sufficient clarity in the language among all team members so that they can effectively implement the rubric. Even though teachers try it out, once they score actual student work, the rubrics often need tweaking and revision, which could conceivably occur during the collaborative-scoring session. Nevertheless, simulating using the rubric is a proactive measure that could lead to identifying and avoiding mistakes that may arise as teams analyze student work.

Crafting descriptors—the most involved of these steps—warrants further exploration. Therefore, teachers should consider the following definitions of performance levels when writing them. Even though teachers might devise these descriptors together, to accurately score students' work, they should participate in collaborative scoring (see page 116) to ensure that all team members interpret them consistently. While reading these suggestions, use figure 4.1 (page 106).

> ▸ The Extends column serves a distinct purpose since, in a PLC, a teacher's obligation is to push or encourage students who already know a skill to extend their learning. Providing students who have already mastered a standard with a descriptor dedicated to extending performance beyond proficient-level expectations upholds this commitment. When crafting this descriptor, discuss what it would look like for a student to extend beyond grade-level expectations when demonstrating proficiency on a particular standard. For example, in figure 4.1, notice that the Extends descriptor for standard RL.3.3 dictates that students can make *inferences* that *go beyond* explicit details and *analyze* how the actions of *two or more characters* propel a story forward. These expectations extend beyond what the standard expects for a proficient third-grade student.

> ▸ The Mastery column signifies the goal for all students, as it reflects grade-level expectations articulated in the standards. To construct this descriptor, teachers use the language of the standard as a guide and discuss what proficiency should resemble. This might include adding further detail for more specificity, for example. For standard RL.3.3, notice that the Mastery column in figure 4.1 indicates that students must use descriptive language to provide a thorough character description. Although this language is not in the language of the standard, the team added the words *descriptive language* to make the mastery expectation more precise.

> ▸ The Developing Mastery column identifies what the initial stages of proficiency look like for a student. Early in the instructional cycle, many students will be at this level, as it demonstrates a partial understanding of the standard progressing toward mastery. Students who are developing mastery typically require prompting and support from the teacher because they are not yet independently demonstrating proficiency. Notice in figure 4.1 that students who are developing mastery of RL.3.3 provide character descriptions that are vague or limited, which indicates

that they aren't yet proficient in fully comprehending the text and meeting the skill independently. Additionally, these students may be able to explain a character's actions but are not yet be able to articulate how the action contributes to the story's sequence. At this level, students have grasped some concepts necessary for mastery but are still working to reach the full expectation of the standard.

▸ The Novice column reflects when students are still unable to demonstrate a partial understanding of the standards, despite adult guidance and prompting. The descriptions tend to be far from proficient and typically indicate deficits, as a student's responses are inaccurate or missing. This student still needs additional differentiated opportunities to learn and master the material. For standard RL.3.3 (figure 4.1, page 106), our team indicated that a student's character description at this level is limited or inaccurate, and he or she cannot yet explain how a character's action is related to a story's sequence.

In the early elementary grades (typically grades preK–2), the criteria descriptors often include language generic enough that teams can apply the rubric to either oral or written work. The goal is to create a rubric suitable for multiple assessment situations, such as small-group discussions, conferences with students, or cases where students complete a task or written response. This leads to efficient collection of student performance data. Once your team has a completed rubric, it should turn its attention to the ways it can effectively use the rubric as an instructional tool for students.

EXERCISE

Develop a Common Analytic Rubric

Using the steps from this section, work as a team to design a grade-level common analytic rubric. Then try out the rubric prior to scoring students' work.

Use the following questions to guide this exercise.

★ What point scale will we use on the rubric?

★ Do the rubric's performance levels include numbers as well as phrases, such as *novice, developing mastery, mastery,* and *extends*?

★ What are the scoring criteria and associated descriptors for the common formative and common summative assessments?

★ Is there a rubric we currently use that we can adjust to ensure the rubric includes the essential components?

Rubrics as an Instructional Tool

Intentionally utilizing rubrics during instruction—that is, using rubrics when introducing new concepts, modeling a strategy or skill, embedding time for independent practice, or providing intervention for students—allows students to assume responsibility for their learning and contribute to achievement. To ready students to address the full scope of a common analytic rubric, teachers conduct a series of direct instruction lessons yielding formative assessments that focus on specific learning targets represented as line items on the rubric. During instruction, teachers can isolate these learning targets by asking students to locate and circle them to direct their focus. To capitalize on using the rubric as an instructional tool for improvement, teams can review the following suggested student actions together and determine how they will have students exercise them. When reviewing these suggestions, teams might decide that teachers use selected suggestions for in-class formative assessments in preparation for the common assessments.

▸ **Set goals and track progress:** Rubrics can equip students with the information necessary to make strides in their learning by setting goals over time and tracking their progress. Students, teachers, and parents or guardians can review a student's past performance and celebrate growth throughout a unit, semester, or school year. By using the rubric as an instructional tool, teachers provide students with consistent feedback and growth opportunities throughout instruction and prior to a summative assessment. Self-monitoring enables students to take charge of their learning and advocate for themselves as they progress.

▸ **Understand task expectations:** As previously stated, rubrics communicate success criteria to students so they are aware of the expectations of assignments they complete. Popham (2007) writes that it is essential that students understand the evaluative criteria the teacher team will judge them on, stating, "How can students make decisions about the effectiveness of their progress in mastering a particular curricular outcome if they don't know the factors by which their performance is to be evaluated?" (p. 80). Having criteria foremost in their minds early in the unit via a rubric sets the stage for success, as students progress with a keen focus on desired outcomes.

▸ **Discern strong from weak writing samples:** During instruction, teachers deliver learning experiences in which students compare strong and weak anonymous student writing samples based on specific target areas. For instance, in a social studies lesson focused on comparing how people adapt to different environments around the world, teachers present written responses that provide thorough evidence to compare how people from different environments have adapted to their unique surroundings, as well as vague responses that lack textual support. Students score the papers against the line item on the rubric for comparing key details only and notice what constitutes proficiency. This exercise of using rubric sections to assess writing allows students to discover what qualities constitute optimal performance so they can strive to achieve it. Matching criteria with concrete examples helps students understand how the rubric supports their growth.

▸ **Self-assess:** To help students self-assess, teachers familiarize students with the rubric elements and format, plus model how students can optimally use rubrics. For example, as students complete a rough draft of a longer piece of writing (an original narrative story or opinion piece, for example), they can use the rubric to assess their efforts, realize which areas of their papers need attention, and make adjustments as needed.

▸ **Conduct peer feedback:** Rubrics also serve as a tool that classmates use to give feedback to each other. During peer feedback in grades 2 and 3, a rubric acts much like a detailed checklist as students use it for crosschecking their partner's work to ensure they have all the necessary components in their writing. Additionally, students use the criteria listed to provide guidance on how their partner might improve in a particular area. For example, suppose that a line item on a second-grade opinion writing rubric states that students must include a topic sentence, and to achieve mastery, both the topic and the writer's opinion on the topic must be clearly stated. A peer feedback partner will look to see that his or her partner has written a topic sentence (the skill identified in the rubric) and will also check to see if he or she has a clearly-stated opinion (the criteria for mastery). If he finds that one of these is missing, he can refer to the rubric while offering suggestions for improvement. Generally, peers will not provide teacher-level feedback, but offering this type of peer interaction emphasizes the importance of feedback and revision, allows students to feel a sense of responsibility, and helps to establish a collaborative classroom community. When students review each other's papers, they can also apply what they learn to improve their own papers.

▸ **Solicit teacher feedback:** Teachers use rubrics to note areas where students must stretch or make improvements and then offer pertinent strategies to meet these areas for growth or extension. Students record the strategies and practice applying the necessary skills to their drafts; the teacher feedback acts as a revisionary tool during the writing process.

For rubrics to be effective as an instructional tool, the language in them must be accessible to students. Typically, grades 2–3 teams create a student version of their rubrics. The student-accessible version breaks down the standard's expectations in student-friendly language. When creating a student copy, teams must be cautious to ensure that the rigor and intention of the newly worded performance descriptors mirror the original at each proficiency level. In many cases, teams may choose to maintain much of the same academic language with students and conduct lessons to introduce the rubric's academic vocabulary and format.

Student Checklists

Checklists are companion pieces to the scoring criteria in a rubric. Whereas a rubric defines the quality of each scoring criterion, a checklist itemizes an assignment's requirements. Teachers can refer to items on the rubric and the checklist as they conduct lessons to make a connection between learning experiences and expectations. Unlike a rubric, teachers do not use a checklist for scoring or reporting purposes; rather, the list serves as a guide and self-checking tool for students as they work to complete a task to demonstrate their learning. For example, when creating a checklist for writing a summary of a science passage, a teacher team should refer to the descriptors in the team's common rubric and include line items such as, *I name the title and the author of the text, I tell the main idea of the passage,* and *I explain the supporting details in the passage.* Figure 4.2 shows an example student checklist for a writing assignment that measures student proficiency on a reading standard based on a social studies text. Rather than using checklists as an afterthought, students should use them in real time as they work. Therefore, teams should write checklist line items using first-person pronouns and present-tense verbs that engage students' reading skills.

Writing prompt: Describe two important people in our community. Use evidence from the article to explain why they are important.

☐ I include a topic sentence with the title and author of the text.

☐ I name two important people in the community.

☐ I describe two people by telling who they are and what they do.

☐ I include evidence from the text to explain why both people are important.

☐ I use complete sentences in my response.

Figure 4.2: Student checklist for a writing assignment.

With a definitive checklist in place, both teacher and students maintain parallel expectations for the requirements of students' end product. Teachers conduct lessons around many items on the checklist since they match the learning targets on the rubric, but this isn't necessarily the case for all line items. Some requirements might be reminders for students of what to include in their writing and represent skills previously taught, like *I spell words correctly* or *I include a creative title.*

Once teams create a checklist, they should present it to students in an engaging way to generate student ownership and familiarity with items. Consider the following exercises to effectively share it. These exercises serve a dual purpose: (1) they expose students to elements of the writing that they will produce (regardless of content area), and (2) they set up the expectations for their task (Glass, 2017).

1. Ask students to read and compare exemplary samples of writing (either published or student-written) to identify elements that are common among them. For example, teachers could pose the following group task, in which they distribute the writing samples on cards: *Inside the envelope in front of you are cards with excerpts of different writing samples. Read all*

the cards once. Then, read them again to figure out what common elements you notice among them all. Make a list of these elements to share with the class. Before students begin the activity, teachers can model the activity using excerpts from a different genre. Note that you can use samples of text from a variety of content areas, which serves the dual purpose of fostering knowledge of the topic and enhancing literacy growth.

2. Have students work collaboratively to create a class-generated list. For example, prior to writing an informative paragraph about volcanoes, a teacher may ask the students to work with a partner or small group to generate a list of the characteristics of well-written informative articles. They might even browse a variety of informational texts—either print or digital—to help identify these characteristics. Groups share their ideas to generate a class list. The class should then review the master list to collapse items, delete unnecessary ones, and add other items, as needed.

3. Have small groups of students create their own unique checklist, and then distribute a teacher-prepared checklist. Have the student groups compare the teacher-created checklist with their group-generated one and identify what is missing on either list. Allow groups to discuss whether items should be added to or deleted from the teacher-prepared checklist, and facilitate a whole-class discussion about their findings.

After some practice with teacher-generated checklists and even rubrics, students may cocreate either tool prior to writing. Doing so promotes critical thinking as students glean the requirements of completing a complex task consistent with the expectations of the grade-level team.

Whether they have a rubric, a checklist, or both, students must be keenly aware of learning expectations. This way, they know what it takes to produce quality products that demonstrate their literacy skill growth, and, depending on the task, they also understand what content-area knowledge they must accumulate. Students can use checklists as a guide while they write to ensure they are including the designated items in their work. Rubrics make them cognizant of the criteria, including the levels of performance, for a given assignment. In addition, rubrics are tools to formatively and summatively assess students' work. Explicitly modeling how to use these instruments throughout instruction can contribute to student improvement.

The following section illustrates how teams conduct a collaborative scoring session to ensure that they consistently evaluate students' work in accordance with the rubric.

EXERCISE

Create Student Checklists

Once your team's common rubric is complete, collaborate to design an accompanying student writing checklist for a common assessment. Write items in first-person point of view with present-tense verbs and accessible language so students can use the checklist as a guide while they address the formative or summative writing task. The questions that follow can guide you in revising an existing checklist or steer you in creating a new one.

Use the following questions to guide this exercise.

★ Are items on the checklist aligned to standards and the rubric?

★ Is each sentence written in first-person point of view and with present-tense verbs?

★ Is the assessment task written at the top of the checklist?

★ How will we introduce the checklist so it captures students' attention and they use it as a useful tool to guide their writing? When might we give students an opportunity to create their own checklists?

Collaborative Scoring

Just as team members must collaborate to determine priority standards, assessment types, and learning progressions, they must also work together to ensure consistency of scoring. This requires that teams calibrate *how* they will score students' work. We refer to this process as a *calibration session*.

While scoring, all teachers aim to arrive at the same score for each criterion. However, this does not always occur. Distribute identical copies of a student-completed assessment and its accompanying rubric to a team of teachers, and it is possible that teachers' scores may vary. While rubrics certainly promote more accurate and informative evaluation of student work, teachers may also interpret the rubric somewhat differently or embrace expectations of student mastery that deviate from each other. This challenge is just as common in less-subjective subjects, such as mathematics, as it is for English language arts or social studies, as teachers unknowingly and unintentionally score student work differently. To close the evaluation gap, teams participate in a calibration session where they align their scoring practices.

When teams convene for a calibration session, they collectively score student work for the same assessment task using an agreed-on common analytic rubric they've designed together. Additionally, uniform scoring requires that teachers administer the task consistently; otherwise, it will have unfair, skewed results. For example, if one teacher assists students with the introduction of an informational writing task and other teachers do not, this support—or lack thereof—will impact student performance, causing an uneven playing field. Use figure 4.3 as a team checklist for the collaborative-scoring process to ensure that team members are aligned in the benefits of calibration.

Calibration Checklist

When we collectively calibrate our team's scoring of students' work, we:

☐ Engage in discussion with colleagues to achieve a common understanding of expectations for student work

☐ Help ensure that team members interpret each level of the rubric consistently and apply the rubric uniformly

☐ Interpret high-inference rubric items using evidence from students' work

☐ Enable reliability and confidence when scoring independently

☐ Collect anchor papers to show levels of performance featured in the rubric

☐ Tap the expertise and input of colleagues

☐ Suggest changes to prompts or rubrics as needed

Figure 4.3: Checklist to calibrate the team-scoring process.

*Visit **go.SolutionTree.com/literacy** for a free reproducible version of this figure.*

During team time, the goal is to reach consensus about student examples of proficiency for each criterion so teachers have consistent impressions of what each level on the rubric means. This ensures that all those scoring student work interpret and apply the rubric uniformly, which increases the assessment data's reliability. To support this endeavor during calibration, teachers collect anchor papers, establish a process for collaborative scoring, and fulfill post-calibration tasks.

Anchor Papers

When teachers review student work as a team in calibration sessions, they determine *anchor papers*—examples of student work that align to each performance level on a rubric. Because teachers can interpret items differently, these anchors give expression to a rubric so that, together, the rubric and anchor papers form a clear picture of what writing at different performance levels looks like.

Since writing-focused rubrics, in particular, contain high-inference items that teachers find difficult to interpret, anchor papers serve as a best representation of what each scoring criterion means. An example of a high-inference item may be one that requires students to provide support for their main ideas in a piece of writing by providing text evidence, examples, or other supporting details. However, teachers may interpret mastery of this skill in a number of different ways. They may be wondering the following.

- How many supporting details are necessary in a student's piece of writing?

- Should evidence from a source be quoted directly or paraphrased?

- Should a student include a combination of text-based evidence and their own thinking?

- What if a student includes only original thoughts?

Anchor papers help to answer questions like these that commonly arise as teachers score in isolation. In this way, they serve as benchmarks for assessing students' writing that contribute to reliability when teachers independently score their students' work. They also aid conversations during parent conferences, as they make family members and guardians aware of how to interpret rubric scores.

Teacher teams can also use their inventory of anchor papers, categorized by levels of performance, for instructional purposes. When teachers conduct lessons using anchor papers, students can capably determine where their writing meets the standard and where they need to focus their attention for improvement. Specifically, students critique and score anchors against the rubric, which challenges them to identify strengths and weaknesses pertinent to targeted writing skills. Teachers also model how to use these sample papers to self-assess and give peer feedback so students can apply these strategies on their own. Teams deem anchors papers that reflect high-quality characteristics that meet or exceed criteria on the rubric as *exemplars*. Along with devising learning activities that ask students to examine weak examples to detect deficiencies and possibly revise them, teachers should also design lessons that give students the opportunity to read, analyze, and emulate exemplars so they can apply elements of good writing to their own work (Graham & Perin, 2007).

The Collaborative-Scoring Process

By participating in a collaborative-scoring process, teachers establish and maintain a shared understanding of the rubric, consistency in their evaluation of student work, and common expectations of mastery for all students in every grade-level classroom. We recommend collaboratively scoring student work at least three times a year for each text type in the curriculum or more throughout an instructional cycle, if time permits. Doing so benefits literacy skill growth for all students as teachers gain clarity around the levels of literacy students must attain to master essential standards. They also gather new ideas for instructing and intervening on key reading and writing concepts. Even singletons (teachers who are without grade-level or content-aligned teammates) can participate in the collaborative-scoring process with colleagues from another grade level, as it is just as important to vertically align student expectations from one grade to the next.

The following sections detail the five steps involved in the collaborative-scoring process that teacher teams should engage in as part of a calibration session.

1. Preselect student samples prior to meeting as a team.

2. Review the task and common rubric.

3. Score the first assignment.

4. Discuss scores and arrive at a consensus.

5. Repeat the process, collect anchors, and take notes.

Preselect Student Samples Prior to Meeting as a Team

In advance of the team meeting, teachers preview their students' papers. They preselect samples that holistically represent a variety of achievement levels, even though the team will ultimately score each line item on the analytic rubric. Specifically, each teacher collects two or three papers at each level—those that appear to meet overall grade-level expectations, those approaching mastery, and those not yet progressing toward mastery—to share with colleagues. If such a sample is available, this collection should also include a paper that seems to extend beyond grade level. Teachers can optionally affix sticky notes to label the general proficiency levels of each pile—*extends*, *mastery*, *developing mastery*, and *novice*, knowing that actual proficiency levels are determined during the team calibration session. Additionally, they should conceal students' names to avoid bias and preserve anonymity during the process. Teachers should devise a system for identifying these papers, such as writing numbers or letters on each paper and generating a class list that matches the code to the students. Teachers then either make enough copies of each sample for every team member or send electronic copies of these preselected papers in advance of the meeting. They will use them to select anchor papers that ground the team in maintaining consistent expectations at each level of proficiency. Teachers should bring the following to the calibration session.

▸ Copies of preselected samples to share with team members (unless they send electronic versions prior to the meeting)

▸ Their entire class set of papers in case there is time to score more than the preselected papers or in the event that the team needs other samples during the discussion

▸ A copy of the common analytic rubric that the team will use to score the assessment

▸ Notetaking tools to collect information about student performance

▸ Charged electronic devices (such as laptops or tablets) to take notes, and to review the papers if everyone is reviewing them electronically

Review the Task and Common Rubric

To begin the calibration process, all teachers review the writing prompt or task that students completed along with the accompanying rubric used for scoring. With a clear understanding of the assessment, teams discuss any high-inference or subjective items on the rubric to clarify expectations. During scoring, a discussion will likely ensue to reach consensus; however, at this point, teachers clarify dubious meanings of any criteria to determine intent. For example, with the standard RL.3.3—"Describe characters in a story (e.g., their traits, motivations, or feelings) and explain how their actions contribute to the sequence of events" (NGA & CCSSO, 2010)—our third-grade team expressly looked for students to use adjectives to describe characters and infer how the characters' actions affected the story's plot. However, questions arose from some teammates, such as the following.

▸ "Will students score a 1 (novice) if they list an adjective as a trait but are unable to explain how characters contribute to the story's sequence?"

▸ "What about students who use phrases and whole sentences to describe characters, rather than specific one-word traits?"

▸ "What if a student explains how a character contributes to the plot at the beginning, middle, and end of a story? Is this student extending beyond grade-level expectations?"

Determining what they expect before scoring as a team well positions teachers to more accurately and consistently assess students' work.

Score the First Assignment

At this step, teams benefit by appointing a facilitator—a teacher on the team or perhaps an instructional coach—who is familiar with the process. The facilitator asks any teacher for a paper preidentified as *extends* (or *mastery*, if no student preliminarily scored in the *extends* level) and reads it aloud. Or, all teachers can read this paper silently since everyone should have a hard or electronic copy. Next, teachers independently score the paper using all criteria on the team's common rubric while taking mental or physical notes about what they notice from the descriptors that match the performance on the student's paper.

Discuss Scores and Arrive at a Consensus

When everyone is ready, the facilitator asks each teacher to share his or her score for one line item at a time. In large teams, the facilitator can record and tally these scores for all to see. If all teachers agree on a score for a criterion, they move on to the next item and repeat the process. The facilitator leads a discussion only for discrepancies in scoring. In these situations, teachers share their impressions of each line item, citing distinct performance indicators from the rubric with textual evidence from the student's work. The team engages in conversation until all teachers agree on a definitive score for the item in question.

During this collaborative discourse, rich conversations emerge about student proficiency and expectations of mastery. This dialogue is a necessary and valuable part of the scoring process. As it develops, teachers often find themselves rethinking and refining their understanding of student mastery and aligning it with their teammates'. If differences of opinion occur, teams should use the rubric language to guide their evaluations, and they may elect to examine additional student examples to make comparisons and further calibrate their scoring practices. If teams don't reach unanimous agreement after further examination, team members must come to accept a majority opinion to continue with the calibration session.

Repeat the Process, Collect Anchor Papers, and Take Notes

Teachers repeat this process for each remaining student paper, forever mindful that the goal is to reach consensus as well as determine which ones qualify as anchors at different performance levels. Sometimes, teams naturally discuss which ones are candidates for anchors as they score papers. Teachers will use these papers when they individually score their class sets of papers after the calibration session.

During the calibration process or after scoring all the preselected papers, teachers need to take notes about how the team can use the selected anchors during instruction. As mentioned previously, teachers may use anchor papers to create learning opportunities where students examine strong and weak samples and notice the elements that account for these differences. They may also have students study exemplars—those papers that are excellent examples—and focus on what makes them stellar so they can emulate the skills the student writer exhibits. Therefore, teachers should leave a calibration session with plans for incorporating anchors into their instructional program, and of course, determine how each teacher can obtain electronic or print copies of these papers. Since it is best to share anonymous student samples, when teachers use these samples for a lesson, they should take off students' names and switch papers with a teacher from another classroom. Or, teachers save the papers to use for the following school year.

While participating in this collaborative process, teachers will also find themselves reflecting on the reliability and validity of the assessment and what changes, if any, the rubric needs. For example, teachers might ask each other the following questions.

▸ "Does the assessment tool provide adequate evidence to determine if a student mastered the standard?"

▸ "Are the questions worded clearly enough to elicit detailed and accurate student responses?"

▸ "Did we format the assessment in a student-friendly manner?"

As teachers consider these factors, they may collectively decide to adjust the assessment for future use or to collect additional formative data so they gain a clearer snapshot of the students' abilities. Either way, participating in the collaborative-scoring process allows teams to develop shared expectations for student achievement and refine assessments to make them as efficient and informative as possible.

Although this process focuses on collaborative scoring of written work, teams can also adapt it for reading or performance tasks in all disciplines. For instance, when teams assess comprehension, teachers can record students reading excerpts. Or, when assessing safety procedures in a science lab, they can videotape precautions students take. These audios or videos then function as the student samples. Using an analytic rubric they have customized for this task, the teacher team members can participate in a modified version of the collaborative-scoring process this section articulates.

Post-Calibration Tasks

After teachers collect anchors during calibration and achieve clarity about student work that aligns to the rubric's proficiency levels, they score the full set of their students' papers. Likely, they need to finish this independently, but teachers might find time available during the team meeting to finish scoring. Afterward, they record their students' strengths and areas for growth to guide future instruction. Additionally, they input all their students' scores onto a spreadsheet or other data-collection tool and reconvene as a group to discuss findings across the grade level and at the classroom level. Read The Data-Inquiry Process section in chapter 5 (page 125) to learn more about how teams use the data from common formative assessments.

EXERCISE
Participate in Collaborative Scoring

Once your team develops a common analytic rubric and issues an accompanying common assessment, engage in collaborative scoring so all team members can independently score their students' papers with consistency against the agreed-on rubric.

Use the following questions to guide this exercise.

★ Are all members aware of the team's calibration session protocol? If not, how can the points in this section be communicated to everyone? (For example, members should know the team's logistic plans for meeting to discuss common formative assessment scores after they issue the assessment.)

★ Who will facilitate our collaborative scoring session?

★ Will we share preselected student writing samples in hard-copy form or electronically?

★ After the calibration session, what are our plans for collecting and sharing anchor papers with students and with members of the team not present?

Summary

Assessments play a critical role in the progression of learning in all classrooms, and to further augment assessments' value, teams in a PLC design effective rubrics and collaboratively score student work to ensure accuracy and consistency when measuring learning. In doing so, second- and third-grade teacher teams emphasize literacy growth as they itemize and agree on the distinct reading and writing skills students must apply to meet the demands of rigorous learning standards across content areas. Analytic rubrics make an abstract learning concept more concrete by explicitly listing the criteria that align to each level of proficiency. When combined with student checklists, students are better able to tackle a literacy task independently, leaning on the checklist as a friendly reminder of the necessary components of the task. These tools assist both teachers and students in ensuring they share consistent expectations for mastery of important skills throughout the year. Embedded calibration sessions further cement the team's collective understanding of learning expectations in all disciplines.

Yet, a team's commitment to student growth doesn't end there. Teachers working in collaborative teams must analyze and respond to the data they collect to determine every student's specific needs in literacy within ELA and across content areas. In chapter 5, the link between data and intervention takes center stage. What do our data tell us about the learning needs of our students? What scaffolds, supports, and other learning opportunities do students need to reach proficiency? How will we appropriately challenge students who are already mastering content? Considering these questions will help sharpen teachers' already-attuned focus on student learning and achievement.

CHAPTER 5

Respond to Student Data to Ensure All Students Learn

A fundamental underpinning of the PLC process centers on the first big idea of a PLC—the belief that all students are capable of learning at high levels. Within this idea reside the two critical questions (questions 3 and 4) that represent this chapter's primary focus: *How will we respond when some students do not learn?* and *How will we extend the learning for students who are already proficient?* (DuFour et al., 2016). To attend to these questions, this chapter demonstrates how teams can use data analysis to determine how they can ensure all students progress in their learning with particular respect to literacy skill development.

As teachers, we are obligated to address each student's unique learning needs. The reality of a heterogeneous classroom is that some students already possess the skills we will teach, while others will require additional time or practice to become proficient. A one-size-fits-all instructional approach does not cater to the needs of all students. Such an approach hinders the learning of students who are ready for more or, conversely, leaves behind students who depend on additional support to learn.

Teacher teams that want to ensure their grades 2–3 students progress in their literacy-skill development, as well as in the rest of the curriculum, need data that confirm that progress. According to Coleman and Pimentel (2012b), "The first three years of instruction (K–2) are the most critical for preventing students from falling behind and preventing reading failure" (p. 3). In preK through second grade, the students who tend to struggle with literacy begin school lacking a strong foundation in language development and foundational reading skills. These students often experience difficulty and frustration while learning to read in the early grades, which continues as they read to learn in later grades. Without adequate data-supported intervention, these students' reading proficiency will continually lag behind while they move from one grade level to the next, as they are never able to comprehend grade-level text. To stop this downward spiral means achieving the fundamental tenet of the PLC process—all students can and will learn at high levels. This requires responsive teaching in the form of intervention.

As we explain in the Learning Progression Timelines section in chapter 3 (page 61), we define *intervention* as the opportunity to remediate skill gaps for students as well as extend learning for those who have already acquired skills. Although the term *intervention* often carries a connotation that implies attending only to those who struggle, we assert that it encompasses both reteaching *and* extension. Therefore, when educators engage in intervention, they meet the needs of learners at all levels of proficiency—those who already demonstrate mastery and are candidates for extension or acceleration and those who haven't yet achieved mastery and benefit from corrective instruction.

In an effort to close achievement gaps and make a profound and long-lasting impact on students' development, educators within a PLC work together to analyze data and use them to provide high-quality, timely, and systematic instruction that targets students' specific needs—in this case, literacy. The team data-inquiry process—a team meeting expressly dedicated to analyzing students' common assessment results—proves essential to this collaboration. Therefore, we begin with this topic, explaining how to implement and prepare for collective data inquiry, and sharing guidelines teachers abide by to respond to data proactively. We address what to do once you have determined when a student or a group of students requires learning extensions or additional time for reteaching.

The Data-Inquiry Process

A recurring public conversation relative to education centers on the amount of time schools devote to assessing students during the school year. When not done well, assessments detract from learning. As a result, critics—including parents and educators—refer to *assessment* as detrimental to students and consider it a distasteful word. However, as discussed in chapter 2 (page 41), when educators issue and use assessments as an effective instructional tool, they can benefit students. Specifically, when teachers systematically collect data, analyze the results, and respond to the ever-shifting instructional needs of students as they strive toward mastery of unit standards, assessment is an altogether powerful contributor to growth. So, it is critical that teams participate in collaborative data inquiry to examine assessment results and use this information to steer instruction intentionally so they push student learning even further.

This section will help guide your understanding of the conversations teacher teams ought to have and the actions they should undertake to further student learning. We support this effort by explaining the team data-inquiry process, establishing how to prepare for a data-inquiry meeting, and providing guidelines for using students' data.

The Purpose of the Team Data-Inquiry Process

Collaborative data inquiry is the foundation of high-performing PLCs, and without it, we cannot ensure high levels of learning for all students. The research of Ronald Gallimore, Bradley A. Ermeling, William M. Saunders, and Claude Goldenberg (2009) finds that when collaborative teams implement an inquiry-focused protocol to address issues with instruction, student achievement significantly increases. This growth only occurs when teams persevere in working on a learning problem until they solve it and realize the correlation between how they teach and positive student gains.

As Jenni Donohoo and Steven Katz (2017) contend, collaborative inquiry helps build teachers' sense of collective efficacy—"the belief that, together, they can positively influence student learning over and above other factors and make an educational difference in the lives of students" (p. 21). Teams that routinely engage in cycles of collaborative data inquiry continuously deepen their knowledge, improve their practice, and impact student success. When teachers can attribute student success to their instructional practices, rather than to outside factors, they shift from the assumption, "I planned and taught the lesson, but they didn't get it," to beliefs, such as, "You haven't taught it until they've learned it" (Gallimore et al., 2009, p. 553). Without evidence, teachers simply hope students learn what they teach rather than guarantee it.

In general, through the data-inquiry process, teachers capitalize on their team members' expertise and learn about instructional experiences that resulted in success for many students. Tapping teammates' knowledge and expertise to generate a wealth of ideas for supporting students during the learning process is a valuable learning opportunity for all team members. Together, team members share ideas on what led to positive outcomes for students. Does a particular teammate have ideas that will enhance instruction for students who are still unclear? Is there a scaffold another teacher used in class that seemed to provide just the right amount of support? Perhaps a teammate suggests a graphic organizer, visual, or hands-on cooperative learning structure that yielded positive results. As teams move through the instructional unit, they continuously collaborate around the informal observational and formal data they collect to refine instruction as needed for students.

Preparing for a Data-Inquiry Meeting

As discussed in chapter 3 (page 61), teams set the stage for their data-inquiry meetings by using their learning progressions to map out core instruction, assessment, intervention, and data-inquiry meeting dates on their team calendar. To ensure your team is prepared for a data-inquiry meeting, use the checklist in figure 5.1 to complete the tasks it lists. Note that you will learn about developing a team data-collection tool in the next section.

Data-Inquiry Meeting Preparation Checklist

☐ Identify the common assessment to be discussed.

☐ Ensure each team member administers and scores all students' assessments in a logical and feasible time frame. (All team members should administer the assessment in their classrooms within a defined and agreed-on window of time; generally, teachers each conduct the assessment within a day or two of their teammates.)

☐ Guarantee all team members have access to the team data-collection tool and are proficient in using it.

☐ Verify all team members enter data (students' results) onto the data-collection tool prior to the meeting. (Teams must be invested in using data-inquiry meeting time to analyze students' results rather than input scores or grade papers. Therefore, teams must emphasize that each teacher enter data prior to the meeting.)

☐ Remind teammates to bring the actual assessments (the task and students' work) to the data-inquiry meeting so teachers can refer to them in conversation.

Figure 5.1: Data-inquiry meeting preparation checklist.

*Visit **go.SolutionTree.com/literacy** for a free reproducible version of this figure.*

Guidelines for Using Student Data in a Data-Inquiry Meeting

To help teachers manage, process, and discuss their results, Tom Many (2009) recommends committing to a set of guidelines, or rules, for using data. Based on his suggestions, we developed three criteria to assist teachers during the data-inquiry process.

1. The data are accessible, easy to manage, and purposefully arranged.

2. The data are publicly discussed.

3. The data are action oriented.

When a teacher team ensures its data meet these criteria, it increases the productivity and utility of the inquiry meeting. The following sections elaborate on each of these criteria.

The Data Are Accessible, Easy to Manage, and Purposefully Arranged

To make data accessible, teams choose and devise a data-collection tool (such as using a print or computer-generated table, chart, graph, or spreadsheet) for sharing and displaying students' results. By serving as a collected representation of data, it is sometimes called a *data wall*—a metaphorical reference if, for example, teachers view data on a computer spreadsheet, or literal if displayed on a wall. Authors and experts on data-based interventions, Austin Buffum, Mike Mattos, and Janet Malone (2018) recommend teams format their data-collection tool to include both individual student results and classroom results for each of an assessment's targets and accompanying scoring criteria.

This tool must also make data easy to manage during the meeting to ensure the inquiry process doesn't become cumbersome and hinder teachers from engaging in the analysis process. Teachers must purposefully arrange data in a format that is complete, accurate, and straightforward (Many, 2009). If not, the team might spend the majority of its meeting working to organize data rather than engaging in the meeting's most critical purpose—collaboratively determining the next steps in instruction for student learning. Displaying data in user-friendly tables, charts, or graphs helps teachers maintain focus on student results and limits potential distractions from a faulty or complicated presentation format.

Teams grant all members—including other professionals who support the students, such as special education teachers, related services providers, teachers of English learners, principals, and assistant principals—access to the data-collection tool. These educators may already be a part of your teacher team and participate in decision making; however, collaborative teams in a PLC can vary depending on the needs of the school. So, inviting invested educators who may not be part of your team to examine the data guarantees that they can responsively support students through their lens.

As discussed in chapter 4 (page 101), teams collaboratively design an analytic rubric that reflects the scoring criteria for a common assessment. In our elements of fiction unit, step 4 of the learning progression includes a common formative assessment that addresses one significant skill: *Describe characters by their traits, motivations, and feelings* (see figure 3.1, page 64). Figure 5.2 shows a portion of our data wall, which includes our third-grade team's common formative assessment and the criteria from our team analytic rubric for the administered assessment. Formatting the data-collection tool as we did helped us clearly display each student's proficiency level for the scoring criteria, highlighting the specific strengths and weaknesses in learning.

Team Common Formative Assessment Data		
Priority standard: Describe characters in a story (e.g., their traits, motivations, or feelings) and explain how their actions contribute to the sequence of events. (RL.3.3)		
Learning target: Describe characters by their traits, motivations, and feelings		
Assessment task: In a two- to three-sentence response, describe a character from a story and use details from the text to support your thinking.		
Student	**Teacher**	**Level of Mastery for the Skill:** Describe a character using details from the story.
Carlos	Teacher A	3.0 (Mastery)
Suzy	Teacher A	2.0 (Developing Mastery)
Latisha	Teacher A	2.0 (Developing Mastery)
John	Teacher B	3.0 (Mastery)
Rohan	Teacher B	2.0 (Developing Mastery)
Anna	Teacher B	3.0 (Mastery)
Ritika	Teacher C	2.0 (Developing Mastery)
Kyle	Teacher C	1.0 (Novice)
Ramon	Teacher C	1.0 (Novice)

Source for standard: NGA & CCSSO, 2010.

Figure 5.2: Team data excerpt for a common formative assessment.

Figure 5.2 provides a modified excerpt of our third-grade team's original work. The original work included many more students. Since this data tool depicts student results for the first common formative assessment of the team's learning progression (refer to step 4 of figure 3.1, page 64), it only includes data for the target skill, *Describe characters by their traits, motivations, and feelings.* Later in the unit, this team will also gather evidence of student proficiency on the full RL.3.3 priority standard: "Describe characters in a story (e.g., their traits, motivations, or feelings) and explain how their actions contribute to the sequence of events" (NGA & CCSSO, 2010). These data then become another column on the tool.

E X E R C I S E
Design a Data-Collection Tool

With your collaborative team, review an upcoming common formative assessment and its common analytic rubric to guide you in designing a data-collection tool that allows for easy access and purposeful management of your team's data.

Use the following questions to guide this exercise.

★ What type of data-collection tool will we use to display our data (for example, a sticky note chart or technology tool)?

★ How will we ensure all team members can access the data-collection tool to record and view student data?

★ What rubric or scoring criteria are we using to measure mastery so we know how to score student work and record this on the data-collection tool?

The Data Are Publicly Discussed

Teams embark on the process of publicly discussing students' results after all teachers enter their data on the tool. To help teammates cultivate a safe, supportive environment conducive for sharing data, education expert and consultant Joellen Killion (2008) suggests using a data-analysis protocol that "keeps the focus on issues rather than people, engages people in an appreciative inquiry approach rather than a deficit approach to a situation, and results in a plan of action that energizes and motivates people" (p. 7).

When teams interact to discuss data, they must determine a set of norms to engage thoughtfully and productively. According to DuFour et. al. (2016), norms represent "commitments developed by each team to guide members in working together. Norms help team members clarify expectations regarding how they will work together to achieve their shared goals." Figure 5.3 has examples of ways to guide a team meeting conversation on developing data-discussion norms. In the first column, teams jot down the overall goals of their data discussions. In this example, we input the guidelines Killion (2008) recommends. In the Avoid This column, teachers brainstorm behaviors that might prevent them from reaching each goal. For instance, to achieve the desired goal of "Keep the focus on issues rather than people," team members might decide that *Blaming each other, Criticizing a teacher's instructional strategies*, or *Refusing to share their data with a teammate* are behaviors to avoid. Therefore, the team adds these to the column. Next, team members discuss how to rewrite the list of behaviors in the Avoid This column into productive actions members might try instead to attain the desired goal. These become the norms in the Try This column. In this instance, teachers might suggest changing *Criticizing a teacher's instructional strategies* to *Reflect on the effectiveness of a teaching strategy*. By turning negatives into positives, teams establish a clear and affirming list of commitment statements all teammates will be inclined to adopt (DuFour et al., 2016).

Tool for Creating Data Discussion Norms		
Goals of Data Analysis	**Avoid This**	**Try This (Norms)**
Keep the focus on issues rather than people		
Engage people in an appreciative inquiry approach rather than a deficit approach to a situation		
Develop a plan of action that energizes and motivates people		

Source for protocol guidelines: Killion, 2008.

Figure 5.3: Tool for creating data-discussion norms.

*Visit **go.SolutionTree.com/literacy** for a free reproducible version of this figure.*

In addition to norms, which include guidelines for communication reflected in the Try This (Norms) column, teams use protocols for examining student data. These protocols delineate procedures that teachers use to examine strengths and weaknesses of their instruction and include time frames for meetings. To determine how long teachers convene, they take into account the length of the assessment and the number of criteria to be assessed. In grades 2 and 3, a team data discussion of a literacy-based common formative assessment typically takes twenty to forty minutes. The third-grade team example in figure 5.2 (page 130) was a thirty-minute, planned conversation. If a team were to address multiple skills within one assessment, that conversation might take closer to an hour because the crux of the conversation centers around planning next steps for students' learning. As a result of these communication parameters, teachers are more likely to benefit from the collective wisdom of their teammates, develop new instructional approaches and strategies, and turn their data into action.

In Kildeer Countryside Community Consolidated School District 96, team members analyze data using the Here's what, So what? Now what? protocol. Through this procedure, teachers identify data trends, determine what led to the results, and ultimately develop an intervention plan to responsively teach particular students by providing corrective instruction for those struggling to meet standards, or extension for those ready for more. The following list breaks down each of this protocol's components.

▶ "Here's what" means that teachers focus on the strengths and weaknesses that the data and student work reveal.

▶ Once teachers critically look at how students perform, they ask, "So what?" to interpret the results and uncover what led some students to succeed and others to miss the mark. Since all teachers strive to gain better results, they endeavor to learn from each other. So this part of the meeting relies on collegial openness and support as teammates share ideas and respond to the following kinds of questions.

- "Does a teammate have ideas that will enhance instruction for students who are still unclear?"

- "Is there a scaffold another teacher used in class that seemed to provide just the right amount of support?"

- "What extension opportunities have helped push students' thinking? Perhaps a teammate might suggest a graphic organizer, visual, or hands-on cooperative learning structure that yielded positive results."

Teachers also examine what might have derailed learning or produced less than desirable results. They might ask these questions to probe for insights.

- "Did our instruction truly align with the priority standards?"

- "Did teachers proactively catch students before they failed?"

- "Did our lessons follow the gradual release of responsibility model to deliberately hand over responsibility to students?" (See chapter 6, page 147.)

▸ Teams conclude by asking, "Now what?" to determine and make a concrete plan for intervention. This section of the protocol is inspired by Buffum and his colleagues (2018) in *Taking Action: A Handbook for RTI*. In this part of the data-inquiry discussion, analysis uncovers which students struggle and need more assistance than others, as well as those who might need extension. Therefore, our third-grade team indicated how we can differentiate to attend to the needs of students who score in the *novice* and *developing mastery* categories on the rubric, as well as those who score in the *mastery and extends* levels. By virtue of attaining the learning target, we coupled *mastery* and *extends* together, although teachers may need to differentiate learning based on students' current level of understanding.

The organizer in figure 5.4 features a template with guiding questions—modeled after Kildeer's protocol—that teams can use to capture the notes from their data discussion. Since teams participate in a continuous cycle of assessment and acting on the data that teams analyze, they can also use this protocol for both common formative and summative assessments. Typically, during these discussions, one team member records the notes using a digital copy of the template that is accessible to the entire team or by recording notes on a hardcopy of the template to be photocopied and distributed to teammates after the meeting.

By working together to analyze student data, teachers are more likely to benefit from the collective wisdom of their teammates, develop new instructional approaches and strategies, and turn their data into action.

The Data Are Action Oriented

As the term explicitly states, *action oriented* simply means that teachers proactively support students based on the data they collect and analyze because, frankly,

Data-Inquiry Discussion and Recording Template

Learning Target

Here's What

Based on the student data and work samples for this assessment, identify specific trends, observations, or outcomes. (Five minutes)

What strengths do students demonstrate that reflect proficiency?

What weaknesses do the data reflect?

So What?

Interpret the results, and determine what led to the results. (Fifteen minutes)

What instructional strategies help proficient students master the learning target?

Why might some students struggle with these concepts or skills?

Now What?

Develop an intervention plan to address the trends or patterns in the data that you've collected. (Fifteen minutes)

What will our team do next to address the trends or patterns in the data that we collected? (Use the following columns to answer.)

continued →

Figure 5.4: Data-inquiry discussion and recording template.

Skill or Standard Addressed	Novice	Developing Mastery	Mastery and Extends
Criterion:	Students:	Students:	Students:
	Instructional plan:	Instructional plan:	Instructional plan:
Criterion:	Students:	Students:	Students:
	Instructional plan:	Instructional plan:	Instructional plan:

Visit **go.SolutionTree.com/literacy** for a free reproducible version of this figure.

that is our job, and it is what common sense dictates. Otherwise, why collect the data? The whole crux of the data-inquiry conversation is to ascertain the next steps in instruction for students, knowing they are each at varying levels of proficiency. As Thomas Guskey (2010) argues, "It would be foolish to charge ahead knowing that students have not learned key concepts or skills well" (p. 55), just as it would be a shame to hold students back knowing they have already mastered the learning.

Therefore, as part of the unit-planning process discussed in chapter 3 (page 61), teams embed dedicated time for responsive teaching into their unit calendar to address the needs of struggling learners and to extend the learning of those students who are ready for more advanced coursework. Building this time into the instructional cycle gives teachers and students the ability to participate in further honed literacy. They indicate this time on the team calendar by inputting *Intervention: Corrective instruction or extension* (see figure 3.8, page 89). Instruction continues during this time; however, teachers must be cognizant of students who need more scaffolding as well as challenge.

To make prudent instructional decisions and select appropriate support for students, teams should also consider alternate forms of data to augment the common assessment results. This means utilizing formal or informal literacy-connected data from across disciplines to ascertain students' performance and to assist with planning scaffolds and extensions. Since students experience a wide range of texts across content areas and write for myriad purposes, teachers can, for example, analyze data from a social studies assessment to predict what support students might need to master a reading or writing standard. As well, teachers may utilize previous writing data from an assignment other than the common assessment to inform their next moves. Considering these results enable teachers to amass a more complete picture in which to create a well-constructed plan for supporting, scaffolding, and individualizing learning, and for forming flexible, instructional groups of students with similar needs.

Figure 5.5 (page 138) shows entries our third-grade team recorded onto the Data-Inquiry Discussion and Recording Template for the common formative assessment we issued. In the *Here's What* section—although we kept our focus on describing characters by their traits, motivations, and feelings, which is the learning target for this common formative assessment—we noted what we saw in student work when we applied the scoring criteria to the work.

Data-Inquiry Discussion and Recording Template

Learning Target: Describe characters by their traits, motivations, and feelings.

Here's What

Based on the student data and work samples for this assessment, identify specific trends, observations, or outcomes. (Five minutes)

What strengths do students demonstrate that reflect proficiency?

- Students use descriptive adjectives to describe characters.
- Many students can make inferences about the characters.
- Students use details from the story to understand how a character is feeling.
- Some students understand that dialogue tags provide hints as to how a character is feeling.
- A few students can support their descriptions with story details. (These students are ready for extension.)

What weaknesses do the data reflect?

- Students need to be clear about which character they are referring to.
- Some students explain a character's action rather than his or her traits or feelings.
- Students need extra practice to understand the concept of motivation.

So What?

Interpret the results, and determine what led to the results. (Fifteen minutes)

What instructional strategies help proficient students master the learning target?

- Students annotated the text to mark details about characters.
- Students highlighted details that describe a character's personality or feelings.

Why might some students struggle with these concepts or skills?

- Students need support in choosing precise vocabulary terms to describe characters (character traits).
- Students need support in using text details to make inferences.

Now What?

Develop an intervention plan to address the trends or patterns in the data that you've collected. Write your answers in the following columns. (Fifteen minutes)

What will your learning team do next to address the trends or patterns in the data that you've collected? (Use the following columns to answer.)

Skill or Standard Assessed	Novice	Developing Mastery	Mastery or Extends
Describe a character using details from the story.	**Students:** Kyle Ramon	**Students:** Suzy Latisha Rohan Ritika	**Students:** Carlos John Anna
	Instructional Plan: Conduct a small-group lesson on the reading strategy of visualizing. Model visualizing by pointing to and thinking aloud about specific details. Explain how those details create a picture of the characters in the reader's mind. Then observe students as they try it with a partner.	**Instructional Plan:** Model for students how to make inferences about characters beyond what is explicitly stated. Demonstrate how details help to support the inferences. Encourage repetition with guided practice.	**Instructional Plan:** Teach students to compare characters with other characters they have encountered based on their traits. Demonstrate how multiple characters (major and minor characters) impact a story's plot.

Figure 5.5: Completed third-grade data-inquiry discussion and recording template.

Students Who Need Extension

The teacher team discusses steps for students who demonstrate a clear understanding of essential learning standards that teachers have addressed or are currently addressing during instruction. Teachers must strive to engage advanced learners in valuable, meaningful learning experiences, rather than simply having these learners bide their time with extra homework, busywork, or time fillers (Guskey, 2010). As Buffum et al. (2018) explain, teachers can provide extended learning opportunities to encourage advanced learners to dig deeper into current content based on standards. To accomplish this differentiated approach, teachers challenge students to:

> look at things from different perspectives, apply skills to new situations or contexts, look for many different ways to solve a problem (not just looking for the correct answer), or use skills learned to create a new outcome or product. (Buffum et al., 2018, p. 180)

For example, our third-grade team's data-inquiry discussion and recording tool (figure 5.5, page 138), which we filled out after our common formative assessment, shows that students we identify as needing extension will tackle more sophisticated levels of thinking. To deepen understanding, we decided these students will learn to compare characters with other characters they have encountered based on their traits. Additionally, they will examine how multiple characters impact a story's plot. These extensions position students to think more deeply about the characters and events in a story without moving ahead to the next topic of instruction. No matter your approach for providing ways to extend learning, keep in mind that all students deserve the opportunity to achieve at high levels.

Students Who Need Additional Time and Support

For students who lack mastery, teams spend additional time implementing instructional scaffolds (temporary support structures) or teaching other strategies to help them understand a concept or perform a task they could not typically achieve on their own (Northern Illinois University, n.d.). The following sections explore each of these approaches.

Establishing Scaffolds

When implementing scaffolds, teachers break down concepts into comprehensible chunks and implement strategies, perhaps offering a structure or a tool of some kind, to guide them in achieving the expected outcome. For example, our third-grade team considered the scaffolding strategies a teacher could use in instruction listed in figure 5.5 (page 138) as options for students who needed additional time and support to describe characters. We decided students would try the strategy of visualizing to help them form a mental image of what they read. We also decided to implement the encouraging-repetition strategy to help students focus on significant passages of a text. Using this strategy, the teacher directs students' attention to precise text details and, over time, releases responsibility to the students so they reread as a means to gain the information they need. In essence, the teacher becomes the scaffold in this scenario.

Providing scaffolds during the reading process helps readers shift from experiencing frustration with a text to feeling successful and capable, thus building their perseverance for when they encounter complex text. In her article "Building Stamina for Struggling Readers and Writers," Paula Bourque (2017) encourages teachers to choose scaffolds that help students build stamina for reading engagement. She offers the following questions to guide teachers in choosing effective and appropriate scaffolds.

▶ Does the scaffold encourage students to employ stamina to stick to a complex text?

▶ Does the scaffold allow students the opportunity to struggle a bit but still find success?

▶ Does the scaffold invite problem solving, or does it require continued support?

▶ Will the scaffold allow for transfer of a strategy to another text or task?

▶ Will the scaffold eventually fade or become obsolete with experience and practice?

Providing scaffolds during the reading process helps readers shift from experiencing frustration with a text to feeling successful and capable, thus building their perseverance for when they face complex text. The following list includes a variety of scaffolding strategies teams can use to support students' learning. Teams can also adapt and apply these scaffolds during interdisciplinary units.

▶ **Build and access prior knowledge:** Struggling readers sometimes lack prior knowledge on the subject matter of a text; therefore, sharing background knowledge on the subject through a read aloud, short video, or quick discussion can give students the information they need to make sense of a text (Coppola, 2014). Teachers can also guide students to use their related experiences or prior knowledge to prepare them for the subject matter in the text.

▸ **Provide stair-step texts:** Texts can be difficult to read when students lack sufficient background knowledge on a topic. To help increase students' ability to grasp the information in a challenging text, teachers can first ask them to read an easier apprentice text on the same topic. Encountering important information in the easier text will help students notice and pay attention to it when they read about it in the challenging text (Shanahan, 2019).

▸ **Encourage repetition or close reading:** When students encounter rigorous texts, a single reading is usually not enough. Teachers should encourage students to reread the texts (or parts of texts) multiple times to make sense of them. Reading a text more than once will make it more accessible (Fisher & Frey, 2012).

▸ **Provide a meta-cognitive demonstration or model:** The purpose of this is to provide a model for students on how to do the task using a strategy. This should always close with giving students explicit steps for being able to independently apply the strategy when they practice or need to employ the skill in another context (Marzano, 2017).

▸ **Help with coherence:** Coherence refers to the way words, ideas, and sentences are connected in a text. When authors use features such as pronouns, synonyms, and ellipses to connect ideas across a text, they sometimes cause confusion for young readers, especially when ideas are far apart and references are not repeated (Shanahan, Fisher, & Frey, 2012). For example, take a look at this simple passage: *Anne and her dog walked in the woods. They saw many different animals. It was a great adventure. They can't wait to do it again soon.* Readers need to know that the word *they* in the second and fourth sentences refers to Anne and her dog from the first sentence. They also need to remember that the third and fourth sentences refer to the experience of walking in the woods mentioned in the first sentence. Since this can be tricky for second- and third-grade readers, teachers can help by marking the text to show connections between words or replacing pronouns with their antecedents.

As students acquire a skill and learning continues, teachers remove the scaffolds to advance pupils to the next level in the learning progression. The key is to select the appropriate scaffold to facilitate productive struggle and then gradually release the scaffold so that students do not become too dependent. Over time, students should be able to employ the strategy or perform the skill without the need for additional support; however, for students with a severe disability, the scaffold can stay in place and serve as an accommodation.

If a scaffold allows the students to accomplish a task too easily, the support is probably too enabling. Instead of providing this level of scaffolding, teachers should encourage productive struggle, offering cues and prompts to support students without giving them the answer outright. In a classroom where a teacher promotes productive struggle, students feel empowered to persist despite a healthy struggle since the teacher encourages determination and curiosity. Students gain a sense of accomplishment as they try and try again to tease out something challenging. They feel the struggle is worthwhile because they can sense that by pushing through, success will come. This learning environment adopts the growth mindset philosophy—believing that intelligence is something that can be developed, rather than a fixed trait (Dweck, 2016).

The absence or mismatch of scaffolds or supports can lead to a destructive struggle for students. When confronted with this type of struggle, students feel overwhelmed and frustrated. Subsequently, learning is disrupted due to missed learning opportunities. Overcoming these consequences requires immense teacher effort in terms of reteaching students and likely rebuilding their self-efficacy. To be clear, teachers are obligated to ensure productive struggle with students so they have the opportunity to grow academically and become more confident in general. To accomplish this, we position our students for success through teaching and assessing at rigorous levels, mindful that scaffolds might be necessary.

Applying Learner Strategies to Rigorous Text

At this point in time, your team might be grappling with holding students accountable for reading and comprehending rigorous text when you might have some students that are not yet proficient in reading grade-level text. It has often come up in our team discussions when teachers indicate students can do the skill when the text is not as complex. So, we would like to show you how teaching students to use and apply strategies to their reading beyond the use of scaffolds you provide will help your team to maintain expectations for how students apply literacy skills to rigorous text.

Let's consider a second-grade student who cannot yet independently and fluently read second-grade text. However, the teacher will assess this student using that level of text; therefore, data is indicating the student is not yet proficient on the skill. This student is most definitely still building necessary foundational skills, such as the ability to decode to become a proficient reader. Professor of literacy education Timothy V. Rasinski (2012) reminds us that readers need to read not only accurately but also automatically. He notes that when students read in a word-by-word, robotic fashion, they may struggle to remember what they've read. This struggle with decoding ultimately leads to a breakdown in making meaning and comprehending text.

At this juncture, the team would turn its attention to the nature of the small-group work. Many teachers use a guided reading structure at the small-group table; however, in this scenario, the student with a specific deficit in fluency will strongly benefit from a fluency-focused small-group experience in addition to continued work on comprehension. The question is not of which the teacher should focus on but rather how he or she can find the time to focus on both. As Rasinski (2012) indicates, improving grade-level reading fluency will improve comprehension as well. During this time, the teacher models an explicit strategy to help the student strengthen fluency skills. Jennifer Serravallo (2015), author of *The Reading Strategies Book*, explains that for small-group lessons to function well—with the teacher providing individualized support to each learner—the learners must have a clear strategy to support their practice. Teachers must define and state the strategy for the group at the beginning of the lesson and explicitly teach it during the small-group session.

So, as we look at the second grader in this scenario, we want to determine which strategy will best address his fluency-skill deficit. Serravallo (2015) shares a multitude of strategies, such as "Say Good-Bye to Robot Reading." This strategy—inspired by educator, author, and presenter Sharon Taberski (as cited in Serravallo, 2015)—teaches readers to "scoop up" a few words at a time, instead of reading word by word, which is a student friendly way of saying, "Pay attention to phrases or chunks of words at a time rather than a single word." Applying a strategy, such as this one, positions students for success because it supports them during the learning process and supplies them with a concrete action they can take when practicing fluency. Students then take ownership of this strategy and use it to improve their reading abilities until they eventually outgrow the need for the strategy, which is the goal. This concept applies to students mastering all standards and not only reading fluently. Students need to be explicitly taught strategies they can apply in order to acquire a skill.

Given intense focus of instruction from the classroom teacher for multiple purpose, there might still be situations in which a student needs more. In that case, we suggest consulting dedicated RTI resources such as *Taking Action* (Buffum, Mattos, & Malone, 2018) as essential for implementing intervention practices to both support and extend learning.

EXERCISE

Participate in a Team CFA Data-Inquiry Discussion

After entering common formative assessment data into your data-collection tool, you and your team are ready to discuss student results, share instructional strategies and ideas, and develop a responsive teaching plan.

Use the following questions to guide this exercise.

- ★ What are our logistics for meeting as a team? For example, have we set a date and location for our team data discussion?

- ★ How will we guarantee all team members complete the necessary steps prior to the meeting?

- ★ Which data-discussion protocol will we use to help each other focus on student results in a safe, nonthreatening environment?

- ★ What expertise (personnel or published) can we tap into to inform our conversation about designing instruction for students?

- ★ Where will we record ideas for providing scaffolds for students who need additional support to master skills and extending the learning for those who have already mastered them?

Summary

In a PLC, collaborative teams are committed to finding ways to support all students in achieving at high levels. A heterogeneous group of second- and third-grade learners will undoubtedly bring to the classroom a wide range of background knowledge and skills. Some will have solid foundational skills in place, and some may still be working to solidify these skills. Some will enter the classroom already applying a variety of reading strategies to comprehend, and some will need explicit instruction on how to make meaning of a text. From reteaching critical concepts in new ways to ensure mastery to extending concepts for students who have already mastered essential skills, the work of responding to data is essential for guaranteeing all students transition from learning to read to reading to learn in these grade levels.

To uphold this promise, teams review and analyze data from a common assessment to find trends in students' performance. With this information, they capitalize on the findings and each other's expertise to devise ways to support struggling learners and extend the capacity of those who have achieved mastery. To help ensure that teachers speak candidly and feel comfortable to share and discuss data in a safe place, they establish norms. Additionally, teams must develop a robust and systematic data analysis protocol—like Here's What, So What?, Now What?—so they have a procedure for sifting through, analyzing, and acting on what the data reveal.

When a team meets to analyze data and ultimately draws the conclusion that some students struggle with a particular target or skill, team members must dig deep into the reasons for this struggle and develop a concrete action plan. As well, they must formulate learning opportunities for students ready to broaden and deepen their understanding of a skill. By working through an ongoing, continuous cycle of data inquiry, teams deliver the quality core instruction and targeted interventions needed to ensure all students can read and write at grade level, fostering a love of literacy to carry them throughout their school-age years and beyond.

In chapter 6, readers will learn how to reach these goals by designing high-quality lessons using *gradual release of responsibility*, a research-based instructional model. When teachers devise lessons through this framework, they position students well to achieve desired goals.

Design Lessons Using the Gradual Release of Responsibility Instructional Framework

Teachers' commitment to their students' reading and writing skills necessitates the planning and delivery of a literacy-focused, guaranteed, and viable curriculum (DuFour & Marzano, 2011). In the preceding chapters, collaborative teams engaged in a deep-dive process to determine priority standards, developed a literacy-focused learning progression (complete with accompanying assessments and rubrics), and established a process to gather and collaboratively assess data. This work is all vital to offering the curriculum grades 2–3 students deserve, but ensuring that all students learn depends on more. It requires that teachers use the data they collect to inform their classroom instruction each day. Figure 6.1 (page 148) illustrates how each step in this process has brought us to this point.

Dovetailing from chapter 5's focus on collecting and responding to data, this chapter continues with a focus on how teams use the assessment data they gather to inform instruction that addresses critical questions 3 and 4 (*What will we do when students haven't learned it?* and *What will we do when students already know it?*; DuFour et al., 2016). To attend to these queries, this chapter explores gradual release of responsibility as an ideal model for providing differentiated instruction that, used appropriately, enhances students' growth when learning any new skill, strategy, or procedure.

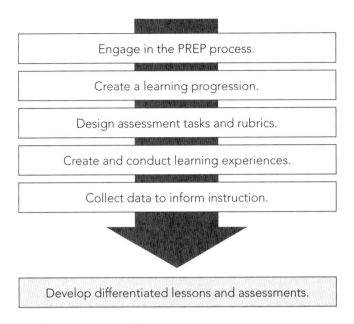

Figure 6.1: Overview of the instructional process.

Proficient readers employ a variety of thinking as they make meaning of text. Second- and third-grade readers engage in reading differently than they did in kindergarten and first grade. A critical emphasis shifts from the word-level skills of decoding and identifying high-frequency words to applying a range of comprehension strategies to make sense of increasingly complex text across disciplines (Castles, Rastle, & Nation, 2018). Similarly, the demands of writing increase as teachers expect second and third graders to weave together complete sentences to convey ideas clearly. As they learn these new essential strategies and skills, students benefit from a gradual release approach in which they observe and listen to their teacher explain a strategy, and then practice it over time with guidance and collaborative support, leading to independence. This cycle of absorbing, processing, and applying small doses of new information allows students to progress in their learning at an appropriate pace. We begin by introducing this instructional framework then follow with a discussion of the model's flexibility; we conclude with an example of gradual release of responsibility in action.

Gradual Release of Responsibility

Teachers have at their disposal an array of strategies but should judiciously employ appropriate ones for the express purpose of meeting learning outcomes. During instruction, teachers must collect evidence of student learning via formal and informal formative assessment (as discussed in chapter 2, page 39) and adjust their teaching based on how well students grasp the targeted skills. As straightforward as that seems, it is no easy task to implement effective instruction.

Direct instruction entails a purposeful interaction between the teacher and students in which the teacher explicitly models a strategy or skill, reinforces concepts, and facilitates feedback as the learning is taking place. This approach aims to provide clear, explicit teaching that is unambiguous for all learners, and research reveals that this model can produce desired effects when teaching a new skill, strategy, or procedure (Magliaro, Lockee, & Burton, 2005). It's an approach that "assumes all students can learn new material when (a) they have mastered prerequisite knowledge and skills and (b) the instruction is unambiguous" (Stockard, Wood, Coughlin, & Rasplica Khoury, 2018, p. 2).

Therefore, to design and execute effective lessons, we recommend teams use *gradual release of responsibility*, an instructional framework that originated with P. David Pearson and Margaret C. Gallagher (1983). It involves an orchestrated, graduated cognitive shift from teachers modeling new learning to students employing the new skill, strategy, or process independently:

> When the teacher is taking all or most of the responsibility for task completion, he is "modeling" or demonstrating the desired application of some strategy. When the student is taking all or most of that responsibility, she is "practicing" or "applying" that strategy. What comes in between these two extremes is the gradual release of responsibility from teacher to student. . . . The hope in the model is that every student gets to the point where she is able to accept total responsibility for the task, including the responsibility for determining whether or not she is applying the strategy appropriately (i.e., self-monitoring). But the model assumes that she will need some guidance in reaching that stage of independence and that it is precisely the teacher's role to provide such guidance. (p. 35)

Douglas Fisher and Nancy Frey (2014c) identify the following four phases of gradual release of responsibility inspired by Pearson and Gallagher's (1983) model. Together they contribute to an effective and fluid learning experience that can yield student achievement and contribute to high-quality instruction.

1. Focused instruction ("I do it.")

2. Guided instruction ("We do it.")

3. Collaborative learning ("You do it together.")

4. Independent learning ("You do it alone.")

When introducing a new learning target, lessons must include all four components of gradual release of responsibility—focused and guided instruction and collaborative and independent learning—to maximize its effect and to increase the likelihood that students will achieve mastery. However, there is flexibility in how teachers use it. For example, they can rearrange or repeat parts of the model based on their expertise of how the lesson should unfold, taking into account their students' needs. For more simplistic skills, teachers can incorporate abbreviated forms of the four components within a typical class period. When addressing more sophisticated learning targets, such as *quote accurately from a text when drawing inferences* or *support reasons with facts and details*, teachers will likely need to extend the model across two or more days. Teachers might omit parts only if they are reinforcing or reviewing a learning target for which students have received direct instruction in a previous or current school year.

Timothy Shanahan (2018) humorously, albeit realistically, addresses decisions about how quickly or gradually teachers relinquish support to students. He also illustrates the potentiality of this model to be iterative:

> Those decisions are hard because they need to be made on the spot. And, when they are wrong—that is, when it turns out that the kids can't take the reins successfully—the teacher has to take back the responsibility, for the time being, that is.
>
> That's why I think of gradual release as: I do it, we do it, I do it again, we try to do it again but this time a little differently, we do it, we do it, oops, I have to do some of it with more explanation, you do it (no, not quite like that), you do it, we do it again, okay now you can do it. (I know it isn't catchy, but it is more descriptive of how the process really tends to work). (Shanahan, 2018)

Teachers must use their professional expertise and knowledge of their students' characteristics to determine how to choreograph the steps of this model so they best suit the needs of all students in their classrooms.

The following sections explain each of the four phases of the gradual release model, adapting the concepts laid out in Pearson and Gallagher (1983) and Fisher and Frey (2014c).

Focused Instruction—"I Do It"

During focused instruction, teachers take on most of the responsibility, which accounts for the first-person phrasing of "I do it." They establish the learning target, provide context, and show students what the skill, strategy, or process entails.

While conducting focused instruction, teachers unobtrusively assess to determine how best to support students later during guided instruction. This portion of the lesson might last around fifteen minutes.

1. **Set the purpose for learning**: Teachers state the lesson's purpose at the outset by posing and posting the learning target (using an *I can* statement) and perhaps a guiding question in student-friendly language. Or, teachers might wait to reveal the learning target and guiding question after teachers engage students in a brief activity. For example, in a lesson that focuses on using sensory details to describe a narrative's setting, teachers might read two paragraphs—one rich with imagery and the other blandly written. They ask students to identify which one is more effective and to justify that choice. After students respond—for example, by articulating that the stronger paragraph has descriptive details, uses sensory words, and helps them visualize the setting—teachers confirm the students' impressions. The teachers then present the goal for the lesson: "Today, we will focus on the guiding question, *How do writers use sensory details to describe settings?* and address the learning target, *I can use sensory details to write descriptive settings for my story.*" To provide context for the work, teachers connect the learning to what students have done previously, what they already know, or how they will use the new learning.

2. **Model or demonstrate and think aloud:** After teachers establish the purpose, they model or demonstrate the new learning to present how to perform the task and what constitutes quality. As part of this instruction, the teacher provides a visual of the text or task (whether it be an excerpt from a poem, a paragraph from a science article, or a mathematics problem) and couples it with a verbal explanation of the thinking he or she employs to accomplish the modeled skill. Teachers can also explicitly model via a think aloud when composing a writing sample. This direct explanation is a critical component of focused instruction, especially for second- and third-grade students who benefit from repeatedly hearing and seeing what expert readers and writers think and do. The more these students can learn from the actions and thought processes expert readers and writers employ, the more they can add to their own literacy repertoires as they develop into capable readers and writers. In addition to using think aloud to make text-dependent thoughts transparent, teachers also talk about pitfalls to avoid, misconceptions to fend off, and how to deal with the challenging aspects of the task.

3. **Invite minimal participation:** Teachers check for understanding at this early stage in the lesson. While modeling or demonstrating the task, they unobtrusively observe students. Additionally, they might invite students to actively respond to a question or prompt by signaling with a thumbs-up (*yes* or *true*), a thumbs-down (*no* or *false*), or a fist (*I am not sure*). Or, to allow time for students to process and synthesize the new learning taking place, teachers might ask students to turn and talk with a neighbor or elbow partner. All the while, teachers collect information to lead guided instruction.

During focused instruction, teachers provide context by presenting the learning target to students and connecting it to what they will be doing. They explicitly show and narrate what proficiency looks like to prepare students for what they will eventually do on their own. They also reveal any errors students might be prone to make so they avoid these mistakes. Teachers attentively assess, albeit informally, in preparation for guided instruction.

Guided Instruction—"We Do It"

During guided instruction, teachers differentiate by arranging students purposefully in pairs, trios, or small groups of four based on similar needs. They work on a different task from the one they previously modeled so that students can practice the new learning and apply it in a novel situation. While students practice how to transfer this skill, teachers supervise and provide guidance. They circulate around the classroom, constantly formatively assessing and offering pointed feedback by way of questioning, prompting, and discussing, to support students in achieving mastery. They differentiate to redirect, remediate, or repeat information, as needed. Additionally, they might scaffold instruction, which serves myriad purposes: "to provide support, knowledge, strategies, modeling, questioning, instructing, restructuring, and other forms of feedback, with the intention that the student comes to 'own' the knowledge, understanding, and concepts" (Hattie, 2012, p. 144). Teachers might also differentiate by offering extension opportunities for those who would benefit from an additional challenge. If need be, teachers regroup students and allow them to work at different paces. For example, if the teacher observes that some students have fully grasped the concept quickly, he or she may discretely ask them a more challenging question or present a more rigorous task, probing them to apply deeper thinking, analyzing, or problem solving.

Collaborative Learning—"You Do It Together"

By discussing and actively engaging in a task with peers, students derive deeper meaning and perhaps new insights based on the learning target. Together, they seek validation and clarification, articulate their thoughts, and question each other (Fisher & Frey, 2014c). This collective involvement spurs students toward clarity and understanding and develops critical-thinking and communication skills.

Collaborative learning is an opportunity for students to work with partners or in small groups around targeted skills. When they do this, students' output becomes stronger than what they would have produced on their own. To be clear, it represents an important component of gradual release of responsibility that teachers should not overlook:

> When done right, collaborative learning is a way for students to consolidate their thinking and understanding. Negotiating with peers, discussing ideas and information, and engaging in inquiry with others gives students the opportunity to use what they have learned during focused and guided instruction. (p. 7)

After students participate in a collaborative exercise, teachers determine the next instructional moves, such as lead a debriefing session, conduct another formative assessment, return to guided practice for particular students as needed, or move to independent learning.

Independent Learning—"You Do It Alone"

Within the gradual release of responsibility model, students eventually assume full responsibility for the cognitive load and independently demonstrate an understanding of their new learning. To accomplish this, each student applies the skill, strategy, or procedure in a unique situation to show that he or she can transfer learning and provide evidence of mastery. For example, if, during collaborative learning, students practiced writing a setting that includes sensory details, they would apply this skill of writing descriptive settings to their own narratives. If some students still exhibit difficulty with application, teachers reteach relevant phases of the instructional model accordingly or group students together to provide differentiated support.

An Example of Gradual Release of Responsibility—Describing Characters

This section provides a specific example of a lesson using gradual release of responsibility that teachers can conduct to support students in describing characters in a story. It addresses step 4 in the learning progression developed in chapter 3 (figure 3.1, page 64), which we excerpt here in figure 6.2. Although this example presents instruction of an English language arts standard, teams can easily adapt it for second- and third-grade learners across all content areas. The benefit of the gradual release model is that it is applicable to a wide variety of learning situations. The lesson presented in the section ahead prepares students to ultimately describe characters by their traits, motivations, and feelings.

Step	Learning Progression	Assessment	Text for Assessment
Step 4	**Learning Target (Skill)** Describe characters by their traits, motivations, and feelings.	**Common Formative Assessment: Short Constructed-Response Assessment** In a two- to three-sentence response, describe a character from a story and use evidence from the text to support your thinking. (Formative and formal)	*The Sign* (Wrang, 2015)

Figure 6.2: Learning progression excerpt—Step 4.

Note that this featured lesson on describing characters is merely *one* lesson among others within the full learning progress, which itself is just one progression within the Exploring Elements of Fiction unit. Prior to this lesson, students have gained essential knowledge about character traits, feelings, and motivations, and they are ready to apply their knowledge to the skill of describing characters in a variety of ways.

To begin a lesson that positions students to eventually compose a short constructed response that describes a character from a story (as indicated in figure 6.2, the third-grade teacher builds background knowledge and connects current learning to prior knowledge gained throughout the previous steps of the learning progression. The teacher might accomplish this by displaying for students a series of pictures, such as photographs of people or illustrations of characters in which the subjects demonstrate varied traits, feelings, or motivations based on the details in the visuals. Around each picture, the teacher posts examples and nonexamples of accurate character traits and descriptions, allowing him or her to explicitly instruct what constitutes a suitable answer backed by distinct evidence from the visual. The teacher thinks aloud as he or she considers each trait, while also pointing to

Figure 6.3: Picture illustrating character trait examples and nonexamples.

the specific evidence within the visual that allows him or her to arrive at appropriate conclusions.

Figure 6.3 illustrates one example picture the teacher might use with students to build background knowledge and activate prior knowledge about character traits. The teacher might also invite class participation or allow students to practice with a partner using subsequent visuals presented after the explicit teacher model. For this portion of the lesson, the teacher may use a total of two or three visuals as a warm-up to set the stage for learning. Additionally, the teacher builds students' vocabulary knowledge by teaching or reviewing the descriptive adjectives' meanings or referring to a class-created anchor chart of character traits created during a previous lesson.

This brief introduction to a lesson on describing characters demonstrates for students how they can use evidence to support inferences about characters' traits, feelings, and motivations, while also exposing them to a breadth of descriptive adjectives that promote more precise and accurate character descriptions. As another example, in a science unit exploring animals' habitats, teachers might instead provide a series of pictures of animals that live in different environments around the world. These images spark students' thinking about why certain animals live in different habitats and what characteristics help them to survive in that particular environment.

The following sections detail how our team approached using gradual release of responsibility so we could position students to be able to describe characters by their traits, feelings, and motivations as well as support their descriptions with evidence from the story. These sections all use the same learning target (*Describe characters by their traits, motivations, and feelings*) and guiding question (*How can readers describe characters in a story?*) to demonstrate each step in the process.

1. **Focused instruction ("I do it"):** The teacher demonstrates how to describe characters by their traits, feelings, and motivations, and how to identify textual evidence to support one's thinking.

2. **Guided instruction ("We do it"):** With teacher guidance and support, students match character descriptions to preidentified pieces of evidence within a shared story; the class collectively adds new traits to a class-generated list.

3. **Collaborative learning ("You do it together"):** With a partner, students work to annotate character descriptions and highlight textual evidence that supports each character inference.

4. **Independent learning ("You do it alone"):** Individually, students describe a character and support their answers by highlighting evidence from the story.

Focused Instruction—"I Do It"

The teacher begins by explaining the purpose of the day's lesson, which is to describe characters in a story and support descriptions with evidence from the text. On an interactive whiteboard or under a document camera, the teacher then displays a passage from a complex text that features descriptive character details. He or she purposely chooses a passage that allows the reader to gather both explicit and implicit information about the characters. For example, the teacher might use an excerpt from the same resource our team used, *The Sign* (Wrang, 2015):

Jess tried to steady his trembling legs. It wasn't easy to do with the strangers in the house. They were searching every room and surrounding Ma, who stood there bravely.

"A slave?" she was saying. "We have no slaves on our farm."

"We're looking for a runaway named Orion," said a bearded man. "If you're hiding my slave . . ." (p. 1)

After reading the passage aloud, the teacher says:

Today in our lesson, we will focus on the guiding question—How can readers describe characters in a story?—*and address the learning target,* I can describe characters by their traits, motivations, and feelings. *This story is about a boy and his mother who are helping a runaway slave. As you read, think about how you would describe each character.*

During this portion of the lesson, the teacher models what students will do: underline details from the passage that reveal a character's traits, feelings, or motivations, and provide corresponding annotations in the margin that describe the character. Concurrently, the teacher thinks out loud to explain what details he or she noticed as he or she read and how those details help him or her make inferences about the characters. For example, the teacher might read the excerpt we used here to point out details she notices, like Jess's "trembling legs" and the fact that there are "strangers in the house" who are "searching every room."

As the teacher underlines and recalls these details aloud, he or she verbalizes his or her thinking by explaining how this evidence suggests to the reader that Jess is experiencing the feeling of nervousness. The teacher also points out the author's use of the word *bravely* to describe the character of Ma. The author's use of this word provides a direct character trait for the reader. Some might call this a "right there" answer. In the case of Jess, however, the reader must use details from the text to infer that he is nervous. By modeling how to draw a distinction between these two character descriptions, the teacher helps students begin to understand the difference between explicit and implicit details within a story and the process readers go through to make meaning of these types of story details.

During the remainder of the focused instruction portion of the lesson, the teacher features another passage and underlines and explains details in it that suggest a character's traits, feelings, or motivations. After thinking aloud to demonstrate a few examples for the class, the teacher may invite students to attempt the remaining examples with a partner. This activates student engagement during focused instruction and embeds essential time for processing and applying the new learning that just took place.

Guided Instruction—"We Do It"

During guided instruction, teachers begin to relinquish their explicit modeling and transfer some of the responsibility to the students. For this lesson on describing characters, teachers may facilitate an exercise that allows students to practice the skill with support, such as the following matching activity with preselected character descriptions.

1. The teacher displays the next paragraph or section of the class's complex text that features descriptive character details. This example continues with *The Sign* (Wrang, 2015). The teacher has already highlighted details he or she preselected within the text.

2. The teacher pairs up students and hands them index cards with a character trait, feeling, or motivation listed on each one. For students who are ready for more of a challenge, the teacher can include both examples and nonexamples of accurate character descriptions within the stack of cards. This allows these students to differentiate and identify appropriate answers from those that evidence in the story does not support.

3. Together with their partner, the students read each highlighted detail from the story and match the appropriate character description to the corresponding highlighted evidence. Students take turns matching one detail at a time while articulating and explaining their thinking aloud to their partner.

4. While the students work together, the teacher unobtrusively assesses and provides support by listening to student responses, asking probing questions to elicit thinking, pointing out pertinent details that students may have missed, and scaffolding the learning for students as needed.

With a scaffolded matching activity, students are able to practice their new learning with the guidance of their teacher and peers, steering their way toward independence. As a culminating activity for this portion of the lesson, the teacher may invite the students to convene as a class to offer character traits and descriptive adjectives to a class-generated list facilitated by the teacher.

Collaborative Learning—"You Do It Together"

Working collaboratively raises students' awareness, clarifies their thinking, develops critical-thinking and communication skills, and results in students learning more together than they would have individually.

During collaborative learning, students work with a partner to apply the learning acquired from the previous two steps of the lesson. Together, using a final passage of the complex text *The Sign* (Wrang, 2015), they practice underlining details that reveal aspects of characters and noting inferences about the characters' distinct traits, feelings, and motivations in the margin. If the whole class shares the passage via an interactive whiteboard or document camera (instead of each student or pair having copies), student pairs can record their findings on paper or individual whiteboards. Figure 6.4 depicts how a pair of students might annotate the excerpt's text. (The text is blurred to protect the publisher's copyright, but the purpose for this example is to observe how students annotate.)

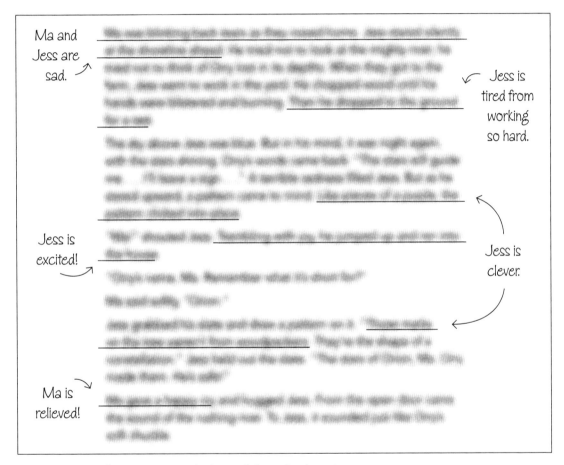

Figure 6.4: Student responses during collaborative learning.

When all student pairs are finished, the teacher invites pairs to share their findings with another pair sitting nearby, or with the whole class. As they share, the teacher encourages students to articulate their thinking using complete sentences that explain both the inference they made about a character and the evidence they found to support their inference. Carefully verbalizing their reasoning positions students to eventually provide more detailed and thoughtful answers on the formative written assessment.

Note that, although the three steps we have illustrated so far (focused instruction, guided instruction, and collaborative learning) utilize the same fiction story, instruction at each of these steps could revolve around separate texts as students work to apply the skill to a variety of literary works. To appropriately move through the gradual release model, students practice applying their learning using new material, whether different portions of the same text or a collection of separate (but aligned) texts.

Independent Learning—"You Do It Alone"

By gradually releasing instructional support throughout the lesson, the teacher has prepared students to independently apply their learning to show what they know and can do. Here, students perform the skill on their own to demonstrate their current level of proficiency, and the teacher formatively assesses students to inform his or her next instructional steps.

To complete the gradual release of responsibility for the sample lesson on describing characters, the teacher provides students with a new story or story excerpt, a highlighter, and a pencil. Individually, students highlight evidence that reveals a unique character trait, feeling, or motivation, while annotating to describe the character in the margin. As students work to highlight and annotate independently, the teacher walks around the room to observe students' performance and offer in-the-moment feedback as needed. When doing this, it's important for the teacher to recognize that some productive struggle is necessary as students cross the bridge to independence. The teacher should also take anecdotal notes on specific students' strengths and areas for growth, which will aid the teacher in grouping students with similar needs for small-group instruction or in planning future whole-class lessons. (Chapter 7, page 165, provides an in-depth look at small- and whole-class instruction during a literacy block.)

The instruction embedded throughout each step of this lesson equips students with the essential knowledge and skills necessary to meet the demands of the learning target: *Describe characters by their traits, motivations, and feelings*. From here, ensuing instruction, scaffolds, and differentiated support position students to eventually meet the rigor of the common formative assessment that the team has chosen to measure this target within the learning progression: *In a two- to three-sentence response, describe a character from a story and use evidence from the text to support your thinking*. If, at the end of this lesson, students can independently generate a well-supported character description based on details within a story, they are well on their way to crafting a thorough written response for the common formative assessment.

Additional Lesson Ideas for Describing Characters

Before or after the featured lesson in this chapter, teachers might develop one or more of the following ideas into a gradual release of responsibility lesson on describing characters or use the lesson ideas to create extension activities for those students who have mastered the skill.

Writing Original Character Descriptions

To fully comprehend how authors artfully craft story elements—such as dynamic characters—students must experience firsthand what it takes to be a writer. In their report *Writing to Read: Evidence for How Writing Can Improve Reading*, Graham and Hebert (2010) examine the positive impact writing instruction has on students' reading abilities. They suggest teachers "teach students the writing skills and processes that go into creating text" to strengthen students' comprehension (p. 5).

Timothy Shanahan (2017) also emphasizes the interconnectedness between reading and writing and the benefits of embedding continuous instruction into both literacy domains when he asserts:

> Readers, who are writers, can end up with insights about what authors are up to and how they exert their effects, something of great value in text interpretation. Likewise, writers, by being readers, can gain insights into the needs of other readers.

When students compose their own novel descriptions, including the characters involved, they acquire a new lens from which to discern character development, and they develop a keen eye for recognizing important character details. During a class lesson, students can partake in this learning experience by crafting character descriptions that depict a particular trait. Teachers can either provide students with specific traits to utilize in this lesson or allow students to select traits from the class anchor chart. From there, students can engage in a class activity where they share their descriptions with peers and allow others to determine the traits being described.

Matching Character Descriptions

After explicit instruction on describing characters by their traits, feelings, and motivations, students can practice the skill by matching a variety of story excerpts with specific character traits or descriptions. Prior to the lesson, the teacher pre-pares a set of cards featuring story excerpts that reveal aspects of character, and a corresponding set of cards featuring character traits, feelings, or motivations. With a partner, in a group, or individually, students work to match each character description to the corresponding text excerpt, identifying specific evidence within each excerpt that justifies and supports the trait or description.

Comparing and Contrasting Characters

When students have mastered the skill of describing characters, they can begin comparing and contrasting two characters in a story by their traits, feelings, and motivations. Using a graphic organizer, students can record unique character descriptions and accompany each description with evidence from the story. Or, they can note character descriptions in the margin of the text and utilize two differ-ent colored markers or highlighters—one color for each character—to highlight or underline the corresponding evidence that supports each character inference. Those students who are ready for an additional challenge can synthesize the information on their graphic organizer to craft a short constructed response that describes both characters from the story, noting their similarities and differences.

EXERCISE
Explore Gradual Release of Responsibility

This chapter provides a research-based model for building well-orchestrated lessons—gradual release of responsibility. Chapters 7 (page 165) and 8 (page 205) will dig deeper into instructional planning, addressing aspects of high-quality literacy instruction and myriad instructional strategies. At the end of chapter 8, teams can participate in an exercise to design lessons implementing gradual release of responsibility (page 225). For now, discuss this model with your colleagues, and record ideas your team can revisit after reading the upcoming chapters.

Use the following questions to guide this exercise.

★ What gradual release of responsibility lessons have members of our team taught with success? Share specifics.

★ Which learning progression line items would benefit from a gradual release of responsibility lesson?

★ How can we strengthen an existing lesson by incorporating gradual release of responsibility? Share specific ideas.

★ How can we plan instruction that gradually relinquishes teacher support and addresses each step in the gradual release of responsibility model?

Summary

When acquiring a new skill, strategy, or procedure, any learner benefits from a direct instruction model, such as gradual release of responsibility. This instructional framework is predicated on four components that teachers use to plan lessons in an orchestrated way that promotes successful mastery. Although teachers can change the order of these phases, when teaching something new, educators must capitalize on each of them to cement learning. In the subsequent chapters, readers will shore up their toolbox for teaching literacy. Once armed with a collection of effective ways to instruct and assess, teachers will use gradual release of responsibility to work with team members to design solid, cohesive lessons that address learning targets.

CHAPTER 7

Plan High-Quality Literacy Instruction

Although this book emphasizes that teacher teams need to establish an instructional focus on literacy in all content areas, delivering high-quality and comprehensive instruction in second and third grade requires that the busy school day include ample dedicated time for the teaching of reading and writing. This critical teaching occurs during what we refer to as the *literacy block*, a specific and sacred segment of time built into the daily schedule. *Specific* implies this time is intentionally devoted to the teaching, refinement, and practice of literacy skills and standards. *Sacred* implies this time is of utmost priority and is safeguarded as a fundamental part of a student's day.

To this end, teams carve out a large portion of the school day for the specific teaching of literacy or what some might call English language arts. Due to scheduling demands at each grade level, this time may occur as one continuous block of time (for example, ninety or more minutes in the morning), or may exist as separate segments of learning time (perhaps sixty or more minutes in the morning and an additional thirty or more minutes in the afternoon). In either case, it constitutes a significant portion of a classroom teacher's contact time with students, typically at least ninety total minutes (Underwood, 2018) and sometimes two hours or more (Morrow, Kunz, & Hall, 2018)

As we've affirmed throughout this book, teams can and should build literacy into the teaching of other disciplines as well. Though educators often view reading and writing instruction as synonymous with English language arts, one cannot possibly achieve levels of proficiency in subjects like science, social studies, or even mathematics without adept literacy skills. Knowing the wide-reaching effects of literacy knowledge across the curriculum, teams of teachers make commitments to embed the teaching and reinforcement of literacy skills throughout the school day. This may occur during content-specific, disciplinary instruction, or teams might combine instruction of multiple content areas into interdisciplinary lessons. For the purposes of this chapter, we focus primarily on planning high-quality instruction during the literacy block, commonly referred to as English language arts. During this time, embedded classroom structures, routines, and engagement opportunities help establish a comfortable and familiar learning environment focused on accountability and student growth.

A well-organized and structured literacy block has multiple components, each of which we cover in this chapter. During this time, students know precisely what they are learning and when, why, and how their learning is taking place. Students engage in explicit, systematic literacy instruction, articulate the purpose of their learning, and work as a classroom community toward the common goal of becoming independent comprehenders, communicators, and writers. To support teams in strengthening literacy instruction, this chapter focuses first on the process of planning for literacy instruction in a PLC. It then establishes the vital components of a literacy block and details how teams piece these individual components together. It concludes with an examination of the role of vocabulary instruction in the literacy block.

Literacy Instruction in a PLC

Delivering a guaranteed and viable curriculum that meets the needs of all students requires a well-thought-out, collaborative plan. To ensure high-quality instruction across all classrooms, collaborative teams work closely together to construct and uphold an all-encompassing literacy block—a daily time for deep and intentional teaching, thinking, and practice. To support the literacy block, teams accomplish the following.

▸ Meet regularly—weekly if schedules permit—to collaborate on a variety of important tasks: collectively discuss forthcoming curricular materials and instructional plans, develop or choose common formative assessments, analyze student data, and share strategies for instruction and intervention based on evidence of student learning.

▸ Utilize the PREP process to complete the PREP template (page 246) and establish learning progressions (page 250). Through this process, examine and develop the curriculum to ensure it meets the demands of second- and third-grade learning standards and overall objectives. As teams work through these protocols, they also consider how they plan to integrate and reinforce literacy skills across disciplines or even weave literacy instruction and other content areas into interdisciplinary units.

▸ Familiarize themselves with the complex texts they deliberately chose for each instructional unit, and identify the elements of the texts that will lead to authentic teachable moments in developing reading, writing, vocabulary, and foundational skills. In second and third grade, teachers ensure that the texts they choose for instruction have qualities that invoke thinking, typically require some level of close reading, and allow for a reasonable amount of productive struggle. Although texts should be appropriate for second- and third-grade learners, they must also allow for new experiences with reading that stretch the mind and lead to the acquisition of new skills and strategies.

▸ Discuss plans for explicit teaching, modeling, differentiating, and assessing, as well as possible scaffolds and opportunities for student engagement. In second and third grade, teachers may find that some students already have a wide range of prerequisite skills and abilities, while others are still working to solidify foundational phonics skills. With an array of student needs, it becomes paramount to collaborate about topics, like modeling, differentiating, and scaffolding.

Teachers will undoubtedly apply their own unique teaching styles within their individual classrooms and adapt instruction to meet their students' diverse needs; however, working as a team allows team members to capitalize on each other's expertise and collective thinking so they plan high-quality instruction that ensures advantageous learning experiences for all students. As teachers collaborate over upcoming literacy instruction, they can use the questions in figure 7.1 (page 168) to guide their thinking and discussions.

As your team plans for its approach to dedicated literacy instruction, it must contend with the many (often quite literally!) moving parts that compose the literacy block. Step inside any classroom, and you're sure to find an impressive array of authentic and active learning experiences taking place, whether as a whole class, in small groups, or independently during literacy-skill application time. Each component of a literacy block plays a distinct role in developing skilled readers and writers, and teachers are better prepared when they collaborate to establish quality learning experiences across all classrooms.

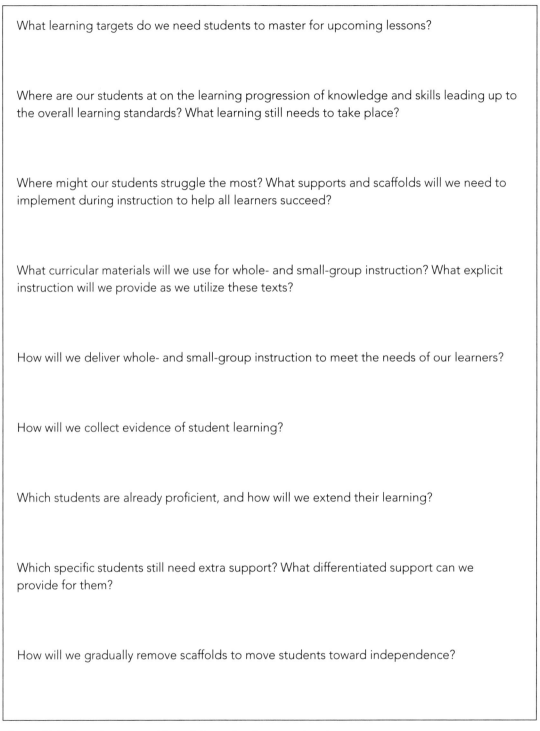

What learning targets do we need students to master for upcoming lessons?

Where are our students at on the learning progression of knowledge and skills leading up to the overall learning standards? What learning still needs to take place?

Where might our students struggle the most? What supports and scaffolds will we need to implement during instruction to help all learners succeed?

What curricular materials will we use for whole- and small-group instruction? What explicit instruction will we provide as we utilize these texts?

How will we deliver whole- and small-group instruction to meet the needs of our learners?

How will we collect evidence of student learning?

Which students are already proficient, and how will we extend their learning?

Which specific students still need extra support? What differentiated support can we provide for them?

How will we gradually remove scaffolds to move students toward independence?

Figure 7.1: Questions to guide collaborative literacy planning.

*Visit **go.SolutionTree.com/literacy** for a free reproducible version of this figure.*

Literacy Block Components

Within the literacy block, students partake in varied learning. All components of the block serve different purposes yet share the same goal of strengthening literacy skills within and beyond the classroom. Though the structures, timing, and procedures for each component may vary by classroom, school, and district, we recommend that literacy blocks include the following components. Building these experiences into the classroom daily creates a well-balanced literacy block that meets the needs of a diverse group of second- and third-grade students.

- ▸ Whole-group reading
- ▸ Small-group reading
- ▸ Whole-group writing
- ▸ Small-group writing
- ▸ Literacy-skill application

A teacher's ultimate goal is to help students develop into independent thinkers, meaning makers, and producers of well-crafted written works. To help students reach this level of proficiency and sophistication, teachers, working as collaborative teams, facilitate instruction that interweaves the domains of reading, writing, speaking, and listening. They provide ample time for the development of these essential skills, guide students in making natural connections among them, and honor the reciprocity of literacy by cultivating a classroom of well-equipped readers and writers.

Though we explore each component of a literacy block separately throughout this chapter, maintaining a well-balanced, interconnected, and data-informed approach to the teaching of all things literacy is the key to amplifying comprehension and writing abilities. The graphic in figure 7.2 (page 170) illustrates the key components of a sample literacy block. It provides time for whole-group and small-group instruction as well as time for students to practice and apply newly learned skills.

In figure 7.2, notice how the shapes overlap, signifying the interrelation of the five learning experiences within the larger literacy block. Additionally, certain concepts of study, such as vocabulary, word work, and foundation skills, appear across multiple whole-group, small-group, and independent learning opportunities. The recurrence of these concepts in the visual is intentional, confirming their importance in delivering continuous comprehensive instruction across all domains

Whole-Group Reading

- Shared texts
- Modeled fluent reading
- Think alouds
- Choral, echo, and partner reading
- Student discourse and engagement
- Explicit instruction related to:
  - Reading standards
  - Comprehension strategies
  - Vocabulary and word work
  - Foundational skills

Whole-Group Writing

- Modeled write-alouds
- Mentor texts
- Student discourse and engagement
- Explicit instruction related to:
  - Writing standards
  - Writing skills and strategies
  - Spelling and conventions
  - Vocabulary and word work
  - Foundational skills

Small-Group Writing

- Guided modeling and student practice
- Differentiated supports and scaffolds
- Student discourse and engagement
- Explicit differentiated instruction and guided practice with:
  - Writing standards
  - Writing skills and strategies
  - Spelling and conventions
  - Vocabulary and word work
  - Foundational skills

Small-Group Reading

- Carefully selected texts
- Students grouped according to skill needs
- Differentiated supports and scaffolds
- Student discourse and engagement
- Explicit differentiated instruction and guided practice with:
  - Reading standards
  - Specific strategies
  - Comprehension skills
  - Vocabulary and word work
  - Foundational skills

Literacy-Skill Application

- Independent and cooperative practice
- Reading-skill application
- Writing-skill application
- Standards-aligned practice
- Hands-on learning
- Individual accountability
- Vocabulary and word work
- Foundational skills

Figure 7.2: Components of a literacy block.

Visit go.SolutionTree.com/literacy for a free reproducible version of this figure.

of literacy *throughout* the block. You'll also notice in figure 7.2 that vocabulary instruction is not featured as a separate component but is embedded into each of the five areas of the literacy block. We like to think of vocabulary not as an isolated entity but as a valuable asset to learning across the literacy block (and in all disciplines). To capture its importance in a student's learning, we detail vocabulary instruction at the end of this chapter. The image in figure 7.2 serves as a sample representation and partial depiction of the many multifaceted instructional approaches, strategies, and areas of study within a well-balanced block of literacy instruction. The following sections cover each of the five components shown in the figure.

EXERCISE

Plan for a Literacy Block

Using the literacy block graphic in figure 7.2 to guide your thinking, facilitate a collaborative discussion about the current structures and literacy-learning experiences that occur within your school day. If your team does not have a consistent and dedicated block of time for literacy, imagine what yours might look like based on the information presented in this chapter so far. Use the worksheet in figure 7.1 (page 168) to direct your initial collaborative discussions.

Use the following questions to guide this exercise.

★ What literacy structures and experiences are built into our current literacy block?

★ How much time do we allot to whole-group, small-group, and independent learning?

★ What refinements might we need to make to our current literacy block?

★ Do we embed literacy instruction into other disciplines, such as science and social studies? Or do we facilitate interdisciplinary lessons or units that combine instruction of two or more content areas?

★ When will our team meet to collaboratively plan and discuss upcoming lessons for the literacy block? On what regular schedule can we establish this meeting?

Whole-Group Reading

Although many different instructional frameworks for whole-group reading exist, whole-group reading's purpose remains unwavering: during this portion of the literacy block, teachers share with students not only the experience of reading but also their knowledge of *how* to read and comprehend. Teachers become models for students as they demonstrate and verbalize the cognitive processes good readers deploy to comprehend complex text (Fisher & Frey, 2015). Students tune in to their teachers' fluent and expressive voices, watch closely as they deliver explicit instruction on specific reading standards, and listen intently as they orally make their thinking concrete. Then, students try it out for themselves through echo reading and choral reading, and they actively engage in thoughtful discourse with their peers to practice the complex art of making meaning. They come to recognize strategies that good readers use and soon muster up the confidence to try them independently.

A whole-group reading lesson is a daily staple that usually spans fifteen to thirty minutes. The lesson's purpose is twofold: (1) it provides direct, teacher-modeled instruction on itemized learning standards and targets, and (2) it gives students continuous exposure to the myriad of effective reading strategies and foundational skills critical to the development of proficient independent readers. A shared reading experience does many things (Fountas & Pinnell Literacy Team, 2019):

- Provides enjoyable, successful experiences with print for all students
- Promotes the development of all aspects of the reading process
- Builds language skills and enhances vocabulary
- Provides opportunities to engage in expressive, meaningful, fluent reading
- Builds understanding of various types of texts, formats, and language structures
- Builds a community of readers

The following sections focus on four specific aspects of the whole-group reading experience: (1) considerations for complex texts, (2) student engagement, (3) gradual release of responsibility, and (4) close reading.

Considerations for Complex Texts

During a whole-group lesson, students engage in the same shared text, which teachers carefully select as a collaborative team for this essential learning opportunity. Whole-group texts are rich, grade-level texts (or beyond-grade-level, if students are ready) from a variety of genres and content areas. All students engage in the complex text with their teacher's careful guidance, allowing for the explicit teaching of the knowledge, skills, comprehension strategies, and vocabulary necessary for continued reading growth.

Though some students in the class may not yet read grade-level material independently, professor of reading Katherine A. Dougherty Stahl (2012) writes that during this teacher-guided lesson, "novice readers with instructional levels that tend to be limited by their decoding abilities are able to stretch into texts containing more words, richer vocabulary, and more sophisticated themes" (p. 48). This whole-group experience allows all students to engage in a text together, deepen their thinking, and exercise their reading brains in new and powerful ways.

When selecting texts for this purpose, teams consider both qualitative and quantitative measures. (See Discuss Options for Complex Texts, page 84.) When choosing texts for second- and third-grade students who are rapidly widening reading repertoires, teachers look closely at the language, syntax, vocabulary, and inferential levels of meaning and consider the focus skills and learning standards (Serravallo, 2018). Since teachers are there to guide the lesson, the texts should be challenging enough that they elicit deep thinking and present new learning. As Tim Shanahan (2020) explains in his blog on text complexity, "Our job as teachers is not to teach kids how to read books they can already read reasonably well . . . , but to enable them to make sense of texts that they can't already read." If texts are too simple, students aren't afforded opportunities to grow, and their reading abilities typically plateau.

Optimal instruction using a complex text requires collaborative preparation ahead of the lesson as well. Team members must have an upfront understanding of the text's nuances that present valuable learning opportunities for students and an intentional plan for how to deliver instruction that is purposeful, robust, and engaging. To maximize time and amplify the learning experience, teams also devise a distinct plan for lesson delivery that embeds engagement opportunities for students.

In districts that use a purchased reading program, it is equally important that teams carefully review the details of the text prior to a whole-group reading lesson. Teams ensure ahead of time that the plans and instructions outlined in their program's teachers' manual directly correlate with the literacy standards and lesson objectives they intend to focus on.

Student Engagement

Critical to a whole-group reading lesson's success is each student's ability to actively engage in the text. Just as a bat is a necessary tool in helping a baseball player perfect his or her swing, the text is the tool readers need at hand to sharpen their skill. Without engagement with and constant exposure to the text, little growth can happen. So, whether teachers share the text on a large electronic screen or interactive board, by way of a big book with large font, or as copies distributed to each student, all students should be able to access and view the text effortlessly. This means that students are looking at the text before, during, and after the lesson. Their eyes are on the precise words, sentences, and illustrations that artfully make up the page, and their minds are focused on making meaning.

We cannot expect students to memorize the subtle details of every text after a first or even second read, just as we can't expect a ballplayer to develop a home run–hitting swing after a single attempt. Therefore, to strengthen students' reading skills, teachers should have students reread and revisit a shared text throughout the lesson and over the course of a few successive days. As students dig into the text to answer questions or participate in collaborative discussions, teachers should see them flipping pages, pointing at words, and explaining their thinking as they reference explicit evidence from the text. When students dive back into the text each day, they build on previous learning while also digging deeper to take thinking and learning about the text, and about the art of reading, to the next level.

To maximize each whole-group lesson's impact, teachers have students engage as *active* participants throughout the lesson. A common misconception about whole-group reading is that the teacher reads aloud to the students the entire time. Reading aloud is a piece of the lesson, as listening to proficient readers gives students a sense of what fluent reading should sound like and leads to increased comprehension (Morrow & Gambrell, 2011). But the goal is to produce independent readers and comprehenders, and when the second- or third-grade teacher does all the reading, it limits students' learning to auditory comprehension, restricting the independent practice necessary for students to become masterful readers.

Gradual Release of Responsibility

In chapter 6 (page 147), you learned about gradual release of responsibility. This structure is especially effective during the whole-group reading experience, as the lesson moves from teacher directed to student centered. Consider the following application of gradual release of responsibility to the whole-group reading process.

1. **Focused instruction:** The teacher begins by setting the purpose of the lesson and building background knowledge with the full class. He or she clearly communicates objectives so that students can make connections to previous and current learning, and he or she establishes background knowledge by way of visuals, meaningful discussions, and other scaffolds that establish context for the new learning taking place. From there, the teacher transitions into the explicit modeling of a skill or reading strategy, usually by way of a think-aloud exercise conducted with an initial section of the text. Students listen to the teacher's fluent and expressive reading as they follow along in the text, and the teacher makes his or her thinking visible by explaining precisely *how* he or she makes meaning of the text. Although this initial part of the whole-group lesson is primarily teacher led, the teacher provides for brief moments of engagement that allow students to process and synthesize their learning. For example, the teacher may have student pairs share their thinking at key moments within the text.

2. **Guided instruction:** After the teacher reads aloud and models the target skills with the first section of the text, students take a more active role in the whole-group experience. Here, students dive into the text and begin practicing the skills and strategies with the teacher's continued guidance. Teachers may prompt students by asking questions or facilitating additional tasks that enhance the learning taking place.

3. **Collaborative learning:** Teachers continue to relinquish their support during the collaborative learning step. At this time, students may engage in a think-pair-share to process their learning and practice the skill together. You might see them annotating or locating details that describe characters' traits, listing evidence that answers a text-based question, or completing a graphic organizer to sequence the text's events in chronological order. As the students try the skill out for themselves, the teacher leans in and provides support or extension opportunities as needed. The teacher also encourages peers to directly support each other during this process.

4. **Independent learning:** By the end of a whole-group reading lesson, students take on more responsibility as they connect their learning to independent practice. Jennifer Serravallo (2010) describes this practice

as having the *to*, *with*, and *by* of balanced literacy. She asserts, "There are times when the teacher provides a model to the students, times when the teacher works with the students, and times when students work by themselves" (Serravallo, 2010, p. 9). As students transition to independent practice, they transfer their knowledge and skills by applying their learning in new ways. Whether continuing with the same shared text or using an alternative, independent text, students read closely and integrate strategies, and teachers hold them accountable for their learning by engaging them in meaningful tasks that demonstrate their precise levels of mastery. Often, this independent practice time occurs as students transition to the part of the literacy block that teachers set aside for small-group instruction.

Although this example application moves from teacher-directed instruction to independent practice, the order in which the structures occur will differ from day to day (Fisher, 2008). On some days, teachers may choose to begin with a cooperative component, allowing pairs of students to engage in up-front discoveries or synthesize previous learning. On other days, teachers may want students to first approach a task independently to observe how they grapple with a concept on their own. What is important is that teachers always state the lesson's purpose, model the learning, provide guided support, and set aside time for independent practice.

Close Reading

At times, the whole-group experience calls for a close reading of a story, article, poem, or excerpt of text. Sheila Brown and Lee Kappes (2012) define *close reading* as an experience where students investigate a short piece of text and teachers bring about the following:

> Students are guided to deeply analyze and appreciate various aspects of the text, such as key vocabulary and how its meaning is shaped by context; attention to form, tone, imagery and/or rhetorical devices; the significance of word choice and syntax; and the discovery of different levels of meaning as passages are read multiple times. (p. 2)

Texts that are worthy of a close read are rich with nuanced language and structures and keenly composed with elements of craft. When teachers guide students through a close reading, they examine with students the subtleties and elaborateness of text at a higher level than students would normally do during a typical everyday reading. Fisher and Frey (2013) emphasize the benefits of close reading in acknowledging that "students do not arrive already knowing how to interrogate a text and dig down into its deeper meaning. Teachers have to teach students how to do this, in both informational and literary texts" (p. 46).

The following list provides a few reminders for implementing effective whole-group reading lessons.

- ▸ Explicitly state learning objectives.
- ▸ Build background knowledge.
- ▸ Engage students in complex grade-level texts.
- ▸ Expose students to fluent modeled reading.
- ▸ Align explicit instruction with standards.
- ▸ Ensure shared text is visible to all students.
- ▸ Embed instruction on vocabulary, word work, and foundational skills as needed.
- ▸ Utilize the gradual release of responsibility model.
- ▸ Embed opportunities for student engagement and discourse.
- ▸ Facilitate a close reading of a text (when applicable).
- ▸ Move students toward independent practice.

Whole-group reading is a staple of literacy instruction. With thoughtfully delivered lessons that stretch student thinking and engage students with text, daily delivery of whole-group reading instruction equips students in becoming well-versed readers. As their teacher provides an explicit model of a skill accompanied by a verbal explanation of thinking, students come to realize the kind of thinking readers do to understand what they read. With embedded opportunities for engagement, students also interact with a variety of genres in new and exciting ways. As a whole-group reading lesson comes to a close, students feel more confident and prepared to begin practicing the skill on their own.

Whole-Group Writing

In a well-balanced literacy block, teachers also set aside valuable instruction time for the teaching and modeling of writing skills. During the whole-group writing experience in second and third grade, explicit instruction typically rotates among three distinct genres of writing—(1) informative, (2) opinion, and (3) narrative—

but may also include writing for other purposes, such as letter, poem, or biography writing.

Depending on the lesson's objective, teachers may deliver instruction on myriad writing techniques, from stringing together ideas at the word and sentence level to developing larger compositions, such as an opinion paragraph with relevant reasons and supporting details. Additionally, teachers naturally embed instruction on vocabulary and foundational skills as authentic teachable moments arise while teaching.

Research evidence supports the claim that writing serves as an impactful tool to improve reading: "In particular, having students write about a text they are reading enhances how well they comprehend it. The same result occurs when students write about a text from different content areas, such as science and social studies" (Graham & Hebert, 2010, p. 6). Based on their findings of the correlative influence between writing and reading, authors Graham and Hebert (2010) recommend ways that teachers can use writing to bolster students' reading skills and comprehension and help students learn about subject-matter content. They sort their findings into three core categories.

1. **Teachers ask students to write about what they read:** When students write an extended response based on a text-based task—for example, a personal response, analysis, interpretation, or summary—reading comprehension improves. Additionally, taking notes about text results in positive gains, as this enables students to review the text, determine significant ideas, organize the material, and make connections. (In second and third grade, students may elect to take notes on a graphic organizer or an alternate tool to make the task less cumbersome.) Collectively, these steps yield new insights. Further, when students answer text-dependent questions in writing or design and answer these types of questions, they also deepen their understanding of a text and increase their knowledge of the content. Students derive more benefit from writing questions and answers down than from engaging in question-and-answer discussions.

2. **Teachers conduct lessons around writing skills and processes to create text:** Since writing and reading share common processes and knowledge, teaching students to write well improves their reading skills. Therefore, teachers conduct lessons on the process of writing (planning, editing, revision, and so on), text structures (such as compare–contrast, problem–solution, cause–effect, sequence, and description), sentence and paragraph construction, and spelling.

3. **Teachers increase the amount of writing that students do:** Providing students with more time to write their own texts—such as texts on self- or peer-selected topics, letters to internet pen pals, and journal entries to themselves or peers—correlates with an uptick in reading comprehension.

Teachers should weave these recommendations into learning experiences throughout the school day; however, initial explicit teaching typically begins in the whole-group setting, where teachers employ a number of instructional strategies to facilitate the learning of new writing concepts. As one approach, Fisher and Frey (2008) suggest teachers make the composing process concrete by utilizing write-alouds during explicit writing instruction. Through write-alouds, teachers provide detailed verbal explanations of their thinking as they artfully move through all steps of the writing process (broken down in manageable chunks for second- and third-grade students).

Similarly, teachers might implement interactive writing in their whole-group lessons. Kate Roth and Joan Dabrowski (2014) define *interactive writing* as "a dynamic instructional method during which the teacher and students work together to construct meaningful text while discussing the details of the writing process" (p. 34). This shared writing experience allows for group collaboration and discussion as the teacher guides the students through the writing process's steps and promotes active participation as he or she invites students to share his or her pen at particular points in the lesson.

Finally, it's important that whole-group writing instruction encourage authentic writing experiences. In the article "Reigniting Writers," Norine Blanch, Lenora C. Forsythe, Jennifer H. Van Allen, and Sherron Killingsworth Roberts (2017) assert, "Teachers should take courage in their ability to model authorship, providing ample opportunities to emulate writers and learn from mentor texts through explicit teaching and use of the writing process" (p. 50). To facilitate this when collaborating with and writing alongside a class of students, teachers might articulate and model components of the writing process, such as the following.

▸ Using brainstorming techniques

▸ Interpreting a writing prompt

▸ Using graphic organizers to gather and organize ideas, information, or research

▸ Choosing precise words to impact writing's mood, tone, or message

▸ Combining sentences

▸ Implementing smooth transitions

▸ Using proper conventions of spelling and punctuation

▸ Writing introduction, body, or conclusion paragraphs

▸ Editing or revising

When considering the knowledge and skills necessary to compose a purposeful writing piece, they are indeed plentiful. The preceding list depicts many of the skills and concepts necessary for crafting a writing task from start to finish. When we consider our grades 2 and 3 learners, we understand that many of them just recently learned to apply their knowledge of letter-and-sound correspondence to write individual words during their primary years. To make the writing process comprehensible and attainable at these grade levels, teachers thoughtfully model and deliver writing instruction in manageable chunks that allow for continued growth throughout the year. It is possible that many of the young writers in second- and third-grade classrooms are not yet familiar with all of the skills listed above.

The Study of Mentor Texts

Mentor texts—either published works or student-generated works—are essentially exemplary writing samples that reflect the tenets of strong writing for students to use as a model when crafting their own pieces. Although we focus here on mentor texts for literacy, teams can locate these texts for any content area and use them for a variety of purposes. For example, in social studies, a text that explains how the climate in different regions of the world affects the people who live there can serve as a mentor text for a cause-and-effect writing task. Similarly, a clearly written word problem in a mathematics textbook can become a mentor from which students create their own word problems. In essence, mentor texts help make the complexities of writing concrete. Often, second- and third-grade students who receive a writing task may not yet have a conceptual understanding of what their writing should entail. They frequently have questions such as the following.

▸ "How should I begin?"

▸ "What should my sentences sound like?"

▸ "What precise words should I include?"

▸ "How do I organize my thoughts?"

▸ "Am I on the right track?"

When students see and examine skilled writing, it not only helps them answer these questions but also offers them something to aspire to. Shanahan (2015) writes:

The idea of text modeling is that students must carefully and analytically read texts to identify their key features so as to produce their own version of a genre or a text feature. By engaging in such reading—with an eye aimed specifically at identifying features of craft and structure . . . students can sharpen both their reading and writing skills. (p. 475)

Using mentor texts, students study the way authors apply elements of craft and language. They might, for example, investigate how authors employ figurative language to describe a narrative setting or determine how authors organize facts within an informative article to demonstrate the causes and effects of natural disasters. Depending on the purpose of the lesson, strong mentor texts may have one or more of the following traits.

▸ An organized text structure that students can emulate (such as chronological, cause and effect, or compare and contrast)

▸ A clear purpose backed by supporting details and evidence

▸ Examples of direct quotes or paraphrased information

▸ A variety of text features, such as captions, diagrams, or charts

▸ Descriptive details or figurative language

▸ Strong word choice

▸ An exemplary introduction or conclusion

▸ Evidence of the author's tone or mood

Texts with these traits exemplify the elements of craft students are to create and become exemplars from which students learn and emulate the fundamental, stylistic nuances that exceptional authors include in their writing.

Gradual Release of Responsibility

Gradual release of responsibility is a powerful instructional approach during whole-group writing, just as it is during whole-group reading. Due to the thought processes necessary to formulate coherent ideas and sentences, as well as the physical demand of writing or even typing out a composition, writing is an intricate exercise. Therefore, teachers cannot simply do all of the writing work during focused instruction or even during guided instruction; that would be counterproductive in helping students internalize new skills. Instead, teachers focus on key writing concepts, gradually release their support, and support students as they apply each writing concept, little by little.

Marzano (2017) affirms, "When information is new to students, they best process it in small, understandable increments. This is because learners can hold only small amounts of information in their working memories" (p. 30). This means teachers should deliver writing instruction to developing writers in meaningful and manageable segments while embedding time for collaborative discourse and independent practice. For example, because oracy is the first step in producing language and articulating thinking and is the foundation for producing writing, teachers should give students time to process and verbalize their thinking within the whole-group writing lesson (NGA & CCSSO, n.d.a). Just a few minutes spent articulating ideas with others can lead to more in-depth and focused writing. Immediate opportunities for trial and practice are also essential in helping students actualize learning. After the teacher explicitly models how to craft topic sentences, for instance, students should have the chance to try writing a few of their own, whether individually or with a partner.

Students depart from effective whole-group writing lessons with systematic strategies for planning, crafting, revising, editing, and publishing their written works. Equipped with the knowledge and skills necessary to write for a variety of purposes, students have the wherewithal and confidence to independently apply the strategies to their own original compositions. The following list provides a few reminders for implementing well-designed whole-group writing lessons in second and third grade.

- ‣ Explicitly state learning objectives.
- ‣ Provide instruction on informative, opinion, and narrative writing.
- ‣ Model writing using mentor texts.
- ‣ Conduct write-alouds.
- ‣ Construct interactive writing experiences.
- ‣ Explain and model standards-aligned writing skills.
- ‣ Include vocabulary, word work, and foundational skills in instruction as needed.
- ‣ Follow the gradual release of responsibility model.
- ‣ Embed opportunities for student engagement and discourse.
- ‣ Move students toward independent writing.

As Lesley Mandel Morrow and Linda B. Gambrell (2011) express in *Best Practices in Literacy Instruction*, "Students learn to write when they are surrounded with examples and models, given expectations, allowed to make decisions and mistakes, given feedback, and allowed time to practice in realistic ways" (p. 294). Through explicit modeling and the delivery of manageable increments of instruction, students begin to conceptualize the writing process and how its many moving parts come together to create a well-written composition. Structuring a literacy block that allows for this type of modeling, thinking, and authentic application leads to continued practice and improvement for students.

EXERCISE
Discuss Whole-Group Reading and Writing Lessons

Consider the information provided about whole-group reading and writing instruction, and have a collaborative discussion on the current whole-group experiences within your team's classrooms. Discuss how team members might refine whole-group reading or writing lessons to make a greater impact on student achievement.

Use the following questions to guide this exercise.

★ How can we ensure that the texts we use for whole-group experiences are appropriately challenging for our students?

★ How can we maintain high engagement levels among our students?

★ How will we incorporate gradual release of responsibility during whole-group reading and writing lessons?

★ What texts will we use as mentor texts during writing instruction?

Small-Group Reading

During small-group reading, teachers gather flexible groups of students—individual students that teachers determine in response to recent data—to provide differentiated instruction and support in a more personalized setting. The word *flexible* asserts that these groups are ever-changing and based on evidence of students' learning. Within these groups, which typically include no more than six students, teachers deliver instruction tailored to the students' current needs. They choose these groupings by using data they have gathered on students' growth to determine which students have similar proficiency levels with targeted reading standards. The goal of this is to ensure students receive just the right amount of support at just the right time. On a given day, students may meet with the teacher to work on any of the following.

- Improving reading fluency
- Engaging in word work (such as practicing letter and sound correspondence, spelling words with common vowel teams, or studying prefixes and suffixes)
- Building foundational skills (such as phonics or decoding)
- Engaging in comprehension strategies
- Focusing on standards-aligned skills

As we explore this topic, you'll notice we repeatedly emphasize the notion of flexibility. To be successful, small groups must be flexible in at least three ways.

1. Flexible in *who* is chosen for the small group
2. Flexible in *how long* a small-group session takes
3. Flexible in *what* differentiated support teachers provide

As Carol Ann Tomlinson and Marcia B. Imbeau (2010) put it, "A flexible approach to teaching 'makes room' for student variance" (p. 14). Put another way, flexibility creates space to differentiate instruction for students who are not all learning at the same rate or in the same way. Remember that, in a PLC, time is the variable, and learning must be the constant (DuFour et al., 2016). The following sections explore how teachers answer the questions of *Who?* and *What?* when differentiating small-group reading instruction. (Both sections address the question of *How Long?*)

Determining Who

To establish an effective differentiated classroom that meets every student's needs, Tomlinson and Imbeau (2010) remind teachers that they should continually ask themselves, "What does *this* student need at *this* moment in order to be able to progress with *this* key content, and what do I need to do to make that happen?" (p. 14). Like a catchy new pop song that plays in your head on repeat, this question continuously resonates in teachers' minds. Teachers are eager to find the answers that will provide the needed support to students in a small-group setting. Teachers gather together students who have similar needs and, with the guidance of their teacher, those students intently work to close teacher-identified skill gaps, practice strategies that align with grade-level reading standards, and extend their learning when they are ready for more.

Teachers use a variety of small-group frameworks to address students' reading needs. A small-group framework teachers commonly implement in primary classrooms is a guided-reading approach that groups readers at the same proficiency level or similar proficiency levels. Irene C. Fountas and Gay Su Pinnell (2019) describe leveled *guided reading* as scaffolded instruction that allows students to make "small shifts in processing power every day" by utilizing a text that is just beyond the level at which the group can read independently (p. 2). For students who are one or more grade levels behind, guided reading provides differentiated support by nudging students along in their reading abilities, little by little. However, Tim Shanahan (2020) cautions teachers in limiting students' reading instruction to only a particular Lexile or guided reading level. He asserts plainly that, by the end of the year, students will have to demonstrate proficiency (on state or local exams as well as summative assessments) using grade-level texts. By third grade, students' needs tend to vary by skill or text type as curriculum materials across content areas become more diverse and increasingly complex. While guided reading may provide the support a student needs to make adequate strides in reading abilities, teachers should use caution to ensure that the student doesn't become defined or limited by their current level. The goal, as with any intervention, is to raise these students up to grade-level proficiency, not to allow them to remain perpetually behind (Buffum et al., 2018); therefore, teachers may want to consider other approaches to small-group reading instruction to serve their students' ever-changing needs.

To help students make strides in their reading abilities, teachers may choose to flexibly group students by identifying particular individuals who need extra practice and support with a specific *skill*. We find this strategy especially effective for third-grade students as many of their diverse needs tend to be driven by the current literacy standards and targets being taught, rather than foundational-type concepts that follow a more standardized scope and sequence. For example, perhaps the teacher has identified four students who are struggling to explain the cause-and-effect relationships in a nonfiction text, while six students are still developing the skill of summarizing a fiction story, and three others are working on decoding multisyllabic words. Clearly, the needs of these groups vary greatly. When the teacher gathers them together during small-group instruction, he or she will expertly orchestrate support using differentiated strategies, teaching tactics, and scaffolds. Additionally, knowing that students will eventually need to demonstrate mastery of the skills using texts at their own grade level, the teacher provides guided practice opportunities for them to do so using grade-level texts. Here, the teacher becomes the scaffold as he or she assists students in navigating challenging texts that are currently beyond the small group's instructional level while also teaching explicit strategies that will aid with comprehension.

At each small-group reading session, instruction is highly differentiated with the goal of continuous improvement and growth. The group of students sitting at the small-group table on Monday may be of an entirely different make-up by Wednesday, due to data collected throughout instruction and the students' evolving needs. Additionally, the length of time it takes for students to grasp a skill will also vary. A teacher may need to meet with a few students on several occasions, while others grasp a concept after a brief small-group encounter with the teacher. The *Who?* of small group reading instruction evolves as students demonstrate their learning throughout a unit of instruction.

Determining What

Small groups are flexible in not only *who* teachers choose to meet in each group but also *what* the focused instruction entails in each group. Early childhood literacy experts Gretchen Owocki and Yetta Goodman (2002) emphasize the need for *kidwatching* within the classroom as a way to gather valuable data on students' strengths and areas for growth in order to meet the students where they're at:

> The primary goals of kidwatching are to support and gain insight into children's learning by (1) intensely observing and documenting what they know and can do; (2) documenting their ways of constructing and expressing knowledge; and (3) planning curriculum and instruction that are tailored to individual strengths and needs. (p. x)

Kidwatching leads to informed decision making because it requires that, each day, teachers listen closely to a student as he or she reads with his or her partner, take notes when it seems that a student is struggling with a reading skill during independent practice, or conference with a student to gather valuable input from the student's perspective. The more information teachers have on students, the better they can determine what students need, both improving the accuracy of assignments for small-group work and ensuring students receive the right assistance during small-group instruction.

At the small-group reading table, teachers explicitly teach students strategies for constructing meaning. Shanahan et al. (2010) define *strategies* as a reader's intentional mental actions and deliberate efforts to better comprehend what he or she is reading. They attest that worksheets or exercises are not strategies, as these are merely activities. Moreover, Jennifer Serravallo (2010) defines *strategies* as the "step-by-step how-tos for internalizing skills such as determining importance, questioning, inferring, monitoring for meaning, activating prior knowledge, visualizing, and retelling/synthesizing" (p. 12). In other words, strategies are scaffolds that teachers teach to students and that aid students in conquering the skills needed for proficient reading. Unless teachers couple activities with strategies and direct instruction on the thinking students must employ to make meaning, activities like worksheets and exercises rarely help students become better at reading. These kinds of activities allow students to show what they know at their current proficiency level, but they don't offer any *new* strategic instruction to actuate growth. Thus, in small groups, students practice strategies with the support of their teacher, building toward independence. As Serravallo (2010) asserts, once the needed skill becomes an intrinsic part of the student's reading repertoire, reliance on the corresponding strategy decreases and only activates when the student faces reading difficulties.

Teachers also help students develop and refine literacy skills at the small-group table. The range of students' proficiency levels tends to widen by grades 2 and 3. Some second- and third-grade students may need differentiated small-group support to strengthen foundational literacy skills, such as phonics and fluency, while others in the class forge ahead onto higher-level inferring skills. To broaden students' knowledge and understanding of how language works, teachers also facilitate differentiated word-work lessons, which equip readers with word attack strategies that lead to greater reading independence (Morrow & Gambrell, 2011)

At the small-group table, students may work on several different skills, from spelling words with common vowel teams to reading irregularly spelled words to studying the meanings of prefixes and suffixes. Teachers also gain valuable insights on individual students as they conduct running records (refer to Running Records and Reading Fluency Checks, page 51) and use the data to identify skill gaps to reinforce, such as a gap in a student's ability to decode multi-syllable words or use context to identify unknown words. After leaving the small-group table, students apply newly learned skills during literacy-skill application time since repeated exposure and immediate application is critical to student growth. The following list provides a few reminders for implementing effective small-group reading instruction.

▸ Ensure student groups are flexible.

▸ Provide differentiated texts, supports, and scaffolds.

▸ Offer guided instruction on comprehension strategies, standards and targets, vocabulary, word work, and foundational skills.

▸ Conduct individual running records for all students.

▸ Establish guided practice for identified student skill gaps.

▸ Move students' learning toward independence.

Focused instruction at the small group table equips students with the differentiated tools needed for literacy growth. As teachers flexibly group students together based on data, they can provide literacy instruction and more personalized support to meet the current needs of the students.

Small-Group Writing

Much like small-group reading, small-group writing is a time for focused, differentiated instruction tailored to students' specific needs with the goal of improving their skilled-writing abilities. The authors of "Bring Powerful Writing Strategies Into Your Classroom!" define *skilled writing* as a complex process "requiring extensive self-regulation of a flexible, goal-directed, problem-solving activity. In addition to basic skills, students must also develop knowledge about the writing process, genre knowledge, and strategies for writing and self-regulating the writing process" (Harris, Graham, Friedlander, & Laud, 2013, p. 539). With their focused attention on just a handful of students, teachers can hone in on targeted writing concepts for each student, providing the necessary scaffolding for them to advance their writing abilities.

During small-group writing, teachers bridge the learning that took place during the whole-group experience and assist students in a smaller setting as they craft their ideas into written compositions. As we established in the section Determining Who (page 184), having thorough data about each student will increase small groups' flexibility and inform teachers' decisions about who to meet with and what concepts to address in small groups. With individualized guidance and feedback from the teacher, the small-group writing table becomes a safe and comfortable environment where students find themselves writing with originality and taking risks to express their ideas in thoughtful and creative ways. With their teacher there to support them, students' words flow more easily onto paper, and students begin to see themselves as authors.

To facilitate continuous student growth, teachers provide differentiated instruction on explicit writing strategies at the small-group table. The U.S. Department of Education's Institute of Education Sciences emphasizes the following about writing-strategy instruction:

> Teachers can help students become effective writers by teaching a variety of strategies for carrying out each component of the writing process and by supporting students in applying the strategies until they are able to do so independently. Over time, students will develop a repertoire of strategies for writing. Teachers should explain and model the fluid nature in which the components of the writing process work together, so that students can learn to apply strategies flexibly—separately or in combination—when they write. (Graham et al., 2012, p. 12)

At the small-group writing table, teachers provide differentiated strategy instruction to students with similar needs as they strengthen, fine-tune, and practice composition skills. Additionally, scaffolds teachers put in place—such as sentence frames, graphic organizers, word banks, templates, mentor texts, visuals, and checklists—provide the proper amount of support as students begin to make connections and build on previous concepts.

At times, this specialized writing instruction might also take the form of an individual student conference. During conferences, teachers meet with individual students to discuss current writing projects and provide feedback so students know what precise changes or additions need to occur next so they improve. Especially for second- and third-grade writers, teachers must make their feedback as concrete and explicit as possible. They should avoid vague directives such as, "Add more description" or "Include evidence from the text," which give little direction to students on the precise next steps to take for notable improvement.

Grant Wiggins (2012) suggests key elements of feedback that teachers can incorporate into their instructional program to issue effective feedback and generate successful results. Based on these key elements, feedback should be the following.

▸ **Goal referenced:** Students should establish a clear goal for their work. When teachers or peers provide effective feedback, it gives specific direction in relation to the goal and lets students know if they are on the right track. Given that students likely have goals in many subject areas, teachers typically need to remind students of their goals to establish the focus of their work together and help move learning along in the right direction. For example, after convening together at the small-group table, the teacher might begin by saying, "Remember, our goal is to add transition words to help our ideas flow throughout a paragraph. Let's get to work so we can practice adding new transition words today."

▸ **Tangible and transparent:** The feedback teachers provide must be so obvious to students that they know precisely what they can do to improve. For writing, that means it is specific to a particular sentence, skill, or component of the writing process. Instead of commenting that the writing is "vague" or "confusing," teachers are much more exact in pointing out the particular part of the writing that is causing these results. Sometimes, students don't always recognize the need for feedback. To help them better recognize the need for revision or editing within their own writing, read their writing aloud, or have the student or a peer do it. Hearing one's own writing allows the writer to step outside of the process and experience the writing in a new way, which often leads to new realizations about the value of feedback and revision.

▸ **Actionable:** Students take action on the feedback they receive. Stating goal-related facts allows students to spring into action to revise or perform a task in order to improve performance. Instead of providing vague statements, such as "Great job!" or "Almost there," teachers use evidence from the students' writing to pinpoint one or two things they can do to better their writing. Teachers phrase feedback as observations rather than judgments. For example, the teacher might say, "In this paragraph, you used many pronouns, but it's not clear who each pronoun is referring to. Can you reread this section and clarify who you are referring to in each sentence?"

▸ **User-friendly:** Students must be able to understand the feedback they receive. Using plain and familiar language allows them to conceptualize the feedback and take action on it. Additionally, providing too much feedback can be ineffective and overwhelming for students. Instead, teachers should focus on providing one or two pieces of feedback that will yield immediate results.

▸ **Timely:** Timely feedback—provided as soon as possible—allows students to apply learning while it is fresh in their minds. One of the benefits of small-group writing instruction is that a teacher can often provide feedback at the very moment that students are sitting with him or her, allowing students to apply it right then and there with his or her guidance and support. Individual student conferences, as well as peer feedback sessions, allow for timely feedback on the writing process.

▸ **Ongoing:** Students must have opportunities to use feedback to further their learning. Feedback given on a summative assessment, when writing instruction comes to a halt, does little to help students improve their skills. Formative assessments, on the other hand, provide plentiful opportunities for ongoing feedback, practice, and improvement. Throughout the writing process, teachers check in on students, little by little, to identify areas of need and intervene while the learning is fresh. This way, for example, teachers can provide support on a student's ability to write a topic sentence early on in the process, instead of waiting until the child completes the entire writing assignment.

▸ **Consistent:** To provide feedback that is accurate and consistent, teachers need to maintain common expectations of what high-quality writing looks like. In chapter 4 (page 101), we addressed the value of using rubrics, calibration sessions, and anchor papers to ensure consistency among teammates. If this work is not consistent, teachers may provide feedback to their students that does not align with the team's collective agreement about what skilled writing looks like in second and third grade.

During one-on-one conferences, students who might be intimidated to share with peers can feel comfortable talking alone with the teacher. Plus, even though this dialogue centers on instruction, it concurrently builds a relationship between the student and teacher. Upon the culmination of individual (or small-group) conference sessions, teachers set individual and specific goals for each student and send students off to apply newly learned skills and concepts during independent work time. Students then self-monitor as they work independently, and they report on the progress they've made at their next meeting with the teacher. With ongoing feedback and the explicit teaching of new skills, students continue working toward and refining personal goals as they add skills to their writing repertoires and develop into skilled authors (Serravallo, 2014).

Students may meet as a small group during any step of the writing process, from brainstorming and planning to editing and revising. Just as with small-group reading, teachers form groups flexibly based on students' needs and how they progress.

With a narrowed focus, select students may work with a teacher to refine a number of writing skills, such as the following.

▸ Generating ideas

▸ Planning for a variety of genres

▸ Crafting topic sentences

▸ Gathering text-based evidence

▸ Elaborating or adding descriptive details

▸ Composing complete sentences

▸ Organizing ideas to develop coherence

▸ Inserting dialogue or other narrative techniques

▸ Replacing words with more precise synonyms

▸ Using proper conventions

▸ Editing for capitalization and punctuation

The following list provides a few reminders for implementing effective small-group writing sessions.

▸ Establish flexible groups of students.

▸ Determine a specific strategy for instruction.

▸ Provide differentiated writing supports and scaffolds.

▸ Give guided instruction at various steps in the writing process.

▸ Provide guided practice on identified skill gaps.

▸ Establish periodic student writing conferences.

▸ Provide specific individualized feedback.

▸ Determine individualized writing goals.

Expressing and elaborating on one's ideas in written form requires many steps, which is why many refer to writing as a *process*. When teachers meet with small groups of students or utilize one-to-one conferencing, they are able to pinpoint precise steps or skills within the writing process and provide feedback and support that is straightforward and tailored to students' various needs. Student goals are established, differentiated scaffolds are put in place, and the rather abstract process of writing becomes more concrete and attainable for students.

EXERCISE
Discuss Small-Group Instruction

Consider the information provided about small-group reading and writing instruction, and have a collaborative discussion on the current small-group experiences within your team's classrooms. Discuss how your team might refine small-group reading or writing sessions to make a greater impact on student achievement.

Use the following questions to guide this exercise.

★ What reading and writing skills do students need to master learning standards, and what strategies can we explicitly teach to help them reach proficiency?

★ How will we use data to decide which students to pull together for small-group differentiated instruction for reading and writing?

★ What differentiated supports or extensions do students need to improve their reading and writing skills?

Literacy-Skill Application

During the facilitation of small-group reading and writing instruction, students who are not part of the small group that is specifically working with the teacher typically engage in literacy-skill application time. We've seen teachers refer to this time as *centers*, *workstations*, *rounds*, *rotations*, or *independent learning time*, but we've chosen *literacy-skill application time* to denote its precise purpose within the larger literacy block. As the teacher conducts small-group lessons with select individuals, the rest of the students in the class receive ample time to apply (either independently or collaboratively) the newly learned strategies and skills explicitly taught during whole- and small-group reading and writing lessons. Students try out the strategies for themselves, engage in tasks that allow them to practice and refine the skills, and strengthen the bridge toward independence.

With the teacher's focused attention on small-group instruction, he or she must carefully structure and design the learning opportunities for the other students in the room. To ensure the students not working with the teacher are continuously engaged, teachers often rotate students through independent learning stations, typically following one of two rotation models: (1) the small-group session with the teacher is included *inside* the rotation of independent stations or (2) the small-group session with the teacher is positioned *outside* the rotation. The diagram in figure 7.3 depicts these two approaches to independent learning stations, with the T representing the teacher's position during small-group instruction.

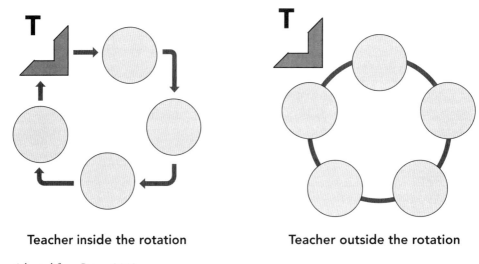

Teacher inside the rotation   Teacher outside the rotation

Source: Adapted from Bates, 2013.

Figure 7.3: Structures for small-group and independent learning.

In our experience, it is better for teachers to remain outside the rotation because it provides for a much more flexible approach to small-group work. When the teacher is included inside a timed rotation, groups of students make their way around the room to a set of predetermined workstations. When the timer goes off (usually after about fifteen minutes), students stop what they are doing and move to the next station, one of which is the small-group reading session with the teacher. While this rotational structure allows for the regimented movement of students in and out of small-group reading and writing sessions, this approach has pitfalls associated with it. First, students cannot always accomplish dynamic, higher-order thinking tasks within the limitations of timed stations. As we know, time is the variable when making learning the constant (DuFour et al., 2010). Not all students move at the same pace, and what one student accomplishes in ten minutes could easily take another student twenty. Second, when teachers position themselves within the cyclical movement of the rotation, they restrict time spent on guided support within each small group to a set duration, *and* they limit their work to only the students who show up to the table in the rotation. This leaves little to no flexible room for pulling individual students based on timely data-driven decisions. Recall that flexibility is crucial for effective small-group work.

Instead of fastening themselves to a rigid rotation structure, we encourage teachers to take themselves outside the independent learning stations. This allows for both flexible groupings of students and flexible timing. Some small groups may need only five minutes with a teacher to quickly receive the differentiated support they need, while other groups may require more intense guided support over the course of fifteen or twenty minutes. Celeste C. Bates (2013), assistant professor at Clemson University, affirms that "flexible grouping allows teachers to call children from centers based on the children's interests and needs, recognizing that as these needs change, so do the grouping arrangements" (p. 30).

With the freedom to move flexibly in and out of small groups—groups they assemble based on data accumulated about students' learning—teachers can make a greater impact on reading achievement and maximize small-group minutes to benefit each student in the room. Table 7.1 summarizes the benefits of positioning the teacher outside an independent station rotation, rather than inside the rotation.

Table 7.1: Positioning the Teacher Inside the Rotation Versus Outside the Rotation

Teacher Is Inside the Station Rotation	Teacher Is Outside the Station Rotation
• The duration of small-group instruction is equivalent and fixed for all groups.	• The duration of small-group instruction is flexible and tailored to each group's needs.
• Small groups are restricted to those students placed together for the rotation.	• Teachers pull students from any workstation on an as-needed basis.
• Homogenous groups of students travel together to all workstations.	• Heterogeneous groups of students can travel or work together at various workstations.
• The duration of each workstation is restricted and dictated by a timer.	• The duration of workstations is flexible and can be adjusted for the task.
• Rotation centers typically involve identical tasks for all students.	• Teachers can differentiate workstations and independent activities based on the needs of students.

Teachers have alternative options besides timed rotation stations that can enhance literacy-skill application time. For example, teachers can implement and display a "must-do, may-do" learning menu of skill-application tasks related to vocabulary, word work, fluency, foundational skills, writing skills, or reading skills.

On the must-do side of the menu, teachers list required learning tasks that students must accomplish during skill-application time. These tasks are a priority, as they are meaningful to the development of current priority standards and aligned with recent whole-group reading and writing lessons. For student accountability, teachers link a distinct piece of evidence of student thinking and learning to each task so that both teachers and students can monitor and measure individual progress. All students must accomplish these tasks first, but students can typically choose the order in which they complete them.

The may-do tasks on the menu are optional activities that students engage in after meeting all must-do requirements. Although these are not priority tasks, they are meaningful and practical in strengthening and advancing literacy skills. They provide learning extensions for students who finish must-do items with time to spare.

A clear and consistent structure during literacy-skill application time allows students to use valuable learning minutes efficiently as they apply and practice essential skills. Though the components of a literacy block will be consistent across teacher teams to ensure guaranteed and viable learning opportunities for all students, the structures individual teachers utilize for learning may vary from teacher to teacher depending on their teaching styles and classroom management preferences. Regardless of the structure, the primary goal of any independent learning framework is to engage students in various relevant, growth-producing learning experiences with embedded accountability measures that help teachers monitor growth and determine next steps for each individual student. When teachers meet with small groups of students, the rest of the class receives time to practice and apply the skills they've learned in whole- and small-group settings. For this component of the literacy block to propel student literacy learning, students must be focused and engaged in the tasks at hand (Guthrie, Wigfield, & You, 2012). The following sections explore critical characteristics of learning across all disciplines: student engagement and creating time for reading.

Student Engagement

Despite teachers' efforts to establish routines and hold high expectations for all students, students don't always have the stamina, attention, or motivation to follow through when working individually at their own pace. The factors that affect these student qualities are highly variable and are frequently not under students' conscious control, particularly in second and third grade. For these young students, minds wander frequently, and distractions are typically abundant as the classroom community is hard at work. For this reason, it is critical that teachers provide students with structure, direction, and clear expectations for all tasks and activities. To optimize literacy-skill application time, some students may require differentiated supports beyond what a teacher provides to the whole class. For example, in addition to a must-do, may-do menu, a student who struggles to maintain focus may benefit from having a detailed, step-by-step checklist on which he or she can track individual progress. Other students may require extra scaffolds or materials, such as graphic organizers, highlighters for locating textual support, sequencing strips, or sticky notes for annotating or tracking one's thinking. Before sending students off to work on their own, teachers must equip them with the various tools they'll need to be independently successful.

Perhaps most critical to the success of independent skill-application time is maintaining continuous cognitive engagement from students. Fisher and Frey (2018) admit what many teachers know to be true: some students pretend to be engaged (though very often unintentionally) when their minds are not actually focused on the task at hand. This requires patience from teachers because, again, students don't always have the self-discipline to engage themselves. To facilitate effective independent work time, teachers must ensure that students are consistently engaged, are self-monitoring their current level of understanding, and are accountable for their learning. If students are not cognitively engaged and actively thinking throughout their independent practice time, valuable minutes within the literacy block are lost, resulting in missed opportunities for student growth.

As you review the engagement strategies in this section, it's important to recognize that what creates engagement in some students may not effectively engage others. Be prepared to differentiate your approach to keeping students engaged, just as you differentiate your instruction. Marzano (2017) illustrates four components of engagement: (1) paying attention, (2) being energized, (3) being intrigued, and (4) being inspired. During independent work time, teachers must be cognizant of wavering engagement levels, refocusing students by refining structures and procedures as needed. Just as teachers often stop and ask themselves *which* students need support, they must as frequently pause to consider just *what* their students are currently doing and precisely *how* it is helping them become skilled independent readers, writers, and thinkers.

Student engagement demands student action and literacy-skill application. To keep students engaged in purposeful cognitive tasks, we suggest teachers use the following activities during literacy-skill application time.

- ▸ Underlining textual evidence

- ▸ Circling descriptive phrases

- ▸ Sorting words

- ▸ Sequencing story events

- ▸ Monitoring progress by way of a checklist

- ▸ Annotating in the margin for a particular purpose

- ▸ Drawing a visual representation

- ▸ Editing or revising in different-colored ink or with electronic tracking tools

- ▸ Jotting down a quick summary after reading a paragraph

Jennifer Gonzalez (2018) of *Cult of Pedagogy* explains the idea of student engagement quite adeptly:

> If we want our students to actually learn the facts and concepts and ideas we're trying to teach them, they have to experience those things in some way that rises above abstract words on paper. They have to process them. Manipulate them. To really learn in a way that will stick, they have to DO something.

When teachers ask students to manipulate materials, underline details, draw a visual, or jot down information, they are attaching a task—an action—to students' performance of a skill. This task not only provides evidence of learning, but it also helps to keep students engaged in their thinking and application of the skill. Think of it this way: if you were to sit back and simply watch a cooking video or tutorial, it's quite possible you would find yourself disengaged at some point or lacking some understanding of how to execute the recipe independently. However, if you actively engaged in the process—utilizing cooking gadgets to skillfully chop, measure, and mix ingredients—you'd likely have a better understanding of the new recipe as well as evidence of your learning in the final result.

Adding a simple engagement task to learning opportunities helps students to stay on track and demonstrate their knowledge in a meaningful way.

Time for Reading

During literacy-skill application time, teachers set aside time for students to read with a partner, to listen to reading, or to read independently. Because the volume of reading students do is linked to increased comprehension and overall reading achievement (Allington, 2014), on most days, teams should ensure students engage in some kind of reading. During this time, teams should give students the freedom to pick a book that interests them, allowing for an element of student choice and the flexibility to choose texts that offer disciplinary learning opportunities. As Nancie Atwell (2007) affirms, "This is a time and a place for students to behave as skilled, passionate, habitual, critical readers" (p. 120).

Although simply reading for pleasure and practice is certainly beneficial, and teachers should offer periodic opportunities for this, teachers will also have students apply newly acquired skills and strategies during this independent reading time. As students read or listen to reading, they practice the concepts they learned during whole- and small-group instruction. Whether students read for pleasure or dig into a text to practice standards-aligned skills, teachers establish expectations and accountability measures (if necessary) to ensure that students remain focused and on the path toward continuous growth.

EXERCISE
Enhance Independent Learning

Consider the information provided about literacy-skill application time, and have a collaborative discussion on the independent learning experiences currently occurring within your team's classrooms. Discuss how your team might refine independent practice time to make a greater impact on student achievement.

Use the following questions to guide this exercise.

★ How will we structure literacy-skill application time to allow for the flexible grouping of students?

★ What engagement structures and activities will we embed into reading time to ensure students are actively and cognitively engaged in their learning?

★ What opportunities can we provide for students to practice skills collaboratively?

★ What accountability measures will students complete to demonstrate progress?

Vocabulary Instruction

To address the question of where vocabulary instruction best fits within the literacy block, we're inclined to begin with a rather simple answer: *everywhere*. Vocabulary plays a prominent role in the development of adeptly literate students across the content areas. In fact, increased vocabulary equates to increased meaning making from text: "There is much evidence—strong correlations, several causal studies, as well as rich theoretical orientations—that shows that vocabulary is tightly related to reading comprehension across the age span" (Beck, McKeown, & Kucan, 2013, p. 1). For this reason, we spend more effort in this section on how teams can design and deliver effective vocabulary instruction for their students.

To comprehend complex texts brimming with rich themes, scientific explanations, or detailed historical accounts, students need word knowledge. With the ability to understand the nuances of language, such as figures of speech, word parts, and connotative language, students can comprehend a range of texts on various topics, as well as artfully tell a story or compose a strongly supported opinion. To communicate clearly and accurately with others, students must be equipped with vocabularies that allow for the effortless exchange of thoughts and ideas. For all these reasons, teachers continuously strengthen and refine students' vocabulary skills throughout the literacy block as well as in other subject areas.

Vocabulary instruction must extend beyond the surface level of teachers providing students with haphazard introductions to new words that appear in various texts. Rather, teachers emphasize expanding word aptitude through direct instruction to bolster students' academic background knowledge. Although reading widely contributes to word acquisition, it does not play as large a role as one might think. Experts in this area admit that reading's impact as a resource for mastering new vocabulary is overestimated.

Isabel L. Beck and colleagues (2013) state that to use a text to learn new words, the reader must be adept at decoding, realize the actual presence of the unknown word, and have the wherewithal to use the context to figure out what the word means. Students who struggle to decipher text in general are ill equipped to successfully use context clues. Plus, to effectively learn the word, students require repeated exposure to it. Therefore, direct instruction proves more efficacious when teaching new words to students:

> The case for direct instruction is strong. From a number of perspectives, the research indicates that wide reading probably is not sufficient in itself to ensure that students will develop the necessary vocabulary and consequently

the necessary academic background knowledge to do well in school. In contrast, direct instruction has an impressive track record of improving students' background knowledge and the comprehension of academic content. (Marzano, 2004, p. 69)

Furthermore, Marzano (2004, 2020) explains that a student's ability and grade level, plus the complexity of the text, dictate the chances of learning a word in context: "A high-ability student has a 19 percent chance of learning a new word in context, whereas a low-ability student has an 8 percent chance" (pp. 67–68).

Not all unknown words need to be taught through direct instruction. Teachers need to carefully select vocabulary words based on various criteria—that words are necessary for students to fully comprehend a text, fundamental to the study of new concepts across disciplines, or enduring in that they are likely to emerge in social or academic settings. To determine how to best choose words for instructional purposes, teachers should be familiar with the three-tier system of categorizing words that Beck and colleagues (2013) devised.

▸ **Tier one:** This tier includes basic words used frequently in conversation. Students acquire these words in everyday life; therefore, explicit instruction is usually unnecessary for native English speakers. Examples include sight words and other common words like *boy, chair, pretty, red*, and *hand*.

▸ **Tier two:** This tier includes words that mature language users commonly use. They are words that often appear in texts but not as frequently in conversation. Examples include *investigate, determine, claim*, and *infer*. These words change meaning based on the context in which they are used. For example, a music teacher might *direct* the school chorus, whereas a teacher teaching a science unit might *direct* students to view a demonstration, and in a literacy unit, a teacher might have students study *direct* characterization.

▸ **Tier three:** Often called *domain-specific words*, this tier refers to words that appear most often in a specific content area and are associated with a particular topic. Examples include *nucleus, genes, treaty*, and *electoral*. Sometimes, these words are so esoteric that people rarely experience them, such as *panjandrum* or *antidisestablishmentarianism*.

Teams plan direct instruction lessons to teach both tier two and tier three. However, Beck et al. (2013) and the Common Core designers (NGA & CCSSO, n.d.a) suggest teachers expend more effort to teach tier two words. For one, most content-area texts assist teachers in their quest to present tier three words since many textbooks or other nonfiction materials use text features to point out their importance—through print features (bold, italicized, or highlighted typeface; subheadings; bullets; and so forth), graphic aids (such as diagrams, graphs, or timelines), organizational support (such as tables of contents, indexes, or glossaries), and illustrations. Plus, tier three words are used repeatedly in the text and explicitly defined, and teachers in content areas focus squarely on these words during instruction. On the other hand, tier two words are more challenging for students to decipher on their own within a text, are used in many contexts, and help provide the pathway to learning tier three words. To help teams select appropriate tier two words, review the following four guidelines. These guidelines originate in Beck and colleagues (2013), but the text is adapted from Kathy Glass (2015). Answering *yes* to most of the listed questions indicates the word is worth teaching.

1. **The word is useful and appears across texts:** Is the word tier two, and is it useful enough to warrant attention and teach students? Will students encounter the word in many texts in other domains, and is it indicative of words mature language users use?

2. **It increases sophisticated word choices:** Are there words familiar to students that are similar to the target word? In this case, it is beneficial for students to learn the new word because it extends their inventory of vocabulary to include more expressive and specific words. This does not include adding synonyms to words already in their lexicon; rather, provide students with new words that are more precise and complex versions of the familiar words they already use.

3. **It aids in comprehension:** Does knowing the word enhance comprehension, and does it serve an important function within the context of the text? Does the word contribute to the student's meaning making? If a student doesn't know the word, will he or she not understand important concepts or find the text confusing?

4. **It connects to other learning:** Does the word relate to other concepts that students are studying? This might include concepts in other subject-matter texts or in other content areas. Does the word have the potential for students to build representations of it and connect to other words and concepts?

To structure strategic vocabulary instruction, Robert J. Marzano and Debra J. Pickering (2005) suggest implementing the following six-step process, which we explain and elaborate on in chapter 8 (page 205).

1. Provide student-friendly descriptions, explanations, or examples of new terms.

2. Ask students to restate the terms in their own words.

3. Ask students to construct a picture, symbol, or graphic representation of the terms.

4. Engage students in structured activities that add to their knowledge of the terms.

5. Ask students to discuss the terms with one another.

6. Involve students in games that allow them to play with the terms.

The first three steps of this process occur on the same day and help students gain familiarity with a new word. Teachers implement the final three steps over several successive days as students engage in multiple activities to discuss, use, apply, and interact with new words.

Summary

Although reading and writing should transpire throughout a student's day, schools must safeguard the specific literacy block as a time for literacy instruction and learning. During this time, those students who haven't yet mastered foundation phonics skills by second or third grade receive differentiated instruction and guidance to develop this essential foundation and close the gap to grade-level learning. In grades 2 and 3, all students learn to decode multisyllabic words, receive ample time to improve fluency, and become word wizards as they broaden their vocabulary knowledge. Also, they learn and apply various strategies to aid with comprehension, and they engage in an abundance of shared reading and writing experiences. They write frequently and passionately, read profusely, and radiate with the motivation to become better each and every day.

When considering the specialized literacy concepts and skills that together compose a well-balanced and complete block of instructional time, teams can easily make the mistake of perceiving these concepts and skills as separate entities—isolated learning experiences that exist within their own realm of literacy instruction. But to develop truly literate students with the capacity for higher-order independent thinking requires a strategically planned and implemented literacy block that honors and celebrates the interconnectedness of reading and writing. Dividing and confining skills and concepts into their own separate chambers of instruction leaves students short of developing all the complexities of literacy. Though teachers will set aside specific times for explicit reading, writing, and vocabulary instruction in both whole- and small-group settings, skillful teachers continuously embed all domains of literacy within their instruction, in every subject area, throughout the day. They guide students in making natural connections between these skills, and work to develop well-rounded, independent readers and writers who have the knowledge and skills to reach new heights in their learning.

In chapter 8, we continue our focus on providing quality literacy instruction by exploring three instructional strategies teams can utilize to facilitate learning throughout a well-balanced literacy block. When teams thoughtfully implement these strategies and teaching tools, they support students in grasping literacy concepts and mastering a variety of complex grade-level targets and standards.

Select Appropriate Instructional Strategies

The PREP process we explained in chapter 1 (page 11) guides teachers in prioritizing standards to create a unit curriculum framework, but when teachers collaborate to plan instruction centered on this framework, they are compelled to ask, "If we expect students to know and be able to do _____, what does the instruction actually need to look like to get them there?" We kicked off the process for answering this question in chapter 6 (page 147), where we detailed gradual release of responsibility. In chapter 7 (page 165), we demonstrated the importance of establishing a literacy block within the school day where teachers conduct lessons in whole- and small-group settings that assist students in acquiring the knowledge and skills necessary to master learning standards. This included making extensive use of gradual release of responsibility for whole-group reading and writing. This chapter continues that journey by giving teams guidance in selecting and implementing appropriate teaching strategies and tools that align with targeted learning outcomes.

When delivering lessons, teachers pair instructional strategies with learning activities since the two go hand in hand. *Instructional strategies* (also called *teaching strategies* or *teaching methods*) are the techniques teachers use throughout instruction—whether it be a structure, procedure, or process—to make learning attainable for all students. *Learning activities* are the tasks students engage in to practice and demonstrate their learning, which results in some form of assessment.

Sometimes a tool teachers employ for an instructional strategy also functions as the activity and even the assessment. For example, a teacher uses a graphic organizer as an instructional strategy to model how to organize research information, to prewrite for an essay, or to demonstrate understanding of a text passage. After modeling for students how to fill it in, the teacher hands students a clean copy of the graphic organizer to complete as a learning activity. Afterward, he or she collects the students' graphic organizers to check for understanding. Sometimes instructional strategies that teachers conduct, learning activities that students participate in, and formative assessment all coalesce to facilitate learning (Glass, 2012).

This chapter features three specific teaching strategies that are effective not only for grades 2–3 literacy instruction within ELA, but also across subject areas: (1) annotation, (2) graphic organizers, and (3) the six-step process for teaching vocabulary we introduced in chapter 7 (page 165). We include a thorough explanation and detailed steps for conducting an activity that relies on the strategy, plus differentiation suggestions to further students' learning goals and contribute to their competency. Because the strategies are transferable, teachers can alter and employ them to teach other standards in a variety of interdisciplinary units. Here, we show how teachers can align each strategy with the priority reading standard, RL.3.2: "Recount stories, including fables, folktales, and myths from diverse cultures; determine the central message, lesson, or moral and explain how it is conveyed through key details in the text" (NGA & CCSSO, 2010). This standard appears on our third-grade team's PREP template in figure 1.1 (page 15).

When perusing the strategies we present and capitalizing on your own inventory of strategies, heed researcher John Hattie's (2012) advice to evaluate the methods you choose before you deploy them: "When students do not learn via one method, it is more likely that it then needs to be re-taught using a different method; it will not be enough merely to repeat the same method again and again" (p. 96). With a wide array of teaching methods in their toolboxes, teachers are better suited to apply different methods as they respond to the needs of their students throughout a unit of instruction.

Annotation

Complex text is precisely as the term denotes—complex. Annotation, a widespread strategy readers typically employ, involves interacting with the text to glean more information from it so that what seems challenging becomes less so. Sometimes, teachers instruct students to return to the text repeatedly to annotate, each time with a new focus. In doing so, they uncover layers of meaning and have the opportunity to appreciate various aspects of a complex text.

To conduct this strategy, teachers ask students to annotate a passage or whole text by posing a question or prompt that is based on a learning target. Students annotate the text by taking two actions that are interrelated: (1) mark pertinent words and phrases (such as by underlining, highlighting, circling) in response to the purpose of the task, then (2) comment about the marked parts—which serves as textual evidence—by explaining, elaborating, analyzing, or drawing an inference. Merely doing one action without the other might render the annotation incomplete. Students can also annotate electronically. If they cannot write in the text, they can draw arrows on a sticky note to point to text they would mark and use another sticky note to explain its meaning.

When second- and third-grade teachers deliberately choose a classroom text, they plan for many learning experiences to address a host of skills related to it. This requires students to dive into the reading several times for different purposes to master each skill. For example, while students use textual evidence to identify what the text states explicitly, they also use evidence to uncover implicit meaning. On other occasions, students might use the text to make predictions, examine the author's craft in using details to establish a setting, identify and interpret figurative language, and analyze characters' interactions or how the characters' actions impact the plot. Teachers can assign annotation tasks to address any of these skills.

Drawing symbols or pictures in the margin (or on sticky notes) adjacent to the marked text can work well both when students first encounter new reading material and when they revisit material for specific purposes. When students annotate using this method, teachers devise a key and share it with students so they have clear directions and know what each symbol means in relation to a specific text. For example, an asterisk can signify something important students want to remember, or it can indicate the main idea of a text. A plus sign can show new information, ideas that agree with a student's thinking, or strong evidence to support reasoning in an opinion paper. A question mark can symbolize parts of the text that students find confusing, or parts that seem untrue or unrealistic. Pictures or emojis can also communicate a student's takeaway or interpretation.

When asking students to annotate, second- and third-grade teachers should target one or two aligned skills at a time and assess student mastery before moving forward to tackle other skills, especially if the skills are challenging. More proficient students can perhaps handle annotating for multiple purposes simultaneously; however, some students might feel overwhelmed and unable to master the necessary skills. In such cases, teachers' eagerness to employ this strategy may backfire by asking too much of students at once. Providing excessive reading tasks concurrently might also interfere with students' enjoyment and meaning making. Plus, it may result in students hastily skimming the text for surface observations rather than doing the deep introspection teachers aim for them to achieve. Therefore, teachers collaborate with their teams and use their own professional judgment and knowledge of current student proficiency levels when determining the purpose for annotation.

The three skills our third-grade team derived from standard RL.3.2 require students to (1) recount the key details in a story; (2) determine the story's central message, lesson, or moral; and (3) explain how key details convey this message, lesson, or moral. We've excerpted this section of our team's PREP template in figure 8.1.

Unwrapped Unit Priority Standards	Knowledge Items	Skills (Learning Targets and DOK Levels)
RL.3.2: RECOUNT stories, including fables, folktales, and myths from diverse cultures; DETERMINE the central message, lesson, or moral and EXPLAIN how it is conveyed through key details in the text.	Stories consist of key elements like characters, setting, and plot. A recount is a recap of the key events and details in a text. The central message, lesson, or moral is what the author wants the reader to learn or understand from the story.	Recount the key events and details in a story. (DOK 1) Determine a central message, lesson, or moral. (DOK 3) Explain how key details convey a central message, lesson, or moral. (DOK 3)

Source for standard: NGA & CCSSO, 2010.

Figure 8.1: Excerpt of priority standard RL.3.2 from the PREP template.

This priority standard necessitates strategic thinking in which students draw conclusions about story details to determine an author's implicit central message and then use evidence to explain their thinking. Accordingly, two of its three skills (or learning targets) require students to think at a DOK 3 level. Due to the complexity of these skills and the higher-order thinking they require, the strategy of annotation becomes particularly helpful as students extract, process, and synthesize details that seem pertinent to a story's overall message. Teachers will need to break down these two reading skills (making inferences about the author's intended message and explaining how story details convey that message) and, through annotation, provide concrete examples of the types of precise story details that typically serve as clues to a message or moral.

A good place to start would be to teach students to pay particular attention to the characters (their actions and traits), the conflict (the main problem), and the resolution (the story's ending). While additional story elements certainly work in concordance to develop an overarching central message, annotating for these three specific details is an important first step in helping second- and third-grade students to master the entire standard. During instruction, students may practice by isolating each element they will annotate. For example, students may make the following three types of annotations one at a time.

1. Students annotate character details by underlining these details.

2. Students annotate content that shows conflict by placing a star in the margin.

3. Students annotate significant details and events occurring in the resolution by circling these details.

From here, the teacher models how to synthesize the story details and draw a conclusion about the central message, lesson, or moral. The following sections further break down this strategy by clarifying how to prepare for and conduct an annotation activity and then adapt it for different purposes.

Preparing for the Activity

Taking the following three steps can help teachers prepare for an annotation activity to ensure that it runs smoothly.

1. **Identify the text that will be used for annotation:** For the purpose of modeling annotation, teachers can consider first using shorter and simpler texts, such as fables, and then leading up to richer, more detailed texts. Using a fable, teachers can demonstrate their annotation of the characters' traits and actions, the main conflict, and the story's ending. With a concrete understanding of annotation and its purpose in pinpointing and processing key details, students begin practicing and applying the strategy with lengthier and more complex stories. Since this particular annotation example prepares third-grade students for determining an overarching central message that develops as a story unfolds, teachers will likely need to use a complete story with a beginning, middle, and end (rather than an excerpt) to teach the strategy and skills. For this exercise, we've chosen to use the story "Treasure in the Field" by Marilyn Bolchunos (2004).

2. **Determine logistics:** After selecting the text, teachers prepare what they'll need to conduct the activity. For example, if explicitly modeling

the activity during instruction, teachers can display the text and make it visible to all students. Teachers can format the text electronically and model for students how to digitally annotate and enter comments if students have devices at their disposal. Or, teachers can provide paper copies on which students annotate with pens, highlighters, or sticky notes. To provide an additional layer of support as students attempt the strategy, teachers may fashion an organizer like the one in figure 8.2, which chunks the story into manageable and meaningful sections for students to annotate in one column and leaves space for students to record their thinking in an adjacent column..

3. **Plan annotation tasks:** Based on the targeted skills, teachers facilitate specific annotation tasks that will occur during the overall annotation activity. Since students will return to the text for several different purposes, teachers plan for all encounters with the text and decide in what order to assign the tasks. Using the Elements of Fiction unit as an example, during the first exposure to a text, students might annotate to comprehend the story's

Selected Text: _____	
Underline, highlight, or circle parts of the story that are clues to the story's central message, lesson, or moral.	**Explain what is important about the parts you annotated.**
Insert first text excerpt. Divide the text students are to read into sections or paragraphs (ranging from about one hundred to three hundred words). Each section provides a stopping point for students to annotate, monitor understanding, and explain their thinking in the righthand column. Teachers may choose to model the annotation and thinking with this first section of text, and then gradually release responsibility to the students with the sections that follow.	Students explain their annotations for excerpt 1. Provide space in this column for students to explain their annotations. Students may jot down a variety of thinking, such as questions, predictions, details they noticed in the text, or the significance of text details.
Insert next text excerpt.	Students explain their annotations.
Insert next text excerpt.	Students explain their annotations.

Figure 8.2: An annotation task.

*Visit **go.SolutionTree.com/literacy** for a free reproducible version of this figure.*

overall plot and use the annotations to support them in recounting the story. On returning to the text on day 2 of instruction (or later on in the literacy block), students might begin annotating to determine the text's central message.

We specifically designed the organizer in figure 8.2 so students can record their thinking in order to meet the cognitive demands of comprehending a story's overall central message (a learning target of priority standard RL.3.2). You'll notice how it facilitates breaking an entire story into sections. Though this example breaks a story into three sections, teachers could divide a text into more sections or fewer sections depending on learning objectives and text length.

Chunking the text in this fashion allows students to think about, annotate, and process one section of the story at a time. Sound comprehension requires focused thinking on the reader's behalf. Too often, students speed through a story, pausing rarely, if at all, to process their thinking and make meaning of the text. Even with the added strategy of annotation, some students may read a story and haphazardly mark the text without fully comprehending the story's details. Therefore, chunking the text provides stopping points for students to pause and reflect. Pausing at the end of a section also affords students the opportunity to reread if necessary, self-repair comprehension, add new annotations, share their annotations with a partner, and establish a firm understanding of the story before reading on.

Further, chunking a story in this way aligns nicely with the gradual release of responsibility model. For example, a teacher could divide a text into four sections and conduct annotations that align with the four components of gradual release of responsibility: (1) focused instruction, (2) guided instruction, (3) collaborative learning, and (4) independent learning.

Conducting the Activity

After teachers identify and prepare the text and annotation tasks, they need to model how students will execute the actual activity. Before students begin annotating, teachers demonstrate aloud how to select which words and phrases to mark based on the task at hand. They explain that, when annotating text, readers should mark specific information that seems significant to the task's purpose, but they must choose information judiciously so as not to mark the entire text, which renders the text one extended underlined or highlighted excerpt. Teachers tell students that they can resist the natural temptation to excessively mark by focusing on what matters most based on the prompt. Finally, teachers note that, although a reader may deem a detail significant at first, not all annotations will ultimately be useful or relevant to the reader's purpose. For example, a reader might annotate a descriptive detail that momentarily seems to be a clue to the story's conflict, but after further reading, he or she might realize it isn't as significant as he or she once thought.

As students apply the annotation strategy, they flag parts of the text they feel are significant by underlining, circling, or highlighting these words and phrases (as in figure 8.2, page 210). To emphasize annotation's purpose as a reading strategy, teachers remind students that readers use annotation to cognitively engage in a text and uncover and think deeply about its meaning or message. As they read and annotate each section of text, students record this precise thinking. Figure 8.2 has students write this thinking in the right column, beside what they marked. In essence, they answer, "Why are the words and phrases that I flagged important to the story, and what do they make me think?" in this column.

Considering Other Annotation Tasks

Teachers can adapt this strategy by having students annotate using a variety of different symbols—triangles, clouds, brackets, and so on—or colored highlighters that each denote something specific aligned with reading skills. For example, students may place clouds around unknown words and brackets around text that provides clues to the words' meaning. Or, they may highlight a main idea in one color and supporting evidence in another. Students can even add pictures to augment their comments and represent their takeaway or interpretation. A picture or specific symbol can reflect what a word means, indicate a character's personality, or show the emotions attached to a character's dialogue.

To differentiate instruction, teachers can pair students homogeneously based on appropriately challenging text they have both read and conduct the following activity.

1. The paired students agree on an annotation task from a teacher-generated list of options.

2. Each student in the pair reads a different passage from a familiar text and annotates according to the agreed-on task's directive.

3. Students swap papers, read their partner's passage and annotation, and then record new information, such as additional annotation responses to extend the partner's entries, a new annotation the partner did not include, or questions.

4. Partners use what they marked and recorded as the basis for discussion.

To scaffold this process, teachers provide more easily accessible reading material and participate as a small-group member to offer support while guiding students through the annotation task. Extensions for this task involve assigning the partners more sophisticated text and annotation tasks that compel them to delve into the text in a more introspective way.

For annotation to be effective, students need to stay cognitively engaged and think critically about the details they are marking. The strategy will do little to help students make meaning of complex texts if they listlessly underline or draw symbols without attaching thinking to each annotation. When students put careful thought into the details they flag and the reasoning behind their selections, they make strides in reading comprehension. Figure 8.3 (page 214) shows a partial list of other kinds of standards-based annotation tasks teachers might assign during instruction.

Although annotation supports students in examining many aspects of a text, teachers might employ additional teaching strategies too; students benefit from having a wide array of learning experiences to fully delve into the richness and rigor of a text. For example, customized graphic organizers are another teaching strategy teachers can implement that will add to their bank of tools. Read on as we discuss how graphic representations can assist students in gathering information, organizing ideas, and demonstrating concepts.

Graphic Organizers

Graphic organizers—visual representations of ideas—are a staple in teachers' repertoire of instructional strategies across content areas. For example, we used a graphic organizer to facilitate an annotation task in this chapter (figure 8.3). Teachers often collect the completed organizers and use them as a formative assessment to determine levels of competency. In literacy, teachers can have students use organizers for myriad reading and writing purposes, including the following.

▸ Identify and explain the structure of a text—compare–contrast, problem–solution, cause–effect, sequence, or description.

▸ Brainstorm and collect ideas for a writing task.

▸ Organize information in a reading selection to deepen understanding.

▸ Demonstrate comprehension and communicate ideas.

▸ Record and categorize research notes.

Skill	What Students Underline, Circle, or Highlight	What Students Write in the Margin or on Sticky Notes	Annotation Task	Next-Step Ideas for Teachers (Partial List)
Ask and answer questions to demonstrate understanding of a text, referring explicitly to the text as the basis for the answers.	Details or information that incite thinking, wonderment, confusion, or questions	A question that they have about the text	After you mark particular details that make you wonder about the text, write the question that you have about the text in the margin.	After they read and annotate the text, have students return to their annotated questions and attempt to answer them. After they read and complete annotations for the text, have students participate in a sharing activity where partners discuss their questions and answers.
Describe characters by their traits, motivations, and feelings	Words and phrases in the story that give clues to a character's personality	A character trait	Underline any words and phrases that help you understand a character's personality. In the margin, write down the personality trait that you feel the character exhibits.	Have students write a paragraph that describes the character in detail. Instruct students to use details from the text to support their answer.
Use sentence-level context as a clue to the meaning of a word or phrase.	Vocabulary words or terms they do not know	What they think the words mean	Underline words that you do not know. Circle any clues that help you learn what the words mean. In the margin, write what you think the words mean as they are used in the passage.	Conduct direct instruction activities that help students learn the new words. Have students apply the new words by using them correctly in an original sentence.
Recount the key events and details in a story	Words or phrases that signal a shift in time or place	The new setting (time or place) in the story's sequence	Underline any part of the text that indicates a shift in time or place in the story. In the margin, note this change in the setting.	Have students: • Use their annotations to assist them in retelling the story to a peer • Use their annotations to assist them in sequencing the main events of the story • Generate a class list of transition words that signal a shift in time or place in a fiction story or narrative
Determine a story's central message, lesson, or moral.	Textual evidence that gives clues to the central message (such as details about the conflict and how it is resolved)	Details about the conflict and the resolution	Underline any words or phrases that help you understand the story's conflict and resolution. In the margin, note important details about these story elements.	Have students share their annotations with a small group and engage in a discussion about the story's central message, lesson, or moral.

Figure 8.3: Sample annotation tasks in a fiction unit.

▸ Learn new words and terms.

▸ Plot the sequence of a text.

In short, a graphic organizer facilitates comprehension, helps students remember content, and provides a model for their writing.

Teachers can find blank organizers online by accessing the following links or design their own to align the organizers to a particular text structure and the purpose of using them.

▸ edHelper.com (www.edhelper.com/teachers/graphic_organizers.htm)

▸ Education Oasis (www.educationoasis.com/curriculum/graphic _organizers.htm)

▸ Freeology (http://freeology.com/graphicorgs)

▸ Houghton Mifflin Harcourt Education Place (www.eduplace.com /graphicorganizer/)

▸ Teacher Files (www.teacherfiles.com/resources_organizers.htm)

▸ TeacherVision (www.teachervision.com/lesson-planning /graphic-organizer)

To differentiate graphic organizers, teachers design or offer choices for students within an overarching structure based on learning style and readiness levels. For example, a Venn diagram typically requires students to compare and contrast two topics or ideas. That might be sufficiently challenging for some students, whereas others would benefit from an extended Venn diagram with three overlapping circles to examine three different subjects. Further, some students prefer a compare–contrast organizer in a column format rather than the traditional circular one.

As you will recall, to meet the learning targets of priority standard RL.3.2 (figure 8.1, page 208), students must be able to *recount* details from a story; *determine* a central message, lesson, or moral; and then *explain* how key details in the text convey that central message, lesson, or moral. Because a work of fiction's central message is typically implicit, students must identify and synthesize the author's carefully crafted details to develop the overall message. Even when a text explicitly states the message at the end, this standard necessitates that students explain how details convey the message throughout the text. Accomplishing this requires multistep processing and higher-order thinking, and a graphic organizer is an effective tool for collecting and organizing the breadth of information students must process to meet the rigor of these skills and the overall standard.

The following sections further break down the graphic organizer strategy by clarifying how to prepare for and conduct an activity using a graphic organizer and then adapt it for different purposes. We will illustrate how students can use a graphic organizer to record text details, organize their thinking, and visually represent their knowledge and skills related to standard RL.3.2.

Preparing for the Activity

To prepare, teams determine a suitable text for their purposes and then select or create an appropriate graphic organizer. For this lesson on standard RL.3.2, our third-grade team had to select a story that conveys a central message, lesson, or moral, so it again selected "Treasure in the Field" (Bolchunos, 2004). It then created its own graphic organizer, pictured in figure 8.4. Students use this organizer to explain how key details from a text convey the central message, lesson, or moral of a story. The team directs students to focus on three key elements of a story: (1) characters, (2) conflict, and (3) resolution (the boxes arrayed across the top of our organizer). Though additional elements of fiction contribute to a story's message, uncovering and synthesizing the nuances of these story details typically leads a reader to uncover the author's overall lesson or moral (the box at the bottom of our organizer). The arrows in the diagram signify the relationships between the story details and the central message and signal to students that they should consider all three elements when determining and explaining that message.

Conducting the Activity

In the Annotation section (page 206), our teachers determined students would use the annotation strategy to identify (recount) significant details within "Treasure in the Field" (Bolchunos, 2004). As part of the exercise, students would determine a central message. While the annotation activity helps students identify and analyze separate details, it doesn't ask them to explain how the details convey the central message, so the team conducted a new activity (using the same text) to facilitate this.

The graphic organizer in figure 8.4 allows students to compile and group similar information to help them explain how the details reveal a central message. The diagram serves as a tool for sorting and displaying the wealth of information students gather from the story, which then assists them in producing an oral or written explanation of how the details convey the central message, lesson, or moral. As with other instructional exercises and teaching tools, teachers first explicitly model for students how to complete the graphic organizer. Since figure 8.4 uses very simple headings to label each box, teachers need to model the type of information students

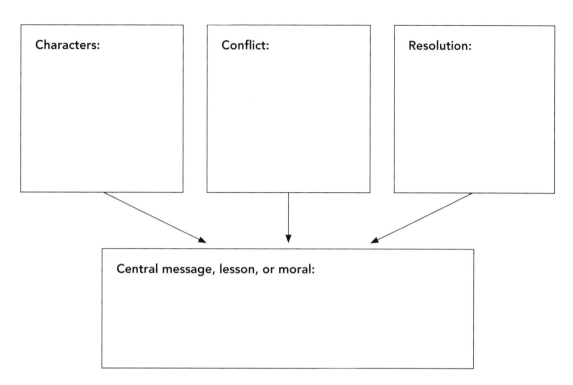

Figure 8.4: Graphic organizer for explaining how details convey a central message.

*Visit **go.SolutionTree.com/literacy** for a free reproducible version of this figure.*

should include in each part of the diagram. For example, in the Characters box, second and third graders may feel inclined to write every detail about a character, such as the color of the character's hair or clothing, even though some character-istics aren't typically pertinent to the lesson an author wishes to express. Teachers might use a think aloud to demonstrate how students can discern trivial details from significant ones in determining and explaining the central message. For stu-dents who are ready for extension, teachers might ask them to add additional boxes to the graphic organizer to record supplementary story details that are also important to the overall lesson.

After explicit modeling, the teacher facilitates the activity following the grad-ual release of responsibility model or a similar structure. The teacher does direct modeling of how to use the graphic organizer to process information from the text, provides guided instruction as students attempt a portion of it on their own, embeds time for collaborative practice, and bridges to independence as students use the organizer as a learning tool. The result of this instruction should allow students to complete the organizer and grasp the skill of explaining how key details convey a central message.

Adapting the Activity

Teams can use the graphic organizer we featured in this section in a variety of ways. Consider the following suggestions.

▸ **Promote cooperative learning:** Have students participate in a partner or group activity where they record details from a story on the graphic organizer. For example, after you explicitly model what to include in the organizer's Characters box, have students first try to fill out the box on their own while you walk around the classroom to observe their performance. Then, direct students to take turns sharing with a partner or in groups of three or four the information they added about characters. After listening to their peers' responses, students add any pertinent information about the characters that they may be missing to their organizers. Repeat the process so the students record details in the graphic organizer's other boxes.

After students record story details in each of the top three boxes on the organizer, have them individually draft a statement that captures the central message, lesson, or moral of the story. This first draft represents each student's initial thinking. To emphasize the importance of rewriting this draft after further investigation, instruct students to record their first draft on a sticky note or on the back of the graphic organizer. Then, have pairs or groups of three or four students take turns sharing their draft statements. After all students have shared their initial thinking, they engage in a discussion to explain their thinking and collectively uncover the author's message. Together, as a pair or group, students then craft a central message that they think best captures the author's intent. For example, as they work together, they may decide to use part of one student's idea with part of another student's wording. Or, they may decide to craft an entirely new statement to better capture the central message. Students each record this collectively written central message in their own graphic organizer. At the end of the activity, facilitate a class discussion where each group shares its agreed-on statement and its work with the class. Then, provide further instruction and reteaching, if necessary.

▸ **Have students independently design graphic organizers:** Once students become familiar with using the graphic organizer, remove the headings from the top boxes, and require students to fill in the headings themselves. This places more responsibility on the students to think critically about a story and pinpoint key details on their own.

As students gain experience using the organizer and show readiness for a greater challenge, distribute a blank piece of paper, and ask them to draw and complete a graphic organizer on their own. To accomplish this, students must employ critical-thinking skills to evaluate the task and illustrate their thinking and learning in an appropriate visual format. Moving them toward independence in this way is an important step in fostering student autonomy.

▸ **Ask students to produce written responses:** Graphic organizers serve as tools to assist students in producing written responses. Writing is a multistep process, and graphic organizers allow students to record and organize original ideas, textual evidence from a science or social studies text, story details from a fiction text, or other important information prior to drafting a variety of content-specific compositions. For example, students might complete a flowchart of key information prior to writing about a class science project.

You may recall from figure 8.1 (page 208) that a learning target embedded within standard RL.3.2 requires students to *explain* how key details convey the central message. Though the graphic organizer allows students to visually display their thinking, teachers may deem it insufficient in accurately measuring students' abilities to explain. Instead, they allow students to use the completed graphic organizer as a tool for writing a well-crafted explanation.

Remember that the ultimate goal is student autonomy. Although graphic organizers are valuable instructional tools that help students acquire and comprehend the knowledge and skills necessary to meet rigorous standards, teachers need to position students to independently analyze a text and its structure and choose the best way to graphically represent a variety of concepts. Further, as they take formative, summative, or high-stakes assessments, students will need to demonstrate their learning without the assistance of scaffolds like graphic organizers.

Vocabulary

In chapter 7 (page 165), we explained why vocabulary instruction is a critical component of the literacy block and of well-balanced literacy learning. Students must continuously work to widen their vocabulary knowledge so they comprehend increasingly complex texts and compose well-crafted written works across content areas. Facilitating effective vocabulary instruction requires that teachers purposefully afford students multiple exposures to words so the words become part of their working vocabularies (Marzano, 2020). To accomplish this, teachers should adopt a six-step process from Robert J. Marzano and Debra J. Pickering (2005), which we introduced in chapter 7.

1. Provide student-friendly descriptions, explanations, or examples of new terms.

2. Ask students to restate the terms in their own words.

3. Ask students to construct a picture, symbol, or graphic representation of the terms.

4. Engage students in structured activities that add to their knowledge of the terms.

5. Ask students to discuss the terms with one another.

6. Involve students in games that allow them to play with the terms.

Before engaging in these steps, teachers identify terms that will become the focus of explicit vocabulary instruction. They carefully select vocabulary words based on a variety of criteria, including the following.

▸ The vocabulary words may be necessary for students to fully comprehend an upcoming text.

▸ The vocabulary words may be fundamental to the study of new concepts across disciplines.

▸ The vocabulary words may be enduring in that they are likely to emerge in social or academic settings.

The Vocabulary Instruction section of Chapter 7 (page 200) also introduced a three-tier system for categorizing words based on their frequency and applicability across content areas (Beck et al., 2013). In choosing words for explicit vocabulary instruction, teachers typically select tier two words (and tier three words when necessary), as these have the most leverage in terms of their applicability to reading, writing, and speaking. Thus, they have the greatest impact on the scope of a student's vocabulary. Most content-area texts assist teachers in locating important tier three vocabulary since many include text features that illuminate tier three instruction—

bold or italicized typeface, highlighted text, labeled diagrams, glossaries, and so on. Because tier two presents more of a challenge for selection, we encourage teams to use the following guidelines to select appropriate words that they should teach second- and third-grade students. Answering *yes* to most of the following questions listed by Kathy Glass (2015) indicates a word is worth teaching:

1. **The word is useful and appears across texts.** Is the word Tier 2? Is it useful enough to warrant attention and teach students? Will it appear across many texts in other domains that students will encounter? Is it indicative of words used by mature language users?

2. **It increases sophisticated word choices.** Are there words similar to the target one that are familiar to students? If so, learning this new word is beneficial since it would extend their inventory of vocabulary to include more expressive and specific words. This does not mean merely adding synonyms to words already in their lexicon. It is about providing students with new words that are more precise or that are complex versions of the familiar words they already use. For example, if students know *salesperson*, then learning the word *merchant* widens their choice of conceptually related words.

3. **It aids in comprehension.** Does knowing the word enhance comprehension? Does the word serve an important function within the context of the text? Does the word contribute to meaning making? Without it, are important concepts lost or confusing?

4. **It connects to other learning.** Does the word relate to other concepts that students are studying, perhaps in this subject or in another content area? Does the word have the potential for students to build representations of it and connect to other words and concepts? (p. 73)

Continuing with our example using "Treasure in the Field" (Bolchunos, 2004), our third-grade team identified the following passages with three key vocabulary words italicized.

▸ "Their neighbor was *astonished* to see. . . ."

▸ "We'll *tend* it just as Father did. . . ."

▸ " . . . the field gave an *abundant* harvest."

Astonished, *tend*, and *abundant* represent tier two words because they aren't tied to a content-specific discipline and students will likely come across them in other texts. By adding these new words to their vocabulary, students are able to communicate—in both speaking and writing—with more accuracy and sophistication. Additionally, knowing these words aids in reading fluency and comprehension.

Delving even deeper into our vocabulary choices, our teachers chose the word *astonished* since it is a more precise word for the widely used adjective *surprised*, and it also helps students better understand the neighbor's reaction in the story. Next, we selected the word *tend* (or *tended*). It is a word students are likely to encounter again and appears three times throughout the story, making it of particular importance to the plot. We used similar reasoning when choosing the word *abundant*. It, too, is critical to comprehending the ending of the story, while serving as a vivid replacement for bland and overused words and phrases within students' writing, such as *a lot* or *many*. With three words chosen for instruction, the teachers on our collaborative team were prepared to begin the six-step process for teaching vocabulary (Marzano & Pickering, 2005).

The following sections break down the six steps and provide an explanation for each. The way we structured this process in the following sections guarantees students multiple exposures to all vocabulary words over several days of instruction. Throughout the year, the team made sure to frequently revisit these words to sharpen students' understanding and secure word ownership.

In your own team's application, teachers can display all vocabulary words on a word wall for easy access during class discussion and activities, or as they work through the steps, teachers might have students record their descriptions and impressions of the words in a vocabulary notebook (Marzano & Pickering, 2005). For each word entry, students would have a place to write the word, describe the word in their own words, draw a visual representation of the word, and rate their understanding on a scale of 1 (little or no understanding) to 4 (complete understanding). (The rating will likely change as students experience multiple exposures to the word.)

Provide Student-Friendly Descriptions, Explanations, or Examples of New Terms

Begin by providing students with a thorough description and explanation of each word to help them develop a keen understanding of the word's explicit and implicit meanings. The goal is to provide enough context and information so students begin to conceptualize each word, and teachers can accomplish this in a variety of ways. For example, for each word, try the following.

> ▸ Use the word in several different sentences.

> ‣ Tell a quick anecdote that includes the word or reveals its meaning.

> ‣ Use visuals that demonstrate the word's meaning, such as video clips, pictures, or other images.

> ‣ Relate the word to current events.

Through multimodal exposures, including both linguistic and nonlinguistic approaches, students begin to develop an initial understanding of each term.

Ask Students to Restate the Terms in Their Own Words

Have students restate each term's description, explanation, or example in their own words. Here, it is important that students do not merely copy what the teacher has said, but rather articulate their understanding of the word in their own way. For each term, students record their descriptions in a vocabulary notebook and then share their thinking with a partner as the teacher monitors students' responses and helps clear up any confusion. If students struggle to provide accurate descriptions, reteach the terms in question, and provide additional support to aid in comprehension.

Ask Students to Construct a Picture, Symbol, or Graphic Representation of the Terms

Here, students must employ a different type of thinking to create a nonlinguistic illustration of the words. The image should be simple and sketched quickly; its purpose is to elicit thinking and allow students to depict their understanding of the word in a new way. Teachers should model this step, as students sometimes tend to draw intricate images that take time away from more meaningful learning activities. Students may also need support in creating a picture or symbol that represents a word's meaning, especially with challenging or abstract terms. After drawing a word in their vocabulary notebooks, students share and explain their illustration with a partner, giving them yet another opportunity to strengthen understanding.

Engage Students in Structured Activities That Add to Their Knowledge of the Terms

Have students engage in activities that help them add to their knowledge of their new words. Recurrent exposure is critical to vocabulary growth, as taking ownership of a word and applying it accurately in context requires repeated experiences (Stahl, 2005). Plan activities such as the following, and frequently embed them into the literacy block.

- Grouping and categorizing words based on similar attributes

- Comparing or contrasting words based on their meanings

- Drawing additional pictures, symbols, or diagrams

- Analyzing or writing analogies

- Matching words with visual representations

- Using words in sentences

As students engage in tasks that promote continuous growth and understanding, encourage them to update or revise their initial descriptions and illustrations in their notebooks to better represent precise meanings and new knowledge.

Ask Students to Discuss the Terms With One Another

Have students discuss vocabulary words with peers. This time for oral articulation further solidifies students' word knowledge. Structure students' discussions in a variety of ways and include cooperative learning strategies such as think-pair-share to ensure all students equally participate. Before having students engage in this cooperative learning, afford them a few minutes of think time to individually review word meanings and prepare their thoughts. Next, pair up students to discuss the words together. Students should discuss with each other their respective original descriptions, reveal and explain their illustrations, or use the words in context. Finally, have students share impressions and new insights about the words as a whole class. As students share, monitor each student's comprehension level, and intervene when necessary.

Involve Students in Games That Allow Them to Play With the Terms

Have students participate in games that further enhance their understanding of new words. While games are engaging and fun for second- and third-grade students, well-structured word games also allow students to interact with words and keep them at the forefront of their minds. Games like charades, memory, bingo, "I have, who has?" matching games, and a host of others help maintain high engagement levels as students continue to add an abundance of words to their working vocabularies. (Conduct an internet search if you want to learn more about these specific games.)

Through this six-step process, students receive frequent, explicit instruction of tier two words that are critical to their vocabulary development (Marzano & Pickering, 2005). With a rich and diverse vocabulary, students are better able to express their ideas through writing and speaking, and they will read with increased fluency and comprehension. It's an ideal method for teachers to foster continuous vocabulary growth that is both productive and motivating for students.

EXERCISE
Design a Complete Lesson

Chapter 6 (page 147) provides a research-based model for building well-orchestrated lessons (gradual release of responsibility), and chapter 7 (page 165) explores the tenets of high-quality literacy instruction. Use the information in these previous chapters, the instructional strategies presented in this one, and those you and your team have acquired through your work and collaboration, to create or enhance a lesson from a team learning progression that utilizes gradual release of responsibility and at least one of the strategies from this chapter.

Use the following questions to guide this exercise.

★ How can our team use line items on the learning progression to design effective lessons? What knowledge or skill will students learn at a particular step, and what type of lesson might help them to learn it?

★ What strategies presented in this chapter meet the needs of our students and align to our team's learning progression?

★ What other strategies can we collectively share as a team to support student learning and embed in lessons?

★ How will we assess student learning in the lessons?

★ How will we differentiate instruction to account for learners who do not master skills and for those who show they are ready for more?

Summary

Within instruction, it is incumbent on teachers to select appropriate strategies that meet the needs of students so their learning moves forward and they master standards based on a learning progression. As Robert J. Marzano (2017) purports in *The New Art and Science of Teaching*, the focus of instruction should rest on student outcomes as opposed to teacher outcomes: "Instructional strategies generate certain mental states and processes in learners' minds which, in turn, enhance students' learning. . . . Without these mental states and processes, a given strategy will have little or no effect on students" (p. 5).

Teachers should also aim to infuse lessons with strategies that pique students' interest and engage them in the task at hand. They should deliberately select strategies expressly designed for students to accomplish a skill and check for understanding to ensure the strategy is producing the desired results. If a particular strategy misses the mark and students are unfortunately still grappling with proficiency, teachers need a different one so students have an alternative avenue to master intended skills.

The next chapter, which focuses on equity, includes information that teachers can use to further engage students in learning. Through literacy education, teachers can endeavor to create a more cohesive and inclusive learning environment.

CHAPTER 9

Consider Equity in Literacy

In thinking about literacy in general, consider for a moment the daily activities that require even the most basic form of reading and writing skills. What percentage of your day or week might you spend reading any kind of text? What literacy skills did you need to get yourself to work today? Did you read signs along the road while driving or consult maps when accessing public transportation? What else in your week required a form of literacy? Did you sign a contract or consent form? Read a list or determine a budget to grocery shop? Peruse a restaurant menu? Fill out a voting ballot? Can you think of a job that does not, in some way, involve written communication?

Now, consider every form of communication you rely on to connect with the people in your life, from the internet and email to social media and text messages. To fully participate in society in the Information Age, teachers must provide *all* students a literacy level that positions them to function effectively in society. They cannot afford to allow even one student to leave their care without guaranteeing he or she can read and write at grade level, as well as engage in fruitful discussions. For example, in second and third grade, literacy skills are the building blocks for and gateway to all future learning.

What does this have to do with equity in learning? Well, if society strives to truly honor the fundamental tenet that all humans are created equal, it must ensure equal access to the necessary skills for all members in that society to aim for success. Literacy is an essential prerequisite for this endeavor and for full engagement in the world. It equips students with the essential building blocks that form the gateway to all learning. Through reading, writing, speaking, and listening, teachers grant their students access to the skills and resources necessary to appreciate a richly diverse society.

Teachers are living and educating students during important times filled with defining movements. From racial- and gender-equality movements to simply understanding and accepting the formation of one's identity, committed people passionately work to generate a society where everyone recognizes and accepts one another for each of our unique qualities. Schools and, more specifically, classrooms provide a venue for students to learn about building toward a more equitable, diverse, and welcoming society. Within the classroom's walls, teachers strive to create a cohesive and inclusive learning environment as a microcosm of a broader, accepting society. In this regard, educators model and teach how to be inclusive of others despite differences—or, rather, *because of* differences.

This approach also helps to create environments in which all students are able and willing to take risks to learn. Teachers aim for this goal but often feel ill equipped to establish it. Therefore, this chapter supports them in this regard and addresses how teachers and administrators can answer the following compelling and difficult questions concerning equitable school practices. These queries require teachers and administrators to be vulnerable and face what could be brutal facts about the current state of equitable practices in their classrooms and schools. Since movements abound, and the richness of a diverse world has expanded, teams should also generate additional questions while reading to examine other issues that affect their students and school.

- ▸ "How can our team and school identify and eliminate invisible biases that might influence our instructional approach to students and affect their trust in us?"

- ▸ "How can our team and school avoid excluding any student from rigorous learning opportunities in curricula and promote high expectations for all students?"

- ▸ "How can our team ensure the resources we select or are asked to use authentically reflect the demographics of our students, diverse perspectives, and the experiences of others?"

The following sections address equity of access to three fundamental aspects of teaching that align to the previously posed questions: (1) instruction, (2) expectations, and (3) resources. These sections act as our final road map to ensuring all second- and third-grade students leave your team's care with a strong foundation in literacy skills that will serve them well in future grades and in life. Educators working together as part of a strong PLC culture have the potential to make a positive impact for students, schools, and society but only if they are willing to step up to do the hard, reflective work on an ongoing basis. It is an educator's obligation, as someone in position to positively influence students, to ensure each student—regardless of gender, race, ethnicity, language, or abilities—feels included in his or her classroom's culture. Your team's approach to literacy instruction can be a critical part of making that happen. Focusing on the material in this chapter can facilitate open conversations and perhaps necessary change for the betterment of your students.

Access to Instruction

Before considering equity in curriculum and resources, your team should begin by examining privately or publicly any internal, personal biases that might be present in how you each approach students. This is not about blame or judgment. It's simply important and valuable to look critically at the intended and unintended messages you each might send to students through your words and actions. This critical introspection might prove challenging, but at the same time might prove rewarding because it fosters growth and perhaps can uncover or lead to areas in instruction that require revision.

Start by inviting team members to share and acknowledge examples of inclusivity within each classroom that most likely occur. Then, ask yourselves how your instructional approaches might foster or inhibit equitable practices in the classroom, particularly as they pertain to literacy. Articulate what existing or new practices lead to more equitable outcomes. While engaging in this discussion, you might discover a sense of vulnerability or the need to confront some uncomfortable issues. Open, honest dialogue is healthy and likely results in identifying one area as a team focus to promote the kind of change that benefits all your students.

To practice, this section offers an examination of factors teams should consider in how their approach to gender might influence their instruction. Although gender represents one defining difference among people, it is not binary—meaning one does not need to identify as either a boy or girl. Rather, researchers state that gender is multidimensional residing somewhere along a continuum or spectrum (Bockting, 2008; Connell, 2009; Harrison, Grant, & Herman, 2012). Students may not explicitly identify solely with one gender, and gender does not always characterize one's inclinations and tastes. For example, women and girls can enjoy sports and play video games, which are often thought of as traditionally masculine preferences. Additionally, men and boys might choose to dress in pink or play with dolls, traits conventionally regarded as feminine.

Transgender individuals might possess a sense that their gender identity misaligns to their physical anatomy even before they enter second grade:

> Research indicates that there is a significant gap between a child's understanding that their gender doesn't conform to expectations and when they communicate with others (namely parents) about it. In one study, the average age of self-realization for the child that they were transgender or non-binary was 7.9 years, but the average age when they disclosed their understanding of their gender was 15.5. (Gender Spectrum, n.d.)

According to Gender Spectrum's Charles Margulis (n.d.), "gender non-conforming behavior in preadolescents is particularly visible . . . most of them are already aware that they do not fit expected gender norms." Furthermore, this source states that while some youth assert transgender or non-binary identity with relative ease or confidence, others feel uncomfortable, experience bullying, and become withdrawn. A teacher's support and understanding can go a long way to mitigate these effects. Consider how you group students currently. Do you separate them by gender? You or other team members may do this with the best of intentions, as this is a seemingly efficient grouping strategy, and it's one you may have experienced as a student or even early in your career if you are a veteran teacher. However, this strategy sends the message that students are defined based on their gender. Avoid singling out gender as a defining characteristic, which signals to students that they ought to identify with all the associated aspects that a particular culture deems as the norm. In fact, grouping by gender, which implies a clear-cut identification of male or female, can be confusing to students grappling with their gender identity. Rather, use themes, colors, or shapes to arrange students into groups; randomly assign them by drawing sticks; or, leave it up to students to formulate their own.

Research shows that "Stereotyping in childhood has wide-ranging and significant negative consequences for both women and men, with more than half (51%) of people affected saying it constrained their career choices and 44% saying it harmed their personal relationships" (Fawcett Society, 2019). In the case of grouping, any students with a nonbinary identification who question their gender may feel forced to select one group or the other. When confronted with such a choice, no safe space exists for these students. Research affirms the damage this causes. Gender stereotyping "is harmful when it limits women's and men's capacity to develop their personal abilities, pursue their professional careers and make choices about their lives" (Office of the High Commissioner for Human Rights, n.d.). This effect often occurs in literacy-based instruction when teachers suggest girls read books with princess or dancer characters while recommending their male counterparts read adventure or sports stories. In this scenario, educators rely on cultural norms to make decisions for students about their interests as well as expectations for them.

Diversity education expert Dana Stachowiak (2018) asserts in the article "The Power to Include" that "literacy classrooms are spaces with unique opportunities to do the work of creating an environment that is gender inclusive" (p. 29). To support teachers in this endeavor, Stachowiak (2018) provides the following six suggestions that teachers of literacy can implement:

1. Learn and understand terms and definitions.

2. Work through your own biases and beliefs.

3. Be proactive, not reactive.

4. Plan to support gender-noncomforming students.

5. Integrate, don't separate, curricula.

6. Commit to growing. (pp. 29–30)

To become more educated about this area so you can strive to create a gender-inclusive classroom environment, consider reading Dana Stachowiak's (2018) full article as well as numerous print and online resources about this expansive topic.

Gender is just one example of many that teams must consider when making instructional choices involving students. Race, culture, and religion are all areas we implore teams to explore when reflecting on how literacy instruction might reflect invisible biases or suppositions that could send overt and covert, unintentional messages to students whose identities are still forming. For example, how does religious diversity among students impact the classroom? Celebrating the month of December with a high emphasis on Christian traditions may confuse or exclude students of other faiths. Further, if your team only celebrates African American history during the month of February, consider the message that sends to black students who deserve to see themselves represented in the curriculum all year long. The following sections examine some of these matters through the lens of curriculum and resources.

Promote High Expectations

It may seem unnecessary to ask, "Should any student be excluded from challenging learning opportunities?" Obviously, the answer is no. Sadly, some educators quickly jump to unfounded conclusions about student capabilities and determine that maybe some students are not ready for or able to participate in rigorous learning experiences. Or, an educator may apply arbitrary reasoning to determine that certain students are not competent enough to learn all the standards that others typically address in their grade level. Both are fallacies. With the exception of those who have a significant cognitive impairment, all students are entitled to and obligated to master all grade-level standards.

Learning opportunities are often withheld, to various degrees, from three different subgroups of students who are able to learn grade-level standards.

1. Students who are evaluated and qualify for an individualized education plan or who are entitled to specific learning goals as a result of having a disability

2. Students who are culturally and linguistically diverse but not yet English proficient and are therefore labeled as English learners

3. Students who begin school disadvantaged in some way, such as economically, or who lacked access to early learning and therefore are unfairly labeled as *low performers*

The students who fit into these groups possess thinking and learning assets. However, some teachers possess limiting beliefs about them, which results in lowered expectations for these students. This dynamic of unfairly setting inappropriate expectations can inadvertently sabotage students' success:

> [Unfounded] judgments about [students'] capability often apply stereotypes about social groups such as about race and gender, reflect myths about development and behavior, confuse what is with what could be, and put too much weight on test scores rather than daily performance as evidence of ability. The actions taken in response to these judgments often determine very different learning opportunities and convey strong messages about capability. (Weinstein, 2002, p. 4)

Consider this common mistake teachers unintentionally make that leads to inherent inequities in access to education: Educators often think a student identified as an English learner lacks skills and cannot achieve the standards. They spend a significant amount of time focusing on those prerequisite language skills and fail to provide instruction in the actual grade-level standards prior to the end of the academic school year. This propels a vicious cycle in which the student cannot catch up, resulting in lost learning opportunities. When this occurs, the teachers miss the importance of having a learning progression to achieve a standard (chapter 3, page 61), and they do not use individual student data to drive instruction (chapter 5, page 125). Further, the teachers neglect to design optimal literacy instruction (chapter 7, page 165). Making inaccurate assumptions that lead to lower expectations may lead teachers to use less-rigorous strategies, groupings, and materials, producing less growth or no growth for students in this population.

Therefore, teachers must realize their influence on students and present possibilities for them. To determine how you and your colleagues can promote high expectations or commit to do so, review these actions together and formulate concrete ways that you can apply them within your classrooms:

- Articulate the belief that students can achieve at high levels
- Create warm social-emotional relationships focused on strengths, funds of knowledge, cultural understandings, and interests/aspirations
- Provide informative feedback on performance to scaffold learning
- Teach content and use tasks with high cognitive demand
- Ask frequent, high-level questions
- Encourage a productive struggle (refraining from giving answers, allowing wait time, guiding to answer)
- Maintain close physical proximity
- Interact frequently
- Use positive nonverbal communication (Budge & Parrett, 2018, p. 81)

Another detrimental situation that aligns to limiting expectations is when we assign labels to students. For example, students with disabilities are often named *SPED* (short for *special education*) or *IEP kids*. Students who work to acquire English are often referred to as *limited* in some way, which is shortsighted since they may understand conceptual ideas but lack the language to articulate them. Further, some students are called *low* due to a disadvantage they encountered at some point in their life that might be ill-defined.

In reality, these students are capable of learning grade-level standards; their learning needs just look different than other students' needs do (DuFour et al., 2016). Unfortunately, no positive asset orientation is associated with these students, as unwarranted expectations and labels cloud teachers' vision, misrepresent students, and communicate what students cannot do rather than what they can.

In their book *Disrupting Poverty*, Kathleen M. Budge and William H. Parrett (2018) provide powerful insight into the negative ramifications of using labels that has merit in this discussion. After reading the following quote, apply the thinking of these authors and discuss with colleagues how to reframe the way educators refer to students in these subgroups since a positive shift in language can correlate to an improved mindset:

> How we think about and refer to our students is an important consideration. . . . Words are powerful, and they often can perpetuate or challenge our beliefs. Have you ever thought about the various ways we describe our students who live in poverty—*Title I kids, free and reduced-priced meals kids, low-SES kids, high-poverty kids*, or *poverty-kids*? What do we mean when we use these labels? What is a "high-poverty kid"? What do the kids and others think when they hear these terms? (Budge & Parrett, 2018, p. 22)

Further, these labels also lead to assumptions about students' abilities. Instead of making assumptions, educators must gain accurate estimations of students' learning needs and knowledge. As John Hattie (2012) presents in *Visible Learning for Teachers*, educator estimates of student achievement have a profound impact on students' learning. In fact, students can yield four years' worth of academic growth in one school year when educators have positive estimates of student achievement, or clear data, as this gives teachers more accurate knowledge of the students in their classes. Accurate knowledge of students results in more-rigorous learning opportunities, learning materials, instructional strategies, and questioning techniques that closely match students' needs, which produces academic growth. Making inaccurate assumptions, in the absence of data, may lead teachers to use less-rigorous strategies, groupings, and materials, producing less growth or no growth for students. Therefore, whatever we think students are capable of will become their ceiling, as we are the drivers who create the ceiling.

Teachers need to ask, "How can our team and school avoid excluding any student from rigorous learning opportunities and promote high expectations for all students?" If there are teaching practices that exclude some students from grade-level learning, teachers must work in collaborative teams to identify how to include all students. For example, can they shift from an English learner pull-out model, in which students are removed from grade-level instruction, to a model that allows these students to work within the classroom? Similarly, teams must address if the needs of students who qualify for an IEP can be met with accommodations or modifications within the classroom.

In our experience, some teachers catalog the obstacles that deter them from supporting these students as a means to justify limiting students' access to the curriculum; for example, they state that programmatic shifts are larger than any one person can consider or implement, that these shifts take time and resources, and that administrators and the board of education generally need to approve them. If discouragement sets in within your team, endeavor to adopt the mindset that change certainly can occur, and begin to educate and engage in supportive, critical conversations as an ally to your most vulnerable students. Remind teachers that they must maintain high expectations for all students within literacy instruction (and across content areas) since the key learning associated with literacy skills supports students in success beyond school. Excluding students risks further marginalizing populations that have been historically treated as peripheral.

Offer Culturally Rich Resources

In addition to providing all students with a high-quality education that prepares them for their futures, teachers should grant students diverse perspectives through access to a plethora of culturally rich resources. It's not enough to simply select reading materials that align to learning targets; teachers must ask and address the crucial question, "How can I ensure the resources I select or am asked to use authentically reflect the demographics of my students, diverse perspectives, and the experiences of others?" To attend to this question, teachers should aim to share a variety of culturally responsive classroom texts that create both mirrors and windows for students. To elucidate this point, reflect on this quote from Aline O'Donnell's (2019) article in *Literacy Today*: "Curriculum can serve as a mirror when it reflects your own culture and identity, as well as a window when it offers a view into someone else's experience" (p. 19).

Critical to student identity development is a sense of belonging and acceptance (Brendtro, Brokenleg, & Van Bockern, 2019). Teachers can help promote this sense of inclusion by ensuring that students see pieces of their identity positively represented in the texts that they read, discuss, and analyze in the classroom. In this regard, teachers invite students to hold up mirrors. Additionally, resources can create windows by exposing them to a breadth and depth of perspectives and experiences that expand their own view of the world. These windows give students an opportunity to appreciate diverse perspectives from their immediate surroundings, the greater community, and beyond. When students of a dominant culture do not experience "windows into the realities of the multicultural world," they are at risk of "developing a false sense of their own importance in the world" in relation to others (Bishop, 2012, p. 9). So, let's be clear about the meaning of *diversity*.

People often use the term *diversity* in reference to race, class, or gender identity or expression; however, it encompasses so much more. It also includes ethnicity, age, sexual or affectual orientation, geographic background, spirituality or religious beliefs, learning style and abilities, marital or partner status, parental or caregiver status, national origin, language, economic status and background, work experiences, personality, and education. The totality of an individual derives from his or her fixed and fluid traits, characteristics, and experiences. As teachers make decisions about selecting diverse texts, they must commit to learning about each individual student, including his or her preferences and experiences. Additionally, they must exercise caution to avoid making assumptions about people who might outwardly appear to possess similar characteristics when they may perhaps differ completely. It is a teacher's charge to use classroom resources to create learning experiences and environments that further the belief that all humans are created equally and that everyone can appreciate what makes each individual unique.

Part of this challenge is that teachers often do not have experience in the vast array of cultures represented by their students. Therefore, they may find it very difficult to know how to successfully incorporate these cultures when choosing resources to support instruction. As a result, teachers commonly make the mistake of believing they must understand *everything* about their students' backgrounds before they can adopt a culturally responsive pedagogy—that is, instruction that helps students connect their learning to their own cultural experience. In "Partnering With Families and Communities," Katherin Garland and Kisha Bryan (2017) explain why this isn't accurate:

> The most successful implementation happens when teachers partner with families and community members to negotiate classrooms' cultures and curricula that actually reflect the communities where students develop and grow. Family and community members can play a major role in teachers' plans to (1) communicate high expectations to all students, (2) help students learn within the context of their cultures, and (3) value students' cultural backgrounds through content integration. (p. 52)

With this in mind, and at the onset of your team's audit of current resources for diverse representation or selecting new resources, consider the fact that the very nuances that we identify by are not monoliths. In other words, one story does not tell the story of all who identify with a cultural group. Not all individuals that identify as female, for example, have similar stories, preferences, or experiences. Therefore, it is impossible and not expected that teachers know everything about all dimensions of diversity that make individuals different from one another. But educators must have a willingness to learn and gain perspective through asking questions of others.

Consider the following example from the principal that leads our third grade team. The principal worked in a suburban school district outside Chicago where Katie Sheridan, Director of Language and Early Literacy, asked each administrator from across the district to interview a parent from a background different from their own. Many families in the school community were immigrants, and this exercise was intended to create connections between the school and home environments as part of a district goal to build cultural proficiency and intercultural skills. The experience would allow administrators to gain insight into their students' cultures and share what they learned with colleagues in the school community so they could positively impact students' involvement at school.

Many administrators wished they had a prepared script of questions to pose, as they felt anxious about approaching parents for a candid conversation on potentially sensitive topics. Intentionally, Katie did not provide a script since she conjectured that the administrators might cycle through a list of questions rather than truly concentrate and engage in effortless dialogue. Instead, they were instructed to begin the conversation by asking, "What do you think I need to know about you—for example, your country of origin, background, family, religion, or culture—that will help me better educate your child or children?" Authentically listening to what parents had to share presented a lesson unto itself.

Based on the reason they selected a particular parent, the administrators each steered the conversation and posed questions. Unsurprisingly, responses were diverse and often centered on differences in education systems in other countries. Some parents pointed out the deficit of diverse resources and the lack of images of people who resembled their families on the school or classroom walls. Parents shared stories of their children feeling uncomfortable in school because teachers used resources that included stereotypes of the children's background. As the administrators probed further to learn more, an easy, fluid exchange of conversation emerged and lasted longer than anticipated.

After the discussions, the administrative team members met to share what they each gleaned from parents to educate one another. At times, they discovered conflicting views among the parents. For example, some parents thought their children's homework lacked rigor because their experience of homework had been different as students. Other parents felt strongly that homework intruded on quality family time in the evenings. In this case, the administrative team admitted it was unable to make changes that catered to every perspective on homework. However, through communication with the administrators, the third-grade team felt empowered to understand reasons some students did not return to school with homework, and the team members could work to create systems that would allow all students to succeed. Additionally, the team members could educate parents who demanded more homework by sharing the research and reaching a compromise about what made the most sense in terms of students' success.

Another recurring concern the administrators learned from families was that many students did not see themselves represented in the school. They took this feedback to heart. As a result, they guaranteed change since the inadequate display of diversity on the walls was unintentional and lacked presence of mind. For the team, this meaningful experience launched a journey to discover what else they had overlooked by neglecting key cultural implications; thus, the team committed to continuous learning and improvement to inculcate diversity into the fabric of the school and across the district.

The most significant outcome from this experience was to refrain from making assumptions, learn about diverse perspectives, and be forthright and comfortable to ask questions. Educators must engage in and commit to the vulnerable act of learning from others. As educators, we sometimes hold back when we have a curious impulse. We recoil from asking questions for fear of offending someone or saying something wrong. In truth, there are those who may not appreciate educating others about their background. But many willingly share about their identities and recognize that helping others learn about myriad cultures creates a more inclusive society for everyone, their children included.

The point of this example is to stress that, as your team continues to audit and augment existing classroom resources, it must take into consideration the demographics of your community. (This aspect of choosing classroom texts aligns with one of the measures of choosing texts highlighted in chapter 3—Discuss Options for Complex Texts, page 84). To expand expertise in this effort, Sharroky Hollie (2019) advises teachers to be cognizant of three types of culturally responsive texts that will assist teachers in wisely choosing core reading material that reflects students culturally and linguistically.

1. **Culturally authentic texts:** This preferred text type refers to fiction or nonfiction that mirrors authentic cultural experiences of a certain group. It might focus on religion, gender, ethnicity, geographic location, or other aspects of culture. (Access www.responsivereads.com to find culturally authentic titles.)

2. **Culturally generic texts:** Although these texts center on characters with racial identities, they include few or superficial cultural details about these characters within the overall storyline.

3. **Culturally neutral texts:** This least-preferred culturally responsive type of text is considered neutral because, although the text focuses on a character of color, the other aspects of the story—its plot, theme, or methods of characterization—are largely traditional or mainstream. Teachers might select these texts for other purposes, such as to focus on the author's strong use of figurative language, vocabulary, or suspense. But in doing so, they should not mistake these texts for culturally responsive texts when their value is predicated on the author's craft.

As mentioned previously, when selecting texts, keep in mind that one story does not tell the whole narrative of all who identify with a gender or cultural group. It is impossible to be an expert about all dimensions of diversity that make us different from one another. Therefore, solicit input from your colleagues, your students, and your students' parents, many of whom are incredible allies and will likely prove willing to educate teacher teams and freely share about their cultures. Be receptive to learning by asking them questions that allow you to gain perspective, as this can ultimately prove useful when selecting texts.

Works from authors of all different cultures and backgrounds artfully bring stories and the world to life that touch on a variety of topics and themes that students might find relevant and interesting. In addition, shine a spotlight on authors since the texts they craft might reflect their own personal experiences and provide an additional dimension into a culture. Of chief importance is your team's awareness of the impact the literature it selects will have on every student in its classrooms. By exposing students to a rich repository of resources, teachers allow students to mirror their own cultures and also afford them opportunities to experience lives different from their own and learn to appreciate diverse perspectives. Presenting an array of rich texts that positively contribute to building students' knowledge, cultural awareness, and acceptance will ensure students grow not only as readers and writers but as human beings.

EXERCISE

Address Important Questions About Access

An educator's job entails creating an inclusive environment in which students appreciate differences. Literacy can serve as a vehicle for expanding students' thinking and exposing them to the richness of the world. Through culturally responsive texts, they experience people, places, and situations perhaps previously unfamiliar to them. Engage in a discussion with your team to determine how you can all make classrooms more inclusive and literacy materials more diverse and culturally authentic.

Use the following questions to guide this exercise.

★ Do we send unintended messages about student identities through our day-to-day instructional practices? If so, how might we reconsider our actions or words?

★ Does our team exclude students from rigorous learning opportunities? Which students are pulled out and do not participate in grade-level classroom instruction as others do, and why do they not? How can we improve this situation?

★ How can we positively shift our collective mindset and language we use when referring to students who need something different? What language can we adopt that shows an asset-based orientation?

★ Do the resources that we select, or that we are asked to use, authentically reflect the demographics of students in our classrooms? Do the resources show a balanced representation of students in our classrooms?

★ Do the resources reflect diverse perspectives and experiences of others? Or, do the texts predominantly reflect one perspective? If they do, how can we positively adjust our plans to be more inclusive?

★ How do we know our resources support diverse cultural experiences? Have we engaged with an ally of that demographic background? Have we considered the author of the text and to what degree the author's experience is authentic?

Summary

We have the opportunity to substantially improve the education experience and outcomes for our students. Literacy instruction is the place to begin this change. Each and every student of a different gender, race, ethnic background, language ability, disability, or other quality contributes uniqueness to the collective composition of a classroom, school, and community. Educators of literacy, in particular, are privileged to provide students with access to learning experiences and resources that highlight and celebrate what each student brings to the classroom and world. With literacy instruction, students read about, write about, talk about, and listen to issues and discussions surrounding equity. Engaging in diverse texts and thoughtful discussions that spawn a change in perspective engenders appreciation for the lives others live and the way they think, which might be different from our own perspectives and experiences. Through teachers' thoughtful guidance, students can transfer what they learn within the class to their communities and make inclusive contributions. This chapter is but a starting point to a potentially rich conversation and a launching point for action through which teams can use literacy as a powerful tool toward inclusivity.

EPILOGUE

Undeniably, possessing strong literacy skills can benefit all members of society. The International Literacy Association (2019) asserts in its position statement, "the ability to identify, understand, interpret, create, compute, and communicate using visual, audible, and digital materials across disciplines and in any context—and access to excellent and equitable literacy instruction are basic human rights" (p. 1).

Whether teaching students to function as generators or receivers of written, digital, or oral discourse, a teacher's obligation is to advance students' literacy capabilities so they can actively and fully engage in our world. Building competencies around literacy instruction is the strongest catalyst for supporting student growth in every area of school curricula. We contend following the steps in this book empowers your team to guarantee each student in your care achieves success in his or her learning.

As schools commit to exemplary instruction to advance learning, educators must not overlook the power of a PLC. Regardless of the structure of teams in your PLC, this work always begins with teaming teachers who are focused on improving their own capacity to impact student learning. Teams dedicate themselves to working collaboratively to position students for success. Specifically, these teams of professionals engage in the PREP process to unwrap standards and identify learning targets, create a learning progression, design assessment tasks and rubrics, develop differentiated lessons, collect and analyze data to inform instruction, and intervene to provide necessary support, all in an effort to move students' learning forward.

While this book speaks directly to second- and third-grade teachers who want to hone their teaching of literacy within their classrooms, this is one installment in a series that supports teacher collaboration and strategic literacy-infused teaching in all elementary grades. Each text in this series focuses on building common instructional and assessment practices with a common language that ensures a literacy focus across academic disciplines. Ultimately, the literacy skills and embedded critical thinking required to master them will prepare grades 2–3 students for the rigor of the next grade level of learning and beyond.

All teachers possess a pressing responsibility to increase students' literacy capacity that opens the doors wide to myriad and boundless opportunities. Teachers working in cohesive, effective, and goal-oriented teams can more capably educate students who will forge ahead with more confidence to meet the next challenge that lies ahead for them. Preparing them amply is our responsibility. Let us embrace this awesome duty.

APPENDIX A:

PREP TEMPLATE AND OTHER TOOLS

This appendix provides a series of reproducible tools your team can use as it works to build literacy-focused instruction through its curriculum. Here, you will find the complete version of the PREP template (including slots for adding essential understandings and guiding principles), the protocol to unwrap priority standards, the learning progression and assessments template, and a tool for measuring text complexity.

PREP Template

Unit: _____ Time Frame: _____

Grade: _____

Unit Standards

Essential Understandings (optional)	Guiding Questions (optional)

Strand (Reading Literature, Reading Informational Text, Writing, Language, and so on):

-

-

-

-

-

Strand (Reading Literature, Reading Informational Text, Writing, Language, and so on):

-
-
-
-
-

Strand (Reading Literature, Reading Informational Text, Writing, Language, and so on):

-
-
-
-
-

Strand (Reading Literature, Reading Informational Text, Writing, Language, and so on):

-
-
-
-
-

Unwrapped Unit Priority Standards	Knowledge Items	Skills (Learning Targets and DOK Levels)

Protocol to Unwrap Priority Standards

Directions: To unpack priority standards, answer the following questions.

1. **What priority standard (or standards) are we targeting?** Record the priority standard in the space provided.

2. **What will students need to do to be proficient?** Find and capitalize (or circle) pertinent verbs in the standard. The verbs—together with the content and context (step 3)—pinpoint the exact skills students need in order to achieve proficiency in this standard. List the verbs in the space provided.

3. **With what content and context will students need to apply these skills?** Find and underline the nouns and phrases that represent the content and concepts to teach, and list them in the space provided.

Learning Progression and Assessments Template

Priority Standard (or Standards):

	Steps	Learning Progression	Assessments
	Step ____	**Priority Standard (or Standards):**	
	Step ____	Learning Target (Skill) or Knowledge	
	Step ____	Learning Target (Skill) or Knowledge	
	Step ____	Learning Target (Skill) or Knowledge	

page 1 of 2

Reading and Writing Instruction for Second- and Third-Grade Classrooms in a PLC at Work © 2020 Solution Tree Press
SolutionTree.com • Visit **go.SolutionTree.com/literacy** to download this free reproducible.

		Learning Target (Skill) or Knowledge	
↑	Step ____	Learning Target (Skill) or Knowledge	
	Step ____	Learning Target (Skill) or Knowledge	
	Step ____	Learning Target (Skill) or Knowledge	
	Step ____	Learning Target (Skill) or Knowledge	
	Step ____	Learning Target (Skill) or Knowledge	
	Step ____	Learning Target (Skill) or Knowledge	

Reading and Writing Instruction for Second- and Third-Grade Classrooms in a PLC at Work © 2020 Solution Tree Press
SolutionTree.com • Visit **go.SolutionTree.com/literacy** to download this free reproducible.

Tool for Measuring Text Complexity

Directions: Use this tool to determine whether or not a text meets rigor demands when considering the qualitative, quantitative, and reader-task information available.

Text to consider: _____

Author: _____

Unit of instruction: _____

Priority standard (or standards) to be instructed with this text:

Students to use this text:

Step 1: Analyze the quantitative measures for second- and third-grade text.

Use multiple measures listed here. Place a check on the measures that indicate the text is within the second- or third-grade band. (Step 1 is not applicable to poetry and drama.)

ATOS	Degrees of Reading Power®	FleschKincaid	The Lexile Framework®	Reading Maturity	SourceRater
2.75–5.14	42–54	1.98–5.34	420–820	3.53–6.13	0.05–2.48

Quantitative Recommendation

Various readability measures indicate the chosen text is:

☐ Appropriate for the grade-level complexity band

  _Or_

☐ Not appropriate for the grade-level complexity band

STEP 2: Analyze the qualitative measures for second- and third-grade text.

Analyze the following features. Circle the items that describe the features of the text. Use the analysis to make a qualitative recommendation.

Features	High Complexity	Low Complexity
Structure	Uses complex, implicit, and (in literary texts) unconventional structures Contains frequent use of flashbacks, flashforwards, multiple points of view, and other manipulations of time and sequence Includes similarly complex graphics that provide an independent source of information and are essential to understanding a text	Uses simple, well-marked, and conventional structures Relates events in chronological order Includes graphics that tend to be simple and either unnecessary or merely supplementary to the meaning of texts
Language Conventionality and Clarity	Relies on figurative, ironic, ambiguous, purposefully misleading, archaic, or otherwise unfamiliar language (such as general academic and domain-specific vocabulary)	Relies on literal, clear, contemporary, and conversational language, which tends to be easier to read.
Knowledge Demands	Makes assumptions about the extent of readers' life experiences and the depth of their cultural, literary, and content knowledge	Makes few assumptions about the extent of readers' life experiences and the depth of their cultural, literary, and content knowledge
Levels of Meaning (Literary Texts) or Purpose (Informational Texts)	Has multiple levels of meaning (literary text) Has a purpose that is partially implicit, hidden, or obscure (informational texts)	Has a single level of meaning (literary text) Has an explicitly stated purpose (informational text)

Qualitative Recommendation

Analysis of the features indicate the chosen text is:

☐ Appropriate for the grade-level complexity band

Or

☐ Not appropriate for the grade-level complexity band

Reading and Writing Instruction for Second- and Third-Grade Classrooms in a PLC at Work © 2020 Solution Tree Press
SolutionTree.com • Visit **go.SolutionTree.com/literacy** to download this free reproducible.

STEP 3: Combine quantitative and qualitative data to determine if the text is complex.

Analysis of combined quantitative and qualitative data indicate:

☐ Both measures indicate the text is complex; we will use it after we consider the readers and task.

Or

☐ One or neither of the measures indicate the text is complex; we will not use it.

STEP 4: Apply reader–task considerations to make a final determination of whether to use the text.

After determining if the text is complex enough for your readers, and to make a professional determination if this complex text is appropriate for your readers, use this section to compare the text to the following.

- Your students' knowledge and experiences

- Your students' motivation relative to the topic

- The purpose and complexity of the task assigned or questions posed

	Will Use This Text	May Not Use This Text
Student Knowledge and Experiences	Text aligns with content that students have some knowledge of or experience with, therefore creating a comprehensible opportunity for the reader.	Students have no knowledge of or experience with this topic, therefore, this text is likely inappropriate at this time.
Motivation About This Topic	Students have some motivation and interest in this topic and, therefore, will engage with the complex text.	Students are not as interested in this topic and, therefore, might reluctantly engage with this complex text.
Purpose, Task or Questions Assigned (Consider the specific students that will be using this text. It might be the whole group or with a small group of students.)	Text aligns with the purpose for reading being assigned (such as close reading, studying to learn new material, or independently practicing a skill or strategy). Text aligns with the type of reading students need to do (such as skim text features to gain new information or follow step by step directions).	Text *does not* align with the purpose for reading being assigned (such as being too long or too short to fully meet the purpose or not having multiple characters to analyze). Text *does not* align with the type of reading students need to do (such as having no text features to analyze when that is the target).

Reading and Writing Instruction for Second- and Third-Grade Classrooms in a PLC at Work © 2020 Solution Tree Press
SolutionTree.com • Visit **go.SolutionTree.com/literacy** to download this free reproducible.

	Text aligns with the intended outcomes (such as acquiring knowledge, finding the solution to a problem, or reading for enjoyment).	Text *does not* align with the intended outcomes (such as not enabling students to find the answer to a problem they are researching).

Step 5: Make your final recommendation.

Text to consider: _____

Author: _____

Unit of instruction: _____

Priority standard (or standards) to be instructed with this text:

Students to use this text:

Our recommendation is to:

☐ Use this text to instruct these students for this purpose

   Or

☐ Not use this text for this purpose

   Optional

☐ Save this text to use during an alternate unit of instruction

Source: National Governors Association Center for Best Practices & Council of Chief State School Officers. (n.d.b). Supplemental information for appendix A of the Common Core State Standards for English language arts and literacy: New Research on text complexity. Washington, DC: Authors. Accessed at www .corestandards.org/assets/E0813_Appendix_A_New_Research_on_Text_Complexity.pdf on April 10, 2020.

APPENDIX B:

PROCESS FOR PRIORITIZING STANDARDS

Teams focus on ensuring a guaranteed and viable curriculum, which this book repeatedly emphasizes as a major doctrine of PLC culture. Because there is simply not enough time within the school year to adequately and deeply teach all the standards listed in a district curriculum guide or provided in a published literacy series, teacher teams must determine which standards qualify as essential. Refer to chapter 1 (page 11) to review and understand the purpose of setting priority standards.

If teacher teams have not participated in a process to prioritize standards, they determine which standards they deem worthy of the priority-standard designation using the process outlined in this appendix. This suggested process includes four steps. Teams might decide to conduct the fourth step earlier if teachers need to familiarize themselves with standards in surrounding grades or with standardized testing expectations.

1. Teams review the task and criteria for determining priority standards.

2. Individuals review standards and critique them against criteria.

3. Individuals share, and the team arrives at an initial list of priority standards.

4. Teams consider vertical alignment and expectations for external exams and finalize priority standards.

Use this appendix in conjunction with the content in chapter 1 to facilitate this process.

Teams Review the Task and Criteria for Determining Priority Standards

Before teacher teams begin to prioritize, they review the preceding four steps to get an overview of the expectations. Then, to begin, they read the following criteria for prioritization and gain clarity about what each point means (Ainsworth, 2017; Reeves, 2007).

- **Endurance:** Are the knowledge, skills, and concepts embedded in the standard critical for students to remember in the future beyond this grade level and course? For example, the ability to coherently summarize complex text is a skill that extends beyond a particular unit of instruction and grade level. Therefore, to summarize is an enduring skill worth teaching.

- **Leverage:** Are the knowledge, skills, and concepts in the standard applicable across several disciplines? For example, summarizing complex text might be taught in language arts when students experience a literary work, but it is equally valuable when reading content in social studies and science.

- **Readiness:** Does the standard include prerequisite knowledge, skills, and concepts necessary to prepare students for the next grade? For example, when students learn the structure and elements of an opinion paper, it equips them with needed skills and knowledge to tackle the more rigorous work of argumentation writing.

- **High-stakes exams:** Will students need to know and apply the knowledge, skills, and concepts of the standard on external exams? For example, district, state or provincial, college, or vocational exams might include questions or writing prompts geared to this standard, so teachers need to prepare students.

Once team members are clear on the task and criteria, they are ready to proceed.

Individuals Review Standards and Critique Them Against Criteria

Individuals on the team review each standard and determine to what degree each meets the criteria. Each team member will be applying professional knowledge and judgment to annotate the standards she or he believes meet one or more of the criteria. For example, electronically or by hand, teachers enter *E* for endurance, *L* for leverage, *R* for readiness, and *H* for high-stakes exams next to each standard. For those that do not meet any of these criteria, no mark is needed. This silent exercise enables think time to foster individual accountability. Special educators should be full participants in this process if they teach the content, and they should approach this process with typical grade-level expectations in mind.

While they will naturally consider their students' current gaps, teachers should not base the process of determining priority standards on individual student considerations. Priority should be based on high expectations for all grade-level students. Teams can set a time limit for this initial activity regarding what standards it should prioritize.

Individuals Share and the Team Arrives at an Initial List of Priority Standards

For the team to arrive at an initial list of priority standards, each teacher shares his or her choices using a round-robin structure. One person begins by identifying a standard he or she chooses as a priority standard, using the criteria—endurance, leverage, and so on—as justification and explanation. Be wary of support that includes individual bias or personal feelings about continuing a long-standing trend. Team members should select only those standards that meet the criteria.

As team members share, a discussion will naturally ensue. Encourage this discussion since it will likely uncover misconceptions about standards as well as provide clarity about them. For this step to be productive, teams can abide by the following.

▸ Assign a scribe to record the standards that are deemed a priority and those that are supporting.

▸ Determine in advance how the team will handle a lack of consensus.

▸ Have each team member share his or her annotated standards until everyone is satisfied with an initial list of priority standards.

Teams Consider Vertical Alignment and Expectations of External Exams and Finalize Priority Standards

Teachers who are unaware of or not well versed in surrounding grades' content standards and standardized tests might move this step up sooner in the process.

However, if they are familiar with grades 1–4 standards and the testing situation, they double-check to ensure how the proposed priority standards align vertically and take into account expectations for external accountability assessments.

For vertical articulation, teams review previous and subsequent grade-level, subject-area, and course standards. In particular, teachers consider future expectations when determining priority standards so they can make certain to amply prepare their students. For instance, in reviewing third-grade reading standards for informational text, a second-grade team realizes that, in addition to teaching students to identify the main topic of a text or paragraph, students will need to determine the main idea and recount the key details that support the main idea in third grade. Therefore, students need to acquire this skill by the end of second grade in order to master the next level of learning. Prudent teams share their initial set of priority standards in person or electronically with other grade-level teams and collect feedback to ensure proper alignment.

Teams also want to pay attention to district, state or provincial, and national accountability assessments to identify the degree of emphasis they should place on particular standards. States or provinces typically release test blueprints or other documents that identify samples of test items aligned to particular standards, the writing tasks students will produce, and holistic rubrics. Teams also consider other district documents or assessment data that reveal grade-level expectations.

Once teams take these factors into consideration, they finalize their list of priority standards. Conscientious teams then share them in person or electronically with other grade-level teams and collect feedback to ensure proper alignment. If the entire school or district participates in this process, all teams or representatives from each grade-level team can work on the vertical progression.

APPENDIX C:

DEPTH OF KNOWLEDGE OVERVIEW

This appendix reviews the thinking levels in Webb's (1997, 1999) Depth of Knowledge. The information is adapted from "Applying Webb's Depth-of-Knowledge (DOK) Levels in Reading" (Hess, n.d.) and "Webb's Depth of Knowledge Guide: Career and Technical Education Definitions" (Mississippi Department of Education, 2009). Briefly, here are the four levels of thinking that comprise DOK.

1. **Recall and reproduction:** Recall a fact, term, principle, or concept; or perform a procedure.

2. **Basic application of skills and concepts:** Use concepts or procedures involving some mental processing.

3. **Strategic thinking:** Show reasoning, developing a plan or sequence of steps to approach a problem; reflect some decision making and justification; and demonstrate abstract and complex thinking.

4. **Extended thinking:** Demonstrate analysis or investigation that requires synthesis, research, and analysis across multiple contexts (such as disciplines, content areas, sources, and so on).

The following tables further elaborate on each of the four levels by establishing high-level traits and verbs associated with the level along with a series of activities that generate thinking at the level. Table C.1 (page 262) begins with recall and reproduction, table C.2 (page 263) shows working with skills and concepts, table C.3 (page 264) aligns to short-term strategic thinking, and table C.4 (page 265) illustrates extended strategic thinking.

Table C.1: Recall and Reproduction

Common Traits	
• Basic tasks require students to recall or reproduce knowledge and skills. • The focus in reading is on initial comprehension rather than analysis or interpretation. • Writing does not include complex synthesis or analysis but does include basic ideas.	• Subject-matter content involves working with facts, terms, and properties. • Students produce a finite answer; the answer doesn't need to be figured out or solved.

Verbs			
Arrange	Find	Memorize	Respond
Calculate	Identify	Name	Restate
Define	Illustrate	Quote	State
Demonstrate	Interpret	Recall	Tabulate
Describe	Label	Recite	Tell
Develop	List	Recognize	Translate
Draw	Match	Repeat	Use
Explain	Measure	Report	

Possible Activities	
• Name and explain each element of literature (setting, character, plot, point of view, theme). • Recite a fact related to an informational report topic. • Make a storyboard showing the sequence of events. • Draw a picture of a character from the author's description. • Describe what a character looks like. • Explain the conflict between the protagonist and antagonist. • Identify examples of methods of characterization. • List adjectives to describe the setting or a character's physical description. • Label the plot elements on a plot diagram. • Brainstorm story ideas. • Outline the main points. • Conduct basic mathematical calculations. • Measure the length and width of an object. • Identify the subject and predicate of a sentence.	• Write a list of key words related to . . . . • Make a chart showing . . . . • Retell the events of . . . . • Develop a concept map showing a process . • List the steps in the writing process. • Recite facts about . . . . • Match vocabulary words with their definitions. • Label locations on a map. • Write a paragraph with varied sentence beginnings. • Label the parts of an opinion or argument paragraph (reason, evidence, elaboration, ending). • Identify misspelled words. • Apply conventional spelling patterns or rules to new situations in writing. • Use resources to correct spelling. • Select or recall appropriate vocabulary to aid meaning.

Table C.2: Working With Skills and Concepts

Common Traits	
<ul><li>This level involves some mental processing and reasoning beyond habitual response.</li><li>In reading, students require both initial comprehension and subsequent processing of text; literal main ideas are stressed.</li></ul>	<ul><li>If students describe or explain, they go beyond the description or explanation of recalled information to describe or explain a result or answer *how* or *why*.</li><li>In writing, students begin to connect ideas using a simple organizational structure and produce short, rough pieces.</li></ul>

Verbs			
Calculate	Demonstrate	Illustrate	Predict
Categorize	Determine cause/effect	Infer	Relate
Classify	Distinguish	Interpret	Separate
Collect and display	Estimate	Make observations	Show
Compare	Graph	Modify	Solve
Compile	Identify patterns	Organize	Summarize
Complete		Paraphrase	Use context clues
Construct			

Possible Activities	
<ul><li>Classify a series of steps.</li><li>Explain the points of view of characters or historical figures.</li><li>Distinguish between fact and opinion.</li><li>Write an explanation about a topic.</li><li>Use details from the text to infer how a character might act.</li><li>State the relationship between two characters or concepts.</li><li>Research, record, and organize information.</li><li>Use an outline or take notes to organize ideas.</li><li>Organize, represent, and interpret data.</li><li>Explain how to perform a specific task.</li><li>Identify the major events in a narrative and write a one-paragraph summary.</li><li>Use context clues to identify the meaning of unfamiliar words.</li><li>Solve routine multiple-step problems.</li><li>State the relationships among multiple concepts.</li></ul>	<ul><li>Cite textual evidence to support a theme.</li><li>Describe the causes and effects of an event or individual's or character's actions.</li><li>Identify patterns in events or an individual's or character's behavior.</li><li>Compare and contrast two topics, events, settings, characters, or historical figures.</li><li>Make informed predictions.</li><li>Paraphrase the ideas in a text.</li><li>Create a character sketch.</li><li>Write a well-structured paragraph.</li><li>Write a passage of dialogue between two characters.</li><li>Write a diary, journal, or blog entry.</li><li>Edit final drafts.</li><li>Show basic understanding and appropriate use of reference materials (print or digital).</li><li>Identify use of figurative language (imagery or sensory details, simile, metaphor, personification).</li></ul>

Table C.3: Strategic Thinking

Common Traits			
• Items demand deep knowledge and use of higher-order thinking processes. • Students must state their reasoning and cite references from sources. • Items can involve abstract theme identification, inferences between or across passages, or application of prior knowledge.		• In writing, students develop multiple paragraph compositions using the writing process; pieces may include complex sentence structures or some synthesis and analysis. • Key processes include: *analyze, explain, support with evidence, generalize, create,* and *connect ideas.*	
Verbs			
Analyze Apprise Argue Assess Calculate Cite evidence Classify	Compare Connect Construct Critique Debate Decide Develop a logical argument	Differentiate Draw conclusions Evaluate Examine Explain phenomena in terms and concepts Formulate Hypothesize	Investigate Judge Justify Predict Revise Use concepts to solve non-routine problems
Possible Activities			
• Use a comparison or contrast graphic organizer to show how two topics are the same and different. • Compare multiple texts and cite textual evidence from them to support a common theme. • Survey classmates to find out their opinions. • Create a graphic organizer to show stages in a process or the sequence of events. • Conduct an investigation to answer a question or address a problem. • Make a brochure about five important rules to convince others of their merit. • Create an advertisement about a new product. • Analyze the various solutions to a problem; choose one and justify your reason. • Create graphs, tables, or charts to display data in an organized way. • Develop a scientific model for a complex situation. • Determine the author's purpose and describe how it affects the interpretation.		• Draw inferences about author's purpose, implied causes and effects, or theme using textual evidence. • Describe how word choice, point of view, or bias affects the interpretation of a reading selection. • Summarize or compare information within and across passages. • Analyze interrelationships among elements of the text (plot, setting, characters). • Develop multiple paragraph compositions (literary analysis, critique) or narrative. • Use appropriate organizational structures (cause and effect, problem–solution). • Use complex and varied sentence construction. • Edit and revise to improve quality of writing. • Summarize information from multiple sources to address a specific topic. • Support ideas with details, examples, quotes, references; include citations.	

Table C.4: Extended Strategic Thinking

Common Traits	
• Items demand complex, higher-order thinking processes, such as plan, develop, synthesize, and reflect over an extended period.	• In writing, students produce multiple-paragraph compositions that demonstrate synthesis, analysis, and evaluation of complex ideas or themes and evidence of deep awareness of purpose and audience.
	• Synthesis and analysis of information from multiple sources can include identifying complexities, discrepancies, or different perspectives.

Verbs			
Analyze	Create	Formulate	Propose
Apply concepts	Critique	Modify	Prove
Connect	Design	Plan	Synthesize

Possible Activities	
• Research to formulate and test hypotheses over time.	• Gather, analyze, organize, and interpret information from multiple print and digital sources for the purpose of writing a report or essay. For example:
• Make multiple strategic and procedural decisions based on new information throughout an event.	• Write a multiple-paragraph research report that requires analysis and synthesis of information from multiple sources.
• Collaborate to identify the problems a particular organization, society, or business faces; define the perspectives of all stakeholders; and formulate a plan of action	• Write a multiple-paragraph argumentation essay based on research that synthesizes information from various sources and that includes a counterargument; draw and justify conclusions.
• Create a marketing plan to sell a product or idea.	• Analyze complex and abstract themes across literary works.
• Conduct a project that requires specifying a problem, designing and conducting an experiment, analyzing data, and reporting results.	• Evaluate the credibility of various sources against criteria.
• Design a mathematical model to inform and solve a practical or abstract situation.	
• Read two or more works by the same author and compare the writer's craft (style, bias, literary techniques, point of view).	

APPENDIX D:

ESSENTIAL UNDERSTANDINGS AND GUIDING QUESTIONS

This appendix provides explanations for and examples of essential understandings and guiding questions. If teams wish to extend the six-step process laid out in chapter 1 (page 11) to include these two additional components, the information here can prove useful. As well, if teams are using a published or existing curriculum that includes these components, this appendix might serve as a vehicle for validating or revising what is in their resources.

Craft Essential Understandings

To craft essential understandings, teams carefully review what they have put into the PREP template (figure 1.1, page 15) to see how the synthesized components weave together to form a unified direction for planning lessons and assessments. In doing so, they focus on formulating deeper conceptual understandings, called *essential* (or *enduring*) *understandings*. These statements enable teams to capture the essence of a unit. Essential understandings are predicated on key concepts that teachers want students to realize, such as the following literacy-focused concepts: figurative language, perspective, patterns, phonemic awareness, and narrative.

Many education icons espouse the value of this aspect of curriculum design. Hattie (2012) states that "conceptual understandings form the 'coat hangers' on which we interpret and assimilate new ideas, and relate and extend them" (p. 115). H. Lynn Erickson (2007) states that the "synergistic interplay between the factual and conceptual levels of thinking" is critical to intellectual development (p. 2). Furthermore, Erickson (2007) writes, "When curriculum and instruction require students to process factual information through the conceptual level of thinking, the students demonstrate greater retention of factual information, deeper levels of understanding, and increased motivation for learning" (p. 2).

Teachers formulate essential understandings by using the unwrapped standards and the foundational information from the knowledge section in the PREP template (figure 1.1, page 15). The following example essential understandings from this book's featured Exploring Elements of Fiction unit help ensure that third-grade teachers fulfill the promise of high-level instruction and assessment.

▸ Readers ask and answer questions as they read to monitor their comprehension.

▸ Authors combine many different elements to tell a story, and these elements interact over the course of the text to express a moral, lesson, or message to the reader.

▸ Informative writers include facts and details about a subject to convey ideas and information.

Review the following points to assist your team in devising essential understandings.

▸ Teachers write essential understandings in adult language to crystallize and articulate the conceptual thinking used to design curriculum.

▸ To write one essential understanding for each standard would be cumbersome and overwhelming. Therefore, each essential understanding can take into account two or more standards.

▸ Essential understandings need to be transferable. To accomplish this, they should not include proper nouns or past-tense verbs, since that would anchor them in a specific situation, context, or time frame. In fact, teachers in grade clusters can use the same essential understandings if they pertain to the content material since they are written in applicable, general terms. In this way, they are similar to themes that can apply across works of literature.

▸ To craft stronger essential understandings, teachers capitalize on action verbs (such as *determine, promote, challenge*, and *support*) instead of forms of the verb *to be*. In the examples from the Elements of Fiction unit, these precise verbs connect concepts embedded in the essential understandings: *ask, answer, combine, interact, include*, and *convey*.

▸ On the PREP template, knowledge items are what students come to *know*; they reflect foundational information. These entries can be vocabulary, people, places, dates, examples, and even a fact; for example, *Authors write memoirs about themselves.* Essential understandings are always complete sentences and represent what we want students to *understand.* These statements push their thinking further to wonder, *So what? What about it? Why is this important?* Therefore, read how this complete and pertinent essential understanding more clearly articulates *why* writing memoirs are important: *Authors create memoirs to share personal experiences with others so they can teach a lesson or explain the truth to the world.* By using essential understandings that go beyond facts, teachers can plan deeper and more meaningful instructional experiences and assessments.

Once teams craft essential understandings, they use them to build guiding questions to frame instruction and assessment. Teams might find, however, that it is beneficial to work on building essential understandings and guiding questions concurrently.

Develop Guiding Questions

Guiding questions establish a purpose for learning, provide an overarching focus that promotes higher-level thinking, and emanate from essential understandings. They are written in student-friendly language rather than solely teacher speak. These questions compel students to engage in the work ahead and make them aware of the connection between what they are doing and learning outcomes. Teachers should post these questions in the classroom so students are grounded in their purpose for learning; this way, they are aware of the value in what they are learning and derive meaning from it. Teachers can use their learning targets (*I can* statements) in conjunction with guiding questions. In fact, the guiding question can show an overarching focus for a cluster of related *I can* statements.

Guiding questions differ from text-dependent questions, which help deepen students' understanding of complex text (for example, *Why doesn't Esperanza want her mother to marry her uncle Tio Luis?*), and from granular questions geared to a specific lesson (for example, *What punctuation marks indicate that a character is speaking?*). Rather, guiding questions focus on overarching concepts. They are broad queries that cannot be answered with a list and typically begin with open-ended words, such as *how, why,* or *is*. Teams can craft guiding questions in third-person point of view or personalize them using first-person pronouns.

In addition, guiding questions are global and transferable—similar to essential understandings that can apply to different units of study across grade levels. For example, in literacy instruction, teachers can design and ask these questions: "How does figurative language enhance setting? How and why do characters change over time? Is a story incomplete without a climax? and Should all stories include dialogue?" Across content areas, teachers might ask, "How can human interaction affect the environment? Is conflict avoidable? How do governments support citizens?"

Each essential understanding holds the answer to an accompanying guiding question. For example, the answer to, *How can a person's story affect readers?* is expressed in the following essential understanding: *A story can inspire readers by showing how people overcome challenges.* For this reason, teachers display the guiding questions to set the stage for learning but refrain from showing the essential understandings since they reveal the answer. Later, teachers can share them or lead a brainstorming session in which students recall the key takeaways from activities and lessons to arrive at the essential understandings based on the learning they acquired.

Guiding questions are purposefully brief because teachers can plan and conduct a series of lessons around these questions where students discover for themselves the deeper meaning embedded in the essential understandings. If a question is leading, teachers offer the answer too easily rather than give students the opportunity to discover answers on their own. Teachers must vigilantly search for and identify what they want students to understand, and the succinctly stated guiding question helps frame and set the purpose for learning. For examples, refer to figure D.1, which shows the pairing of essential understandings and guiding questions.

Essential Understandings (Students will understand that . . .)	Guiding Questions
Readers ask and answer questions as they read to monitor their comprehension.	What questions can we ask ourselves as we read to make sure we understand a text?
Authors combine many different elements to tell a story, and these elements interact over the course of the text to express a moral, lesson, or message to the reader.	How do authors use story elements to tell a story? How do story elements help to express a message?
Informative writers include facts and details about a subject to convey ideas and information.	How do writers use facts and details to give information about a topic?

Figure D.1: Example guiding questions paired with essential understandings.

As you review the figure, notice the following.

- ▶ Teams can use guiding questions across units or grades, so they are purposefully written for this transferability. For example, *What questions can we ask ourselves as we read to make sure we understand a text?* can apply to various complex texts within a school year and across grades.

- ▶ Answers to each guiding question, which teams write using language students can understand, are found in an associated essential understanding.

- ▶ Questions should require open-ended, higher-order responses; beginning them with *why*, *how*, or even *is* can foster such a response. If other question words achieve this goal, use them.

- ▶ Teachers can write the questions in first-person point of view, which personalizes them to the students, or in third-person point of view, as they wish.

- ▶ Like learning targets, teachers should post the guiding questions in the classroom and refer to them to set the purpose for learning.

If teams decide to write and use guiding questions within their instructional program, they should make it a priority to collaborate as a team to develop them, connect the questions to learning targets, and ensure that they transpire from the essential understandings.

APPENDIX E:

LIST OF FIGURES AND TABLES

*Reproducible figures are in italics. Visit **go.SolutionTree.com/literacy** to download free reproducible versions of these figures.*

REFERENCES AND RESOURCES

Ainsworth, L. (2013). *Prioritizing the Common Core: Identifying specific standards to emphasize the most.* Englewood, CO: Lead + Learn Press.

Ainsworth, L. (2017, April 6). *Priority standards: The power of focus* [Blog post]. Accessed at www.larryainsworth.com/blog/priority-standards-the-power-of-focus on March 30, 2020.

Ainsworth, L., & Viegut, D. (2015). *Common formative assessments 2.0: How teacher teams intentionally align standards, instruction, and assessment.* Thousand Oaks, CA: Corwin Press.

Allington, R. L. (2001). *What really matters for struggling readers: Designing research-based programs.* New York: Longman.

Allington, R. L. (2009). *What really matters in response to intervention: Research-based designs.* Boston: Pearson.

Allington, R. L. (2014). How reading volume affects both reading fluency and reading achievement. *International Electronic Journal of Elementary Education, 7*(1), 13–26.

Anderson, L. W., & Krathwohl, D. R. (Eds.). (2001). *A taxonomy for learning, teaching, and assessing: A revision of Bloom's taxonomy of educational objectives.* New York: Longman.

Annie E. Casey Foundation. (2010). *Early warning! Why reading by the end of third grade matters.* Baltimore: Author.

Atwell, N. (2007). *The reading zone: How to help kids become skilled, passionate, habitual, critical readers.* New York: Scholastic.

Bailey, K., & Jakicic, C. (2017). *Simplifying common assessment: A guide for Professional Learning Communities at Work.* Bloomington, IN: Solution Tree Press.

Bailey, K., Jakicic, C., & Spiller, J. (2014). *Collaborating for success with the Common Core: A toolkit for Professional Learning Communities at Work.* Bloomington, IN: Solution Tree Press.

Bates, C. C. (2013). Flexible grouping during literacy centers: A model for differentiating instruction. *YC Young Children, 68*(2), 30–33.

Beck, I. L., & Beck, M. E. (2013). *Making sense of phonics: The hows and whys* (2nd ed.). New York: Guilford Press.

Beck, I. L., McKeown, M. G., & Kucan, L. (2013). *Bringing words to life: Robust vocabulary instruction* (2nd ed.). New York: Guilford Press.

Bennett-Armistead, V. S. (n.d.). *What is dramatic play and how does it support literacy development in preschool?* Accessed at www.scholastic.com/teachers/articles/teaching-content/what-dramatic-play-and-how-does-it-support-literacy-development-preschool on July 14, 2019.

Billen, M. T., & Allington, R. L. (2013). An evidence-based approach to response to intervention. In D. M. Barone & M. H. Mallette (Eds.), *Best practices in early literacy instruction* (pp. 305–321). New York: Guilford Press.

Bishop, R. S. (2012). Reflections on the development of African American children's literature. *Journal of Children's Literature, 38*(2), 5–13.

Blanch, N., Forsythe, L. C., Van Allen, J. H., & Roberts, S. K. (2017). Reigniting writers: Using the literacy block with elementary students to support authentic writing experiences. *Childhood Education, 93*(1), 48–57.

Blevins, W. (2016). *Phonics: Ten important research findings.* Accessed at www.wileyblevins.com/uploads/files/Ten%20Important%20Research%20Findings%20by%20Wiley%20Blevins.pdf on June 15, 2019.

Blevins, W. (2017). *A fresh look at phonics: Common causes of failure and seven ingredients for success.* Thousand Oaks, CA: Corwin Press.

Bolchunos, M. (2004). *Treasure in the field: A Vietnamese folktale.* Columbus, OH: Highlights for Children.

Bockting, W. O. (2008). Psychotherapy and real-life experience: From gender dichotomy to gender diversity. *Sexologies, 17*(4), 211–224.

Bourque, P. (2017). Building stamina for struggling readers and writers. *Educational Leadership, 74*(5). Accessed at www.ascd.org/publications/educational-leadership/feb17/vol74/num05/Building-Stamina-for-Struggling-Readers-and-Writers.aspx on July 8, 2019.

Brendtro, L. K., Brokenleg, M., & Van Bockern, S. (2019). *Reclaiming youth at risk: Futures of promise* (3rd ed.). Bloomington, IN: Solution Tree Press.

Brookhart, S. M. (2013). *How to create and use rubrics for formative assessment and grading.* Alexandria, VA: Association for Supervision and Curriculum Development.

Brown, S., & Kappes, L. (2012, October). *Implementing the Common Core State Standards: A primer on "close reading of text."* Washington, DC: Aspen Institute.

Bruner, J. S., Goodnow, J. J., & Austin, G. A. (1956). *A study of thinking.* New York: Wiley.

Buckley, E. M. (n.d.). *Why personalized learning requires technology and thinking humans.* Accessed at http://hipporeads.com/why-personalized-learning-requires-technology-and-thinking-humans on November 21, 2019.

Budge, K. M., & Parrett, W. H. (2018). *Disrupting poverty: Five powerful classroom practices.* Alexandria, VA: Association for Supervision and Curriculum Development.

Buffum, A., & Mattos, M. (2020). *RTI at Work plan book*. Bloomington, IN: Solution Tree Press.

Buffum, A., Mattos, M., & Malone, J. (2018). *Taking action: A handbook for RTI at Work*. Bloomington, IN: Solution Tree Press.

Buffum, A., Mattos, M., & Weber, C. (2010). The why behind RTI. *Educational Leadership, 68*(2), 10–16.

Buffum, A., Mattos, M., & Weber, C. (2012). *Simplifying response to intervention: Four essential guiding principles*. Bloomington, IN: Solution Tree Press.

Casbergue, R. M., & Strickland, D. S. (2016). *Reading and writing in preschool: Teaching the essentials*. New York: Guilford Press.

Castles, A., Rastle, K., & Nation, K. (2018, June 11). Ending the reading wars: Reading acquisition from novice to expert. *Psychological Science in the Public Interest, 19*(1), 5–51.

Clay, M. M. (1993). *Reading recovery: A guidebook for teachers in training*. Portsmouth, NH: Heinemann.

Coburn, D. (2003). Using graphic organizers. *Science Scope, 27*(1), 46–48.

Coleman, D., & Pimentel, S. (2012a). *Revised publishers' criteria for the Common Core State Standards in English language arts and literacy, grades 3–12*. Accessed at www .corestandards.org/assets/Publishers_Criteria_for_3-12.pdf on May 25, 2019.

Coleman, D., & Pimentel, S. (2012b). *Revised publishers' criteria for the Common Core State Standards in English language arts and literacy, grades K–2*. Accessed at www .corestandards.org/assets/Publishers_Criteria_for_K-2.pdf on July 15, 2019.

Connell, R. (2009, February). Accountable conduct: "Doing gender" in transsexual and political retrospect. *Gender & Society, 23*(1), 104–111.

Coppola, S. (2014). Building background knowledge. *The Reading Teacher, 68*(2), 145–148.

Crawford, J. (2011). *Using power standards to build an aligned curriculum: A process manual*. Thousand Oaks, CA: Corwin Press.

Cunningham, A. E., & Stanovich, K. E. (1997). Early reading acquisition and its relation to reading experience and ability 10 years later. *Developmental Psychology, 33*(6), 934–945.

Darling-Hammond, L. (1999). *Teacher quality and student achievement: A review of state policy evidence*. Seattle, WA: Center for the Study of Teaching and Policy.

Dogan, E., Ogut, B., & Kim, Y. Y. (2015). Early childhood reading skills and proficiency in NAEP eighth-grade reading assessment. *Applied Measurement in Education, 28*(3), 187–201.

Donohoo, J., & Katz, S. (2017). When teachers believe, students achieve: Collaborative inquiry builds teacher efficacy for better student outcomes. *The Learning Professional, 38*(6), 20–27.

DuFour, R., DuFour, R., Eaker, R., & Many, T. W. (2010). *Learning by doing: A handbook for Professional Learning Communities at Work* (2nd ed.). Bloomington, IN: Solution Tree Press.

DuFour, R., DuFour, R., Eaker, R., Many, T. W., & Mattos, M. (2016). *Learning by doing: A handbook for Professional Learning Communities at Work* (3rd ed.). Bloomington, IN: Solution Tree Press.

DuFour, R., & Marzano, R. J. (2011). *Leaders of learning: How district, school, and classroom leaders improve student achievement.* Bloomington, IN: Solution Tree Press.

Dweck, C. S. (2016). *Mindset: The new psychology of success.* New York: Penguin Random House.

Ehri, L. C., & Roberts, T. (2006). The roots of learning to read and write: Acquisition of letters and phonemic awareness. In D. K. Dickinson & S. B. Neuman (Eds.), *Handbook of early literacy research* (Vol. 2, pp. 113–131). New York: Guilford Press.

Erickson, H. L. (2002). *Concept-based curriculum and instruction: Teaching beyond the facts.* Thousand Oaks, CA: Corwin Press.

Erickson, H. L. (2007). *Concept-based curriculum and instruction for the thinking classroom.* Thousand Oaks, CA: Corwin Press.

Fawcett Society. (2019, March 7). *Fawcett research shows exposure to gender stereotypes as a child causes harm in later life.* Accessed at www.fawcettsociety.org.uk/news/fawcett -research-exposure-gender-stereotypes-child-causes-harm-later-life on February 2, 2019.

Fisher, D. (2008). *Effective use of the gradual release of responsibility model.* Accessed at www.mheonline.com/_treasures/pdf/douglas_fisher.pdf on November 21, 2019.

Fisher, D., & Frey, N. (2008). *Better learning through structured teaching: A framework for the gradual release of responsibility.* Alexandria, VA: Association for Supervision and Curriculum Development.

Fisher, D., & Frey, N. (2012). Close reading in elementary schools. *Reading Teacher, 66*(3), 179–188.

Fisher, D., & Frey, N. (2014a). Closely reading informational texts in the primary grades. *Reading Teacher, 68*(3), 222–227.

Fisher, D., & Frey, N. (2014b). Scaffolded reading instruction of content-area texts. *Reading Teacher, 67*(5), 347–351.

Fisher, D., & Frey, N. (2014c). *Better learning through structured teaching: A framework for the gradual release of responsibility* (2nd ed.). Alexandria, VA: Association for Supervision and Curriculum Development.

Fisher, D., & Frey, N. (2015). Teacher modeling using complex informational texts. *Reading Teacher, 69*(1), 63–69.

Fisher, D., & Frey, N. (2018). Building capable kids. *Principal, 98*(1), 14–17.

Fitzgerald, J., & Shanahan, T. (2000). Reading and writing relations and their development. *Educational Psychologist, 35*(1), 39–50.

Foorman, B., Beyler, N., Borradaile, K., Coyne, M., Denton, C. A., Dimino, J., et al. (2016, July). *Foundational skills to support reading for understanding in kindergarten through 3rd grade* (NCEE 2016-4008). Washington, DC: National Center for Education Evaluation and Regional Assistance. Accessed at https://ies.ed.gov/ncee/wwc/Docs/PracticeGuide /wwc_foundationalreading_070516.pdf on November 21, 2019.

Fountas, I. C., & Pinnell, G. S. (2006). *Teaching for comprehending and fluency: Thinking, talking, and writing about reading, K–8*. Portsmouth, NH: Heinemann.

Fountas, I. C. & Pinnell, G. S. (2012). *Genre student: Teaching with fiction and nonfiction books*. Portsmouth, NH: Heineman.

Fountas, I. C., & Pinnell, G. S. (2019). *Level books, not children: The role of text levels in literacy instruction*. Accessed at www.fountasandpinnell.com/shared/resources/FPL _LevelBooksNotKids_Whitepaper.pdfon November 19, 2019.

Fountas & Pinnell Literacy Team. (2019, February 1). *What is shared reading?* [Blog post]. Accessed at https://fpblog.fountasandpinnell.com/what-is-shared-reading on November 20, 2019.

Freeman, D. (1968). *Corduroy*. New York: Viking Press.

Frey, N., & Fisher, D. (2013). *Rigorous reading: Five access points for comprehending complex texts*. Thousand Oaks, CA: Corwin Press.

Fried, M. D. (2013). Activating teaching: Using running records to inform teaching decisions. *Journal of Reading Recovery, 13*(1), 5–16.

Friziellie, H., Schmidt, J. A., & Spiller, J. (2016). *Yes we can! General and special educators collaborating in a professional learning community*. Bloomington, IN: Solution Tree Press.

Furry, A., & Domaradzki, L. (2010) *The value of instructional time and pacing schedules for K–3 reading*. Accessed at https://rmcresearchcorporation.com/tampafl/wp-content /uploads/sites/7/2015/04/Value-of-Instructional-Time-and-Pacing-Schedules.pdf on April 10, 2020.

Gallimore, R., Ermeling, B. A., Saunders, W. M., & Goldenberg, C. (2009). Moving the learning of teaching closer to practice: Teacher education implications of school-based inquiry teams. *Elementary School Journal, 109*(5), 537–553.

Gareis, C. R., & Grant, L. W. (2008). *Teacher-made assessments: How to connect curriculum, instruction, and student learning*. Larchmont, NY: Eye on Education.

Gareis, C. R., & Grant, L. W. (2015). *Teacher-made assessments: How to connect curriculum, instruction, and student learning* (2nd ed.). New York: Routledge.

Garland, K., & Bryan, K. (2017). Partnering with families and communities: Culturally responsive pedagogy at its best. *Voices From the Middle, 24*(3), 52–55.

Gender Spectrum. (n.d.). *Understanding gender and the experience of gender diverse youth and their families*. Accessed at www.genderspectrum.org/policybrief/#myths on March 2, 2020.

Glass, K. T. (2012). *Mapping comprehensive units to the ELA Common Core standards, K–5*. Thousand Oaks, CA: Corwin Press.

Glass, K. T. (2013). *Mapping comprehensive units to the ELA Common Core standards, 6–12*. Thousand Oaks, CA: Corwin Press.

Glass, K. T. (2015). *Complex text decoded: How to design lessons and use strategies that target authentic texts*. Alexandria, VA: Association for Supervision and Curriculum Development.

Glass, K. T. (2017). *The fundamentals of (re)designing writing units*. Bloomington, IN: Solution Tree Press.

Glass, K. T. (2018). *(Re)designing narrative writing units for grades 5–12*. Bloomington, IN: Solution Tree Press.

Glass, K. T., & Marzano, R. J. (2018). *The new art and science of teaching writing*. Bloomington, IN: Solution Tree Press.

Gonzalez, J. (2018, November 4). To learn, students need to DO something. *Cult of Pedagogy*. Accessed at www.cultofpedagogy.com/do-something on November 21, 2019.

Graham, S., Bollinger, A., Booth Olson, C., D'Aoust, C., MacArthur, C., McCutchen, D., et al. (2012, June). *Teaching elementary school students to be effective writers: A practice guide* (NCEE 2012-4058). Washington, DC: National Center for Education Evaluation and Regional Assistance. Accessed at https://ies.ed.gov/ncee/wwc/Docs/PracticeGuide/writing_pg_062612.pdf on November 22, 2019.

Graham, S., & Hebert, M. (2010). *Writing to read: Evidence for how writing can improve reading—A report to Carnegie Corporation of New York*. Washington, DC: Alliance for Excellent Education.

Graham, S., & Hebert, M. (2011). Writing to read: A meta-analysis of the impact of writing and writing instruction on reading. *Harvard Educational Review, 81*(4), 710–744.

Graham, S., & Perin, D. (2007). *Writing next: Effective strategies to improve writing of adolescents in middle and high schools—A report to Carnegie Corporation of New York*. Washington, DC: Alliance for Excellent Education.

Guskey, T. R. (2010). Lessons of mastery learning. *Educational Leadership, 68*(2), 52–57.

Guthrie, J., Wigfield, A., & You, W. (2012). *Instructional contexts for engagement and achievement in reading*. In *Handbook of Research on Student Engagement*, S. L. Christenson, A. L. Reschly, & C. Wylie (eds.). New York: Springer. Accessed at http://citeseerx.ist.psu.edu/viewdoc/download?doi=10.1.1.688.4291&rep=rep1&type=pdf on April 10, 2020.

Harris, K. R., Graham, S., Friedlander, B., & Laud, L. (2013). Bring powerful writing strategies into your classroom! Why and how. *Reading Teacher, 66*(7), 538–542.

Harrison, J., Grant, J., & Herman, J. L. (2012). A gender not listed here: Genderqueers, gender rebels, and otherwise in the National Transgender Discrimination Survey. *LGBTQ Public Policy Journal at the Harvard Kennedy School, 2*(1), 13–24.

Hattie, J. (2012). *Visible learning for teachers: Maximizing impact on learning*. New York: Routledge.

Heritage, M. (2008). *Learning progressions: Supporting instruction and formative assessment*. Washington, DC: Council of Chief State School Officers.

Hernandez, D. J. (2011, April). *Double jeopardy: How third-grade reading skills and poverty influence high school graduation*. Baltimore: Annie E. Casey Foundation.

Hess, K. K. (n.d.). *Applying Webb's depth-of-knowledge (DOK) levels in reading*. Accessed at www.nciea.org/publications/DOKreading_KH08.pdf on April 10, 2020.

Hillsdale County Intermediate School District. (n.d.). *RTI Tier 3 intensive intervention*. Accessed at www.hillsdale-isd.org/cms/lib/MI01001046/Centricity/Domain/15 /RtI_Tier_3_Intensive_Intervention.pdf on November 22, 2019.

Himmele, W., & Himmele, P. (2012). Why read-alouds matter more in the age of the Common Core standards. *ASCD Express*, *8*(5). Accessed at www.ascd.org/ascd -express/vol8/805-himmele.aspx on November 22, 2019.

Hollie, S. (2019, May 22). *Steps to authenticity* [Blog post]. Accessed at https:// literacyworldwide.org/blog/literacy-daily/2019/05/22/steps-to-authenticity on July 14, 2019.

International Literacy Association. (2019). *Children's rights to excellent literacy instruction*. Accessed at https://literacyworldwide.org/docs/default-source/where-we-stand/ila -childrens-rights-to-excellent-literacy-instruction.pdf on March 21, 2020.

Johnson, D. W., & Johnson, R. T. (n.d.). *An overview of cooperative learning*. Accessed at www.co-operation.org/what-is-cooperative-learning on November 22, 2019.

Jonsson, A., & Svingby, G. (2007). The use of scoring rubrics: Reliability, validity and educational consequences. *Educational Research Review*, *2*(2), 130–144.

Kagan, S. (1999). Cooperative learning: Seventeen pros and seventeen cons plus ten tips for success. *Kagan Online Magazine*. Accessed at www.kaganonline.com /free_articles/dr_spencer_kagan/259/Cooperative-Learning-Seventeen-Pros-and -Seventeen-Cons-Plus-Ten-Tips-for-Success on November 22, 2019.

Kagan, S., & Kagan, M. (2009). *Kagan cooperative learning*. San Clemente, CA: Kagan.

Kagan, S., Kagan, M., & Kagan, L. (2016). *59 Kagan structures: Proven engagement strategies*. San Clemente, CA: Kagan.

Killion, J. (2008, February). *Coaches help mine the data*. Accessed at https://learningforward .org/leading-teacher/february-2008-vol-3-no-5/focus-on-nsdcs-standards-coaches-help -mine-the-data on June 17, 2019.

Lapp, D., Moss, B., Grant, M., & Johnson, K. (2015). *A close look at close reading: Teaching students to analyze complex texts, grades K–5*. Alexandria, VA: Association for Supervision and Curriculum Development.

Lee, J., Grigg, W. S., & Donahue, P. L. (2007). *The nation's report card: Reading 2007— National Assessment of Educational Progress at grades 4 and 8* (NCES 2007-496).

Washington, DC: National Center for Education Statistics. Accessed at https://nces .ed.gov/nationsreportcard/pdf/main2007/2007496.pdf on July 5, 2019.

Lesnick, J., Goerge, R. M., Smithgall, C., & Gwynne, J. (2010). *Reading on grade level in third grade: How is it related to high school performance and college enrollment? A longitudinal analysis of third-grade students in Chicago in 1996–97 and their educational outcomes. A report to the Annie E. Casey Foundation.* Chicago: Chapin Hall at the University of Chicago.

Liben, M., & Pimentel, S. (2018, November 7). *Placing text at the center of the standards-aligned ELA classroom.* Accessed at https://achievethecore.org/page/3185/placing -text-at-the-center-of-the-standards-aligned-ela-classroom on July 14, 2019.

MacLachlan, P. (1985). *Sarah, plain and tall.* New York: HarperCollins.

Magliaro, S. G., Lockee, B. B., & Burton, J. K. (2005). Direct instruction revisited: A key Model for instructional technology. *Educational Technology Research and Development, 53*(4), 41–56.

Many, T. W. (2009, July 7). *Three rules help manage assessment data* [Blog post]. Accessed at www.allthingsplc.info/blog/view/53/three-rules-help-manage-assessment-data on November 21, 2019.

Markel, M. (2013). *Brave girl: Clara and the shirtwaist maker's strike of 1909.* New York: HarperCollins.

Marzano, R. J. (2003). *What works in schools: Translating research into action.* Alexandria, VA: Association for Supervision and Curriculum Development.

Marzano, R. J. (2004). *Building background knowledge for academic achievement: Research on what works in schools.* Alexandria, VA: Association for Supervision and Curriculum Development.

Marzano, R. J. (2017). *The new art and science of teaching.* Bloomington, IN: Solution Tree Press.

Marzano, R. J. (2019). *The handbook for the new art and science of teaching.* Bloomington, IN: Solution Tree Press.

Marzano, R. J. (2020). *Teaching basic, advanced, and academic vocabulary: A comprehensive framework for elementary instruction.* Bloomington, IN: Marzano Resources.

Marzano, R. J., & Pickering, D. J. (2005). *Building academic vocabulary: Teacher's manual.* Alexandria, VA: Association for Supervision and Curriculum Development.

Mindset Works. (2017). *The science: Dr. Dweck's research into growth mindset changed education forever.* Accessed at www.mindsetworks.com/science on November 21, 2019.

Mississippi Department of Education. (2009). *Webb's depth of knowledge guide: Career and technical education definitions.* Accessed at www.aps.edu/sapr/documents /resources/Webbs_DOK_Guide.pdf on April 10, 2020.

Morrow, L. M., & Gambrell, L. B. (Eds.). (2011). *Best practices in literacy instruction* (4th ed.). New York: Guilford Press.

Morrow, L. M., Kunz, K., & Hall, M. (2018). *Breaking through the language arts block: Organizing and managing the exemplary literacy day.* New York: Guilford Press.

National Association for the Education of Young Children. (n.d.). *Learning to read and write: What research reveals.* Accessed at www.readingrockets.org/article/learning-read-and-write-what-research-reveals on November 22, 2019.

National Center for Learning Disabilities. (n.d.). *What is RTI?* Accessed at www.rtinetwork.org/learn/what/whatisrti on July 1, 2019.

National Governors Association Center for Best Practices & Council of Chief State School Officers. (n.d.a). *Common Core State Standards for English language arts and literacy in history/social studies, science, and technical subjects: Appendix A—Research supporting key elements of the standards.* Washington, DC: Authors. Accessed at www.corestandards.org/assets/Appendix_A.pdf on November 21, 2019.

National Governors Association Center for Best Practices & Council of Chief State School Officers. (n.d.b). *Supplemental information for appendix A of the Common Core State Standards for English language arts and literacy: New research on text complexity.* Washington, DC: Authors. Accessed at www.corestandards.org/assets/E0813_Appendix_A_New_Research_on_Text_Complexity.pdf on Text Complexity on April 10, 2020.

National Governors Association Center for Best Practices & Council of Chief State School Officers. (2010). *Common Core State Standards for English language arts and literacy in history/social studies, science, and technical subjects.* Washington, DC: Authors. Accessed at www.corestandards.org/assets/CCSSI_ELA%20Standards.pdf on November 22, 2019.

Northern Illinois University. (n.d.). *Instructional scaffolding to improve learning.* Accessed at www.niu.edu/facdev/_pdf/guide/strategies/instructional_scaffolding_to_improve_learning.pdf on July 8, 2019.

O'Donnell, A. (2019). Windows, mirrors, and sliding glass doors: The enduring impact of Rudine Sims Bishop's work. *Literacy Today, 36*(6), 16–19.

Office of the High Commissioner for Human Rights. (n.d.). *Gender stereotyping.* Accessed at www.ohchr.org/en/issues/women/wrgs/pages/genderstereotypes.aspx on February 2, 2019.

Owocki, G., & Goodman, Y. (2002). *Kidwatching: Documenting children's literacy development.* Portsmouth, NH: Heinemann.

Pearson, P. D., & Gallagher, M. C. (1983, October). *The instruction of reading comprehension* (Technical Report No. 297). Champaign, IL: Center for the Study of Reading.

Pikulski, J. J., & Chard, D. J. (2005). Fluency: Bridge between decoding and reading comprehension. *Reading Teacher, 58*(6), 510–519.

Pinnell, G. S., Pikulski, J. J., Wixson, K. K., Campbell, J. R., Gough, P. B., & Beatty, A. S. (1995, January). *Listening to children read aloud: Data from NAEP's integrated reading performance record (IRPR) at grade 4.* Washington, DC: National Center for Education Statistics.

Popham, W. J. (2007). All about accountability/The lowdown on learning progressions. *Educational Leadership*, 64(7). Accessed at www.ascd.org/publications/educational -leadership/apr07/vol64/num07/The-Lowdown-on-Learning-Progressions.aspx on May 10, 2019.

Popham, W. J. (2008). *Transformative assessment*. Alexandria, VA: Association for Supervision and Curriculum Development.

Pressley, M., Allington, R. L., Wharton-McDonald, R., Block, C. C., & Morrow, L. M. (2001). *Learning to read: Lessons from exemplary first-grade classrooms*. New York: Guilford Press.

Rasinski, T. (2014). Fluency matters. *International Electronic Journal of Elementary Education*, 7(1), 3–12.

Rasinski, T. V. (2012). Why reading fluency should be hot! *Reading Teacher*, 65(8), 516–522.

Reeves, D. B. (2002). *The leader's guide to standards: A blueprint for educational equity and excellence*. San Francisco: Jossey-Bass.

Reeves, D. (2007). *Ahead of the curve: The power of assessment to transform teaching and learning*. Bloomington, IN: Solution Tree.

Riley-Ayers, S. (2013). Supporting language and literacy development in quality preschools. In D. M. Barone & M. H. Mallette (Eds.), *Best practices in early literacy instruction* (pp. 58–77). New York: Guilford Press.

Roskos, K., & Christie, J. (2011). The play-literacy nexus and the importance of evidence-based techniques in the classroom. *American Journal of Play*, 4(2), 204–224. Accessed at https://files.eric.ed.gov/fulltext/EJ985588.pdf on November 22, 2019.

Roth, K., & Dabrowski, J. (2014). Extending interactive writing into grades 2–5. *Reading Teacher*, 68(1), 33–44.

Rylant, C. (2008). *Poppleton in winter*. New York: Scholastic.

Schimmer, T. (2019, February 19). *Should formative assessments be graded?* [Blog post]. Accessed at www.solutiontree.com/blog/grading-formative-assessments on July 14, 2019.

Schmitt, B. D. (2014). *Attention deficit/hyperactivity disorder (ADHD): How to help your child*. Accessed at www.summitmedicalgroup.com/library/pediatric_health /pa-hhgbeh_attention on November 22, 2019.

Schwartz, S., & Sparks, S. D. (2019, October 2). How do kids learn to read? What the science says. *Education Week*. Accessed at www.edweek.org/ew/issues/how-do-kids -learn-to-read.html on April 7, 2020.

Searle, M. (2010). *What every school leader needs to know about RTI*. Alexandria, VA: Association for Supervision and Curriculum Development.

Serravallo, J. (2010). *Teaching reading in small groups: Differentiated instruction for building strategic, independent readers*. Portsmouth, NH: Heinemann.

Serravallo, J. (2014). *The literacy teacher's playbook, grades 3–6: Four steps for turning assessment data into goal-directed instruction.* Portsmouth, NH: Heinemann.

Serravallo, J. (2015). *The reading strategies book: Your everything guide to developing skilled readers.* Portsmouth, NH: Heinemann.

Serravallo, J. (2018). *Understanding texts and readers: Responsive comprehension instruction with leveled texts.* Portsmouth, NH: Heinemann.

Shanahan, T. (2006). Relations among oral language, reading, and writing development. In C. MacArthur, S. Graham, & J. Fitzgerald (Eds.), *Handbook of writing research* (pp. 171–183). New York: Guilford Press.

Shanahan, T. (2008). *Teaching students to read complex text* [PowerPoint slides]. Accessed at www.shanahanonliteracy.com/publications/teaching-with-complex-text-1 on June 14, 2019.

Shanahan, T. (2015). Common Core State Standards: A new role for writing. *Elementary School Journal, 115*(4), 464–479.

Shanahan, T. (2016, September 6). *Eight ways to help kids to read complex text* [Blog post]. Accessed at https://shanahanonliteracy.com/blog/eight-ways-to-help-kids-to-read-complex-text on November 22, 2019.

Shanahan, T. (2017, February 23). *How should we combine reading and writing?* [Blog post]. Accessed at https://shanahanonliteracy.com/blog/how-should-we-combine-reading-and-writing on November 22, 2019.

Shanahan, T. (2018). *Gradual release of responsibility and complex text* [Blog post]. Accessed at https://shanahanonliteracy.com/blog/gradual-release-of-responsibility-and-complex-text on June 5, 2020.

Shanahan, T. (2019). *Teaching students to read complex text.* Accessed at www.shanahanonliteracy.com/publications/teaching-students-to-read-complex-text on March 19, 2020.

Shanahan, T. (2020, February 1). *If students meet a standard with below grade level texts, are they meeting the standard?* [Blog post]. Accessed at https://shanahanonliteracy.com/blog/if-students-meet-a-standard-with-below-grade-level-texts-are-they-meeting-the-standard on March 21, 2020.

Shanahan, T., & Allington, R. L. (2014, February 6). *To special ed or not to special ed: RTI and the early identification of reading disabilities* [Blog post]. Accessed at www.cdl.org/articles/to-special-ed-or-not-to-special-ed-rti-and-the-early-identification-of-reading-disabilities on May 25, 2019.

Shanahan, T., Callison, K., Carriere, C., Duke, N. K., Pearson, P. D., Schatschneider, C., et al. (2010). *Improving reading comprehension in kindergarten through 3rd grade: A practice guide* (NCEE 2010-4038). Washington, DC: National Center for Education Evaluation and Regional Assistance. Accessed at https://files.eric.ed.gov/fulltext/ED512029.pdf on November 22, 2019.

Shanahan, T., Fisher, D., & Frey, N. (2012). The challenge of challenging text. *Educational Leadership, 69*(6), 58–62.

Slavin, R. E. (2014). Making cooperative learning powerful. *Educational Leadership, 72*(2). Accessed at www.ascd.org/publications/educational-leadership/oct14/vol72 /num02/Making-Cooperative-Learning-Powerful.aspx on November 21, 2019.

Snow, C. E., Burns, M. S., & Griffin, P. (Eds.). (1998). *Preventing reading difficulties in young children.* Washington, DC: National Academies Press.

Stachowiak, D. (2018). The power to include: A starting place for creating gender-inclusive literacy classrooms. *Literacy Today, 36*(1), 28–30.

Stahl, K. A. D. (2005). Improving the asphalt of reading instruction: A tribute to the work of Steven A. Stahl. *Reading Teacher, 59*(2), 184–192.

Stahl, K. A. D. (2012). Complex text or frustration-level text: Using shared reading to bridge the difference. *Reading Teacher, 66*(1), 47–51.

Stecker, P. M., & Lembke, E. S. (2005). *Advanced applications of CBM in reading: Instructional decision-making strategies manual.* Washington, DC: National Center on Student Progress Monitoring.

Stein, S. (2000). *Equipped for the future content standards: What adults need to know and be able to do in the 21st century.* Washington, DC: National Institute for Literacy. Accessed at https://eff.clee.utk.edu/PDF/standards_guide.pdf on November 21, 2019.

Steinbeck, J. (1939/1993). *The grapes of wrath.* London: Penguin.

Stiggins, R. (2005). From formative assessment to assessment FOR learning: A path to success in standards-based schools. *Phi Delta Kappan, 87*(4), 324–328.

Stockard, J., Wood, T. W., Coughlin, C., & Rasplica Khoury, C. (2018). The effectiveness of direct instruction curricula: A meta-analysis of a half century of research. *Review of Educational Research, 88*(4), 479–507.

TeacherVision. (2007, February 8). *Cooperative learning: Teaching strategies (grades K–12).* Accessed at www.teachervision.com/professional-development/cooperative -learning on November 21, 2019.

Thurber, J. (1950/1978). *The 13 clocks.* New York: Penguin.

Tierney, R. J., & Shanahan, T. (1991). Research on the reading-writing relationship: Interactions, transactions, and outcomes. In R. Barr, M. L. Kamil, P. Mosenthal, & P. D. Pearson (Eds.), *Handbook of reading research* (Vol. 2, pp. 246–280). New York: Routledge.

Tomlinson, C. A. (2000, August). *Differentiation of instruction in the elementary grades.* Champaign, IL: ERIC Clearinghouse on Elementary and Early Childhood Education. Accessed at https://files.eric.ed.gov/fulltext/ED443572.pdf on November 22, 2019.

Tomlinson, C. A., & Imbeau, M. B. (2010). *Leading and managing a differentiated classroom.* Alexandria, VA: Association for Supervision and Curriculum Development.

Tomlinson, C. A., & Moon, T. R. (2013). *Assessment and student success in a differentiated classroom*. Alexandria, VA: Association for Supervision and Curriculum Development.

Trehearne, M., Healy, L. H., Cantalini, M., & Moore, J. L. (2003). *Comprehensive literacy resource for kindergarten teachers*. Vernon Hills, IL: ETA/Cuisenaire.

Underwood, S. (2018) *What is the evidence for an uninterrupted, 90-minute literacy instruction block?: Education Northwest literacy brief*. Accessed at https://educationnorthwest.org/sites/default/files/resources/uninterrupted-literacy-block-brief.pdf on April 10, 2020.

Virginia Department of Education. (2017). *K–12 English standards of learning and curriculum framework*. Accessed at www.doe.virginia.gov/testing/sol/standards_docs/english/index.shtml on February 3, 2019.

Webb, N. L. (1997). *Criteria for alignment of expectations and assessments in mathematics and science education* (Research monograph no. 8). Washington, DC: Council of Chief State School Officers.

Weinstein, R. S. (2002). *Reaching higher: The power of expectations in schooling*. President and Fellows of Harvard College.

Wiggins, G. (2012). Seven keys to effective feedback. *Educational Leadership*, *70*(1), 10–16.

White, E. B. (1952/1980). *Charlotte's web*. New York: HarperCollins.

Wiliam, D. (2018). *Embedded formative assessment* (2nd ed.). Bloomington, IN: Solution Tree Press.

Wrang, L. (2015). *The sign*. Columbus, OH: Highlights for Children. Accessed at www.commonlit.org/texts/the-sign on November 22, 2019.

INDEX

Reading and Writing Instruction for PreK Through First-Grade Classrooms in a PLC at Work®
Erica Martin and Lisa May
Mark Onuscheck and Jeanne Spiller (Editors)

Prepare your collaborative PLC team to fully support and encourage every learner's literacy development. Written specifically for teachers of preK through first grade, this practical resource includes tools and strategies for designing standards-aligned instruction, assessments, interventions, and more.
BKF901

Reading and Writing Instruction for Fourth- and Fifth-Grade Classrooms in a PLC at Work®
Kathy Tuchman Glass
Mark Onuscheck and Jeanne Spiller (Editors)

Prepare students to succeed with increasingly sophisticated reading and writing challenges. Designed for teachers of grades 4–5, this book fully prepares individuals and collaborative teams to establish a rich and robust plan for quality literacy instruction, assessment, and intervention.
BKF902

The New Art and Science of Teaching Reading
Julia A. Simms and Robert J. Marzano

The New Art and Science of Teaching Reading presents a compelling model for reading development structured around five key topic areas. More than one hundred reading-focused instructional strategies are laid out in detail to help teachers ensure every student becomes a proficient reader.
BKF811

The New Art and Science of Teaching Writing
Kathy Tuchman Glass and Robert J. Marzano

Using a clear and well-organized structure, the authors apply the strategies originally laid out in *The New Art and Science of Teaching* to the teaching of writing. In total, the book explores more than one hundred strategies for teaching writing across grade levels and subject areas.
BKF796

Solution Tree | Press

a division of

Solution Tree

Visit SolutionTree.com or call 800.733.6786 to order.

Tremendous, tremendous, tremendous!

The speaker made me do some very deep internal reflection about the **PLC process** and the personal responsibility I have in making the school improvement process work **for ALL kids**.

—Marc Rodriguez, teacher effectiveness coach, Denver Public Schools, Colorado

PD Services

Our experts draw from decades of research and their own experiences to bring you practical strategies for building and sustaining a high-performing PLC. You can choose from a range of customizable services, from a one-day overview to a multiyear process.

Book your PLC PD today!
888.763.9045

Solution Tree